A William S. Hein & Company Reprint

HISTORICAL REPRINTS IN
JURISPRUDENCE AND
CLASSICAL LEGAL LITERATURE

Advisory Editor
Bernard D. Reams, Jr.

ANCIENT LAW

ITS CONNECTION WITH THE EARLY HISTORY OF SOCIETY AND ITS RELATION TO MODERN IDEAS

BY

SIR HENRY SUMNER MAINE

William S. Hein & Company

Buffalo

1983

30-21428

Maine, Sir Henry James Sumner, 1822-1888.

    Ancient law, its connection with the early history of society
and its relation to modern ideas, by Sir Henry Sumner Maine
...with introduction and notes by the Right Hon. Sir Frederick
Pollock, bart. London, J. Murrary 1920

    xxiv, 426 p. 21 1/2 cm.

ISBN 0-89941-249-1

ANCIENT LAW

ANCIENT LAW

ITS CONNECTION WITH THE EARLY HISTORY OF SOCIETY AND ITS RELATION TO MODERN IDEAS

BY SIR HENRY SUMNER MAINE

K.C.S.I., LL.D., F.R.S.

FOREIGN ASSOCIATE MEMBER OF THE INSTITUTE OF FRANCE

WITH INTRODUCTION AND NOTES BY
THE RIGHT HON. SIR FREDERICK POLLOCK, BART.
LL.D., D.C.L.

LONDON
JOHN MURRAY, ALBEMARLE STREET, W.
1920

FIRST EDITION, with Sir Frederick
    Pollock's Notes .   . *January* 1906
Reprinted   .   .   . *August* 1907
Reprinted   .   .   . *June* 1909
Reprinted   .   .   . *July* 1912
Reprinted   .   .   . *July* 1916
Reprinted   .   .   . *April* 1920

PREFACE

———

THE theory of legal development propounded in
this volume has been generally accepted ; but it
has been thought that, in his Fifth Chapter on
" Primitive Society and Ancient Law," the Author
has not done sufficient justice to investigations
which appear to show the existence of states of
society still more rudimentary than that vividly
described in the Homeric lines quoted·at page 110,
and ordinarily known as the Patriarchal State.
The Author at page 106 has mentioned " accounts
by contemporary observers of civilisations less
advanced than their own," as capable of affording
peculiarly good evidence concerning the rudiments
of society ; and, in fact, since his work was first
published, in 1861, the observation of savage or
extremely barbarous races has brought to light
forms of social organisation extremely unlike that
to which he has referred the beginnings of law,

and possibly in some cases of greater antiquity. The subject is, properly speaking, beyond the scope of the present work, but he has given his opinion upon the results of these more recent inquiries in a paper on " Theories of Primitive Society," published in a volume on " Early Law and Custom " (Murray, 1883).

H. S. M.

LONDON: *November* 1884.

PREFACE

TO

THE FIRST EDITION

———

THE chief object of the following pages is to indicate some of the earliest ideas of mankind, as they are reflected in Ancient Law, and to point out the relation of those ideas to modern thought. Much of the inquiry attempted could not have been prosecuted with the slightest hope of a useful result if there had not existed a body of law, like that of the Romans, bearing in its earlier portions the traces of the most remote antiquity and supplying from its later rules the staple of the civil institutions by which modern society is even now controlled. The necessity of taking the Roman law as a typical system, has compelled the Author to draw from it what may appear a disproportionate number of his illustrations ; but it has not been his intention to write a treatise on Roman jurisprudence, and he has as much as possible avoided all discussions which might

give that appearance to his work. The space
allotted in the Third and Fourth Chapters to
certain philosophical theories of the Roman
Jurisconsults, has been appropriated to them for
two reasons. In the first place, those theories
appear to the Author to have had a much wider
and more permanent influence on the thought
and action of the world than is usually supposed.
Secondly, they are believed to be the ultimate
source of most of the views which have been
prevalent, till quite recently, on the subjects
treated of in this volume. It was impossible for
the Author to proceed far with his undertaking,
without stating his opinion on the origin, meaning,
and value of those speculations.

H. S. M.

LONDON: *January* 1861.

CONTENTS

INTRODUCTION

SIR HENRY MAINE's "Ancient Law" is now a
classical text. The object of this edition is to
reproduce it, accompanied by such help to right
understanding and profitable use as a younger
generation may reasonably require. More than
forty years have passed since the book was first
published in 1861. During those years, and to
a great extent under the influence of Maine's
own work, research into the early history of
laws and institutions has been more active,
systematic, and fruitful than it ever was before.
Many new facts have been disclosed ; our knowledge of others has been freed from error and
misconception ; as many, perhaps more, which
were formerly accessible, but neglected as being
insignificant or of merely local interest, have
found their due place and importance in a wider
field of knowledge. The materials thus acquired
enable us to confirm and supplement Maine's
work in many points. If they also show us that
it calls for amendment in some places, no one
who is at all acquainted with the progressive
character of legal and historical learning will
find in this any cause for disappointment. The
wonder is not that Maine's results, after more

than a generation, should stand in need of some correction, but that, in fact, they need so little as they do. Later speculation and research have, on the whole, confirmed Maine's leading ideas in the most striking manner, partly by actual verification of consequences indicated by him as probable, partly by new examples and applications in regions which he had not himself explored.

There is no better witness to the intrinsic weight of Maine's work than the nature of some criticism it has met with, from competent persons on the Continent rather than at home. So far as those learned persons complain of anything, they miss that symmetrical construction of a finished system to which their training has accustomed them. Now it is to be observed that no words of Maine's own ever gave his readers the promise of a systematic doctrine. Not one of his books professed on the face of it to account for the ultimate origin of human laws, or to settle the relations of jurisprudence to ethics, or to connect the science of law with any theory of politics or of social development. Yet it does not seem to have occurred to the critics in question to charge Maine with remissness in not having attempted these things. The disappointment expressed was that he did not fully accomplish them, or that, if he had a solution, he never sufficiently declared it. Regret that Maine's work was not more openly ambitious is legitimate, though I do not share it ; expression of it might have signified much or little. It might have been thoroughly sincere, and due to imperfect understanding of the relations to time, circumstances,

and materials, which determined Maine's manner
of working, and, as I believe, determined it for
the best. It might also have been, in the critic's
intention, the easy compliment of the professional
and disciplined scholar to a brilliant amateur.
Very different from this was the actual criticism.
It assumed that the author had proved himself
a master, and that, accordingly, the highest and
most exacting standard was to be applied both
to his method and to his results. When we
turn from Dareste or Vanni to the original
preface to " Ancient Law," we are astonished
by the studiously modest terms in which Maine
defined his own undertaking : " The chief object
of the following pages is to indicate some of the
earliest ideas of mankind as they are reflected
in ancient law, and to point out the relation of
those ideas to modern thought." In like manner,
on the first publication of the lectures on Village
Communities, he apologised for their fragmentary
character, and in the height of his mature fame
he described " Early Law and Custom " only as
an endeavour " to connect a portion of existing
institutions with a part of the primitive or very
ancient usages of mankind, and of the ideas
associated with those usages." It is worth while
to observe Maine's caution in disclaiming authority
to lay down what ancient usages, if any, are
really primitive—a caution sometimes neglected
by his followers, and often by the champions of
other theories.

Maine's dignified and almost ironical reserve
about his own work has certainly made it rather
difficult for a student approaching it for the

first time to form any general notion of what it has really done for legal and historical science. Although Maine himself was the last person of whom the answer to such a question could be expected, we who are in no way bound to reticence must say that he did nothing less than create the natural history of law. He showed, on the one hand, that legal ideas and institutions have a real course of development as much as the genera and species of living creatures, and in every stage of that development have their normal characters ; on the other hand, he made it clear that these processes deserve and require distinct study, and cannot be treated as mere incidents in the general history of the societies where they occur. There have been complaints, often too well justified, of the historical ignorance prevailing among lawyers. " Woe unto you also, ye lawyers ! " Freeman said—whether in print in those terms, I know not ; but I have heard him say it—when he was grieved at the fictions about mediæval institutions that still passed current for history twenty-five or thirty years ago. But Maine has taught us that the way to impart a historical habit of mind to lawyers is to show them that law has an important history of its own, not at all confined to its political and constitutional aspects, and offers a vast field for the regular application of historical and comparative method. When once a lawyer has grasped this, he is entitled to point out in turn that a historian who is not content to be a mere chronicler can hardly do without some understanding of legal ideas and systems. And the importance of the legal element, so far from diminishing as we retrace the growth of our modern institutions into a semi-historic past, rather increases. Others have shown this besides Maine, but none before him. It is easy to underrate his originality now that his points have been taken up by many teachers and become current in the schools. Any student who harbours doubt as to the extent of Maine's contributions to the historical philosophy of law may do well to ask himself in what books, legal or historical, of earlier date than " Ancient Law," he could have found adequate perception, or any distinct perception, of such matters as these : The sentiment of reverence evoked by the mere existence of law in early communities ; the essential formalism of archaic law ; the predominance of rules of procedure over rules of substance in early legal systems ; the fundamental difference between ancient and modern ideas as to legal proof ; the relatively modern character of the individual citizen's disposing power, especially by will, and freedom of contract ; and the still more modern appearance of true criminal law. Nowadays it may be said that " all have got the seed," but this is no justification for forgetting who first cleared and sowed the ground. We may till fields that the master left untouched, and one man will bring a better ox to yoke to the plough, and another a worse ; but it is the master's plough still.

It will now be proper to consider in a general way what resources were available for Maine's purposes when he wrote " Ancient Law," or rather when he prepared and delivered the lectures

b

of which it was a revised publication (" Early Law and Custom," p. 194). We shall be pretty safe in taking legal and historical scholarship as they stood, for an English student who had not frequented Continental seats of learning, about the middle of the nineteenth century.

First, in Roman law Savigny, then still living, was the person of greatest authority; the historical school which he took a principal part in founding was dominant in Germany and beginning to prevail elsewhere. Savigny's work, as well as that of his contemporaries and immediate followers, dealt only with the Roman materials. Comparative investigation of archaic legal systems had scarcely been undertaken at all, certainly not on any considerable scale, and this may perhaps account for more than one conjecture of Savigny's which has not proved tenable. The work of Rudolf von Ihering, the character of whose genius, individual as it was, perhaps most nearly resembled Maine's in the same generation, was only beginning. His views on the evolution of modern from archaic law coincide remarkably with those of Maine in several points; for example, in the position that all jurisdiction, if we could trace it far back enough, would be found to be in its origin not compulsory, but voluntary. But there can be no question of borrowing either way. Maine had formed his own ideas before any part of Ihering's great work, " Der Geist des römischen Rechtes," was published; and Ihering was never in a position to make much use of Maine's work, even if he had the time; for, as I came to know from himself, he could not read English with any facility.

The literature of Roman law to be found in our own language was, with few exceptions, antiquated or contemptible, and such incidental references to Roman law as occurred in English text-books were almost always crude, often inappropriate or quite erroneous. Blackstone has some very bad mistakes in this kind. For many years after the publication of " Ancient Law " this state of things remained unamended. At the present time it is very different. In our own language Muirhead, Poste, Dr. Moyle, Dr. Roby, and the late Dr. Greenidge have made excellent provision of various kinds both for beginners and for advanced students, and Sohm's Institutes are accessible in Mr. Ledlie's scholarly translation. Professor Girard's " Manuel élémentaire de droit romain " (3rd ed., 1901) is, notwithstanding its modest title, one of the most learned and comprehensive, as well as the most recent, works on the subject. The reader of " Ancient Law " will understand that, as Maine was careful to explain in his first preface, the portions dealing with Roman law were never intended to take the place of an academic treatise. In fact, they assume the elementary knowledge which may be obtained from a good edition of Justinian's Institutes. It would therefore be idle to attempt a detailed commentary on them from a technical point of view which would not be appropriate ; and any reader who thinks he can use Maine's work as a substitute for first-hand acquaintance with the texts and the best commentators, instead of a

companion and aid, must do so wholly at his
own peril. Still less can Maine be censured for
having adopted, at the time, current views of
the highest authorities in Roman legal history
which have since been abandoned.

Germanic legal antiquities had been investigated to a considerable extent ; but the Continental scholars who had done this were still
hardly aware of the wealth or importance of the
material awaiting scientific treatment in England.
On the other hand, those who made their results
known to English readers, John Mitchell Kemble
the foremost, were not learned in the modern
law of England, and had not the means of connecting its later or even its mediæval history with
the earliest monuments of English institutions.
Thus no one had made any serious attempt to
sift the mass of information collected by English
professional writers and antiquaries of the sixteenth and seventeenth centuries, whose indus-
trious labour assuredly deserves all praise, and
whose judgment has in some cases been restored
to credit which it had not deserved to lose. We
need hardly say that Maine, not being a technical
antiquary, did not attempt any such thing himself. Indeed, the work he actually did was
needful to disclose the right lines of antiquarian
research, and rescue it from the state of mere
dilettante curiosity.

English legal history was very imperfectly
known, and what was known was concealed under
huge masses of comparatively modern formalism.
There was much to be learnt (as there still is)
from Blackstone, whose work was admirable in

its day, notwithstanding conspicuous faults of method and arrangement mostly not his own; but Blackstone had ceased to be generally read with attention even by lawyers, and was not a safe guide for any period before the thirteenth century. Whatever was before the Great Charter (and I am taking the earliest possible date) lay under a cloud of thick darkness, pierced only in part by the brilliant lights of Kemble and Palgrave. These fell, moreover, chiefly on the political and constitutional aspects of the common law, leaving in shadow those technical archaisms which we now know for landmarks. Palgrave, again, was often exuberant and fanciful, Kemble not seldom rash; and their work (though its general merit can hardly be exaggerated) is by no means free from positive mistakes, which, considering its novelty at the time, is in no way surprising. In every branch of the law scientific or even well written and tolerably arranged text-books were rare; in some they were wholly wanting. Constitutional law (and that from a political more than a legal point of view) was the only department which could be said to have found an adequate historian. On the whole, historical knowledge of English law before the twelfth century was not to be found, and after the twelfth century was pretty much what Blackstone had left it. In consequence of the general indifference to historical study, besides the real difficulties then attending it, lawyers and judges, even really learned ones, were commonly prone to accept superficial explanations which a little more research, not of a recondite kind, would have proved to be erroneous. In particular there was a strong tendency to exaggerate Roman influence in the formation of English institutions, by no means without plausible excuse. Perhaps it was knowledge of Kemble's work that saved Maine from this rife and dangerous error. Clearly the English materials were not in a fit state, when Maine was writing " Ancient Law," to be used with effect for any purpose of historical generalisation or comparison ; and he had no choice but to leave them alone for the most part, and build on other and at that time safer ground.

Asiatic systems of law were more or less known to Orientalists, but only in so far as their texts were documents of Arabic or Sanskrit literature. On the other hand, it was the duty of a considerable number of British magistrates and officials in India to have some acquaintance with so much of Hindu and Mahometan law as was recognised and applied by the civil courts ; but this was only for the necessities of judicial business. Few men, if any, followed the splendid example of Sir William Jones in combining literary with practical knowledge, as indeed very few can at any one time reasonably be supposed capable of it. As to the Mosaic law, it was still the received opinion that there was an impassable or at least a highly perilous gulf between sacred and profane history. Knowledge of the text of the Old Testament, far more complete and more generally diffused in English-speaking countries than anywhere else, had therefore produced little result for secular learning. Neither the philological nor the official handling of Asiatic law-books caused any appreciable number of scholars to perceive the importance of Asiatic custom for the general study of legal ideas and history. Maine's pointed references to Hindu institutions, at a time before he had or expected to have anything to do with India, could have been made only by a man of quite extraordinary insight. It would be interesting to know from what quarter his attention was first directed that way.

It has been thought proper to reprint the text of " Ancient Law " as last revised by Maine not only without alteration, but without the interruption of editorial footnotes. Such comments as I have been able to add will be found collected in notes at the end of each chapter. As " Ancient Law " touches on a greater variety of matters than almost any modern book of serious learning which is not of an encyclopædic nature, I have perforce omitted some topics, not because they might not have been considered with profit by a person competent in them, but because I was not competent. For the same reason I can by no means vouch for the accuracy in detail, according to the present state of knowledge, of everything I have passed over without remark. But my experience of the points I am qualified to test has led me to presume that such errors as may be discovered by specialists will seldom be found to affect the general course of the argument. I have purposely not dwelt on matters of elementary information which any student capable of profiting by Maine's work is equally capable of verifying for himself with little trouble. Maine did not write, for example, for readers who had never heard of Hobbes or Montesquieu. Such a name as Du Molin's, on the other hand, may well be strange, not only to an educated Englishman (as that of Bracton or Plowden might be to an educated Frenchman), but to an English lawyer who has not made a special study of the Reformation controversies or the revival of classical Roman law ; and in this case it would be vexatious to put off such readers with a bare reference to the French biographical dictionaries.

I have to thank the owners and the editor of the *Edinburgh Review* for permission to make free use of an article entitled " Sir Henry Maine as a Jurist," contributed by me in 1893.

In the second issue of these Notes (1907) some additional references and explanations have been given, which it is hoped will make them more useful.

F. P.

For general information about Maine's life and works the following publications may be consulted : " Sir Henry Maine : a brief memoir of his life," by Sir M. E. Grant Duff, 1892 ; " Sir Henry Maine and his Work," in " Oxford Lectures and other discourses," 1890, by the present writer ; and the articles in the Dictionary of National Biography (1893), and the Supplement to the ninth edition of the Encyclopædia Britannica (1902), by Leslie (afterwards Sir L.) Stephen and the present writer respectively.

ANCIENT LAW

CHAPTER I

ANCIENT CODES

THE most celebrated system of jurisprudence known to the world begins, as it ends, with a Code. From the commencement to the close of its history, the expositors of Roman Law consistently employed language which implied that the body of their system rested on the Twelve Decemviral Tables, and therefore on a basis of written law. Except in one particular, no institutions anterior to the Twelve Tables were recognised at Rome. The theoretical descent of Roman jurisprudence from a code, the theoretical ascription of English law to immemorial unwritten tradition, were the chief reasons why the development of their system differed from the development of ours. Neither theory corresponded exactly with the facts, but each produced consequences of the utmost importance.

I need hardly say that the publication of the Twelve Tables is not the earliest point at which we can take up the history of law. The ancient Roman code belongs to a class of which almost every civilised nation in the world can show a sample, and which, so far as the Roman and Hellenic worlds were concerned, were largely diffused over them at epochs not widely distant from one another. They appeared under exceedingly similar circumstances, and were produced, to our knowledge, by very similar causes. Unquestionably, many jural phenomena lie behind these codes and preceded them in point of time. Not a few documentary records exist which profess to give us information concerning the early phenomena of law; but, until philology has effected a complete analysis of the Sanskrit literature, our best sources of knowledge are undoubtedly the Greek Homeric poems, considered of course not as a history of actual occurrences, but as a description, not wholly idealised, of a state of society known to the writer. However the fancy of the poet may have exaggerated certain features of the heroic age, the prowess of warriors and the potency of gods, there is no reason to believe that it has tampered with moral or metaphysical conceptions which were not yet the subjects of conscious observation; and in this respect the Homeric literature is far more trustworthy than those relatively later documents which pretend to give an account of times similarly early, but which were compiled under philosophical or theological influences. If by any means we can determine the early forms of jural conceptions, they will be invaluable to us. These rudimentary ideas are to the jurist what the primary crusts of the earth are to the geologist. They contain, potentially, all the forms

in which law has subsequently exhibited itself.
The haste or the prejudice which has generally
refused them all but the most superficial examination, must bear the blame of the unsatisfactory
condition in which we find the science of jurisprudence. The inquiries of the jurist are in
truth prosecuted much as inquiry in physics
and physiology was prosecuted before observation
had taken the place of assumption. Theories,
plausible and comprehensive, but absolutely un-
verified, such as the Law of Nature or the Social
Compact, enjoy a universal preference over sober
research into the primitive history of society
and law ; and they obscure the truth not only
by diverting attention from the only quarter
in which it can be found, but by that most real
and most important influence which, when once
entertained and believed in, they are enabled
to exercise on the later stages of jurisprudence.

The earliest notions connected with the conception, now so fully developed, of a law or rule
of life, are those contained in the Homeric words
" Themis " and " Themistes." " Themis," it is
well known, appears in the later Greek pantheon
as the Goddess of Justice, but this is a modern
and much developed idea, and it is in a very
different sense that Themis is described in the
Iliad as the assessor of Zeus. It is now clearly
seen by all trustworthy observers of the primitive
condition of mankind that, in the infancy of
the race, men could only account for sustained
or periodically recurring action by supposing a
personal agent. Thus, the wind blowing was a
person and of course a divine person ; the sun

rising, culminating, and setting was a person and
a divine person ; the earth yielding her increase
was a person and divine. As, then, in the physical
world, so in the moral. When a king decided
a dispute by a sentence, the judgment was assumed
to be the result of direct inspiration. The divine
agent, suggesting judicial awards to kings or to
gods, the greatest of kings, was *Themis*. The
peculiarity of the conception is brought out by
the use of the plural. *Themistes*, Themises, the
plural of Themis, are the awards themselves,
divinely dictated to the judge. Kings are spoken
of as if they had a store of " Themistes " ready
to hand for use ; but it must be distinctly understood that they are not laws, but judgments,
or, to take the exact Teutonic equivalent,
" dooms." " Zeus, or the human king on earth,"
says Mr. Grote, in his History of Greece, " is
not a law-maker, but a judge." He is provided
with Themistes, but, consistently with the belief
in their emanation from above, they cannot be
supposed to be connected by any thread of principle ; they are separate, isolated judgments.

Even in the Homeric poems we can see that
these ideas are transient. Parities of circumstance
were probably commoner in the simple mechanism
of ancient society than they are now, and in the
succession of similar cases awards are likely to
follow and resemble each other. Here we have
the germ or rudiment of a custom, a conception
posterior to that of Themistes or judgments.
However strongly we, with our modern associations, may be inclined to lay down *à priori* that
the notion of a Custom must precede that of a

judicial sentence, and that a judgment must
affirm a custom or punish its breach, it seems
quite certain that the historical order of the
ideas is that in which I have placed them. The
Homeric word for a custom in the embryo is
sometimes " Themis " in the singular—more often
" Dike," the meaning of which visibly fluctuates
between a " judgment " and a " custom " or
" usage." Νόμος, a Law, so great and famous
a term in the political vocabulary of the later
Greek society, does not occur in Homer.

This notion of a divine agency, suggesting
the Themistes, and itself impersonated in Themis,
must be kept apart from other primitive beliefs
with which a superficial inquirer might confound
it. The conception of the Deity dictating an
entire code or body of law, as in the case of
the Hindoo laws of Manu, seems to belong to a
range of ideas more recent and more advanced.
" Themis " and " Themistes " are much less
remotely linked with that persuasion which clung
so long and so tenaciously to the human mind,
of a divine influence underlying and supporting
every relation of life, every social institution.
In early law, and amid the rudiments of political
thought, symptoms of this belief meet us on all
sides. A supernatural presidency is supposed
to consecrate and keep together all the cardinal
institutions of those times, the State, the Race,
and the Family. Men, grouped together in the
different relations which those institutions imply,
are bound to celebrate periodically common rites
and to offer common sacrifices ; and every now
and then the same duty is even more significantly

recognised in the purifications and expiations which they perform, and which appear intended to deprecate punishment for involuntary or neglectful disrespect. Everybody acquainted with ordinary classical literature will remember the *sacra gentilicia*, which exercised so important an influence on the early Roman law of adoption and of wills. And to this hour the Hindoo Customary Law, in which some of the most curious features of primitive society are stereotyped, makes almost all the rights of persons and all the rules of succession hinge on the due solemnisation of fixed ceremonies at the dead man's funeral, that is, at every point where a breach occurs in the continuity of the family.

Before we quit this stage of jurisprudence, a caution may be usefully given to the English student. Bentham, in his " Fragment on Government," and Austin, in his " Province of Jurisprudence Determined," resolve every law into a *command* of the lawgiver, an *obligation* imposed thereby on the citizen, and a *sanction* threatened in the event of disobedience ; and it is further predicated of the *command*, which is the first element in a law, that it must prescribe, not a single act, but a series or number of acts of the same class or kind. The results of this separation of ingredients tally exactly with the facts of mature jurisprudence ; and, by a little straining of language, they may be made to correspond in form with all law, of all kinds, at all epochs. It is not, however, asserted that the notion of law entertained by the generality is even now quite in conformity with this dissection ; and

it is curious that, the farther we penetrate into
the primitive history of thought, the farther we
find ourselves from a conception of law which at
all resembles a compound of the elements which
Bentham determined. It is certain that, in the
infancy of mankind, no sort of legislature, nor
even a distinct author of law, is contemplated
or conceived of. Law has scarcely reached the
footing of custom ; it is rather a habit. It is,
to use a French phrase, " in the air." The only
authoritative statement of right and wrong is a
judicial sentence after the facts, not one pre-
supposing a law which has been violated, but
one which is breathed for the first time by a
higher power into the judge's mind at the moment
of adjudication. It is of course extremely difficult
for us to realise a view so far removed from us
in point both of time and of association, but it
will become more credible when we dwell more
at length on the constitution of ancient society,
in which every man, living during the greater
part of his life under the patriarchal despotism,
was practically controlled in all his actions by
a regimen not of law but of caprice. I may add
that an Englishman should be better able than
a foreigner to appreciate the historical fact that
the " Themistes " preceded any conception of
law, because, amid the many inconsistent theories
which prevail concerning the character of English
jurisprudence, the most popular, or at all events
the one which most affects practice, is certainly
a theory which assumes that adjudged cases and
precedents exist antecedently to rules, principles,
and distinctions. The " Themistes " have too,

it should be remarked, the characteristic which, in the view of Bentham and Austin, distinguishes single or mere commands from laws. A true law enjoins on all the citizens indifferently a number of acts similar in class or kind ; and this is exactly the feature of a law which has most deeply impressed itself on the popular mind, causing the term "law" to be applied to mere uniformities, successions, and similitudes. A *command* prescribes only a single act, and it is to commands, therefore, that " Themistes " are more akin than to laws. They are simply adjudications on insulated states of fact, and do not necessarily follow each other in any orderly sequence.

The literature of the heroic age discloses to us law in the germ under the " Themistes " and a little more developed in the conception of " Dike." The next stage which we reach in the history of jurisprudence is strongly marked and surrounded by the utmost interest. Mr. Grote, in the second part and ninth chapter of his History, has fully described the mode in which society gradually clothed itself with a different character from that delineated by Homer. Heroic kingship depended partly on divinely given prerogative, and partly on the possession of supereminent strength, courage, and wisdom. Gradually, as the impression of the monarch's sacredness became weakened, and feeble members occurred in the series of hereditary kings, the royal power decayed, and at last gave way to the dominion of aristocracies. If language so precise can be used of the revolution, we might say that the office of the king was usurped by that council of chiefs

which Homer repeatedly alludes to and depicts.
At all events from an epoch of kingly rule we
come everywhere in Europe to an era of oligarchies;
and even where the name of the monarchical
functions does not absolutely disappear, the
authority of the king is reduced to a mere shadow.
He becomes a mere hereditary general, as in
Lacedæmon, a mere functionary, as the King
Archon at Athens, or a mere formal hierophant,
like the *Rex Sacrificulus* at Rome. In Greece,
Italy, and Asia Minor, the dominant orders seem
to have universally consisted of a number of
families united by an assumed relationship in
blood, and, though they all appear at first to
have laid claim to a quasi-sacred character,
their strength does not seem to have resided in
their pretended sanctity. Unless they were pre-
maturely overthrown by the popular party, they
all ultimately approached very closely to what we
should now understand by a political aristocracy.
The changes which society underwent in the
communities of the further Asia occurred of
course at periods long anterior in point of time
to these revolutions of the Italian and Hellenic
worlds; but their relative place in civilisation
appears to have been the same, and they seem
to have been exceedingly similar in general
character. There is some evidence that the races
which were subsequently united under the Persian
monarchy, and those which peopled the peninsula
of India, had all their heroic age and their era
of aristocracies; but a military and a religious
oligarchy appear to have grown up separately,
nor was the authority of the king generally

superseded. Contrary, too, to the course of events in the West, the religious element in the East tended to get the better of the military and political. Military and civil aristocracies disappear, annihilated or crushed into insignificance between the kings and the sacerdotal order; and the ultimate result at which we arrive is, a monarch enjoying great power, but circumscribed by the privileges of a caste of priests. With these differences, however, that in the East aristocracies became religious, in the West civil or political, the proposition that a historical era of aristocracies succeeded a historical era of heroic kings may be considered as true, if not of all mankind, at all events of all branches of the Indo-European family of nations.

The important point for the jurist is that these aristocracies were universally the depositaries and administrators of law. They seem to have succeeded to the prerogatives of the king, with the important difference, however, that they do not appear to have pretended to direct inspiration for each sentence. The connection of ideas which caused the judgments of the patriarchal chieftain to be attributed to superhuman dictation still shows itself here and there in the claim of a divine origin for the entire body of rules, or for certain parts of it, but the progress of thought no longer permits the solution of particular disputes to be explained by supposing an extra-human interposition. What the juristical oligarchy now claims is to monopolise the *knowledge* of the laws, to have the exclusive possession of the principles by which quarrels are decided.

We have in fact arrived at the epoch of Customary Law. Customs or Observances now exist as a substantive aggregate, and are assumed to be precisely known to the aristocratic order or caste. Our authorities leave us no doubt that the trust lodged with the oligarchy was sometimes abused, but it certainly ought not to be regarded as a mere usurpation or engine of tyranny. Before the invention of writing, and during the infancy of the art, an aristocracy invested with judicial privileges formed the only expedient by which accurate preservation of the customs of the race or tribe could be at all approximated to. Their genuineness was, so far as possible, insured by confiding them to the recollection of a limited portion of the community.

The epoch of Customary Law, and of its custody by a privileged order, is a very remarkable one. The condition of jurisprudence which it implies has left traces which may still be detected in legal and popular phraseology. The law, thus known exclusively to a privileged minority, whether a caste, an aristocracy, a priestly tribe, or a sacerdotal college, is true unwritten law. Except this, there is no such thing as unwritten law in the world. English case-law is sometimes spoken of as unwritten, and there are some English theorists who assure us that if a code of English jurisprudence were prepared we should be turning unwritten law into written—a conversion, as they insist, if not of doubtful policy, at all events of the greatest seriousness. Now, it is quite true that there was once a period at which the English common law might reasonably have been termed unwritten. The elder English judges did really pretend to knowledge of rules, principles, and distinctions which were not entirely revealed to the bar and to the lay-public. Whether all the law which they claimed to monopolise was really unwritten, is exceedingly questionable ; but at all events, on the assumption that there was once a large mass of civil and criminal rules known exclusively to the judges, it presently ceased to be unwritten law. As soon as the Courts at Westminster Hall began to base their judgments on cases recorded, whether in the year-books or elsewhere, the law which they administered became written law. At the present moment a rule of English law has first to be disentangled from the recorded facts of adjudged printed precedents, then thrown into a form of words varying with the taste, precision, and knowledge of the particular judge, and then applied to the circumstances of the case for adjudication. But at no stage of this process has it any characteristic which distinguishes it from written law. It is written case-law, and only different from code-law because it is written in a different way.

From the period of Customary Law we come to another sharply defined epoch in the history of jurisprudence. We arrive at the era of Codes, those ancient codes of which the Twelve Tables of Rome were the most famous specimen. In Greece, in Italy, on the Hellenised sea-board of Western Asia, these codes all made their appearance at periods much the same everywhere, not, I mean, at periods identical in point of time, but similar in point of the relative progress of each community. Everywhere, in the countries I have named, laws engraven on tablets and published to the people take the place of usages deposited with the recollection of a privileged oligarchy. It must not for a moment be supposed that the refined considerations now urged in favour of what is called codification had any part or place in the change I have described. The ancient codes were doubtless originally suggested by the discovery and diffusion of the art of writing. It is true that the aristocracies seem to have abused their monopoly of legal knowledge ; and at all events their exclusive possession of the law was a formidable impediment to the success of those popular movements which began to be universal in the western world. But, though democratic sentiment may have added to their popularity, the codes were certainly in the main a direct result of the invention of writing. Inscribed tablets were seen to be a better depository of law, and a better security for its accurate preservation, than the memory of a number of persons however strengthened by habitual exercise.

The Roman code belongs to the class of codes I have been describing. Their value did not consist in any approach to symmetrical classification, or to terseness and clearness of expression, but in their publicity, and in the knowledge which they furnished to everybody, as to what he was to do, and what not to do. It is, indeed, true that the Twelve Tables of Rome do exhibit some traces of systematic arrangement, but this is probably explained by the tradition that the framers of that body of law called in the assistance

of Greeks who enjoyed the later Greek experience
in the art of law-making. The fragments of the
Attic Code of Solon show, however, that it had
but little order, and probably the laws of Draco
had even less. Quite enough too remains of these
collections, both in the East and in the West, to
show that they mingled up religious, civil, and
merely moral ordinances, without any regard to
differences in their essential character; and this
is consistent with all we know of early thought
from other sources, the severance of law from
morality, and of religion from law, belonging
very distinctly to the later stages of mental
progress.

But, whatever to a modern eye are the singularities of these codes, their importance to ancient
societies was unspeakable. The question—and it
was one which affected the whole future of each
community—was not so much whether there
should be a code at all, for the majority of ancient
societies seem to have obtained them sooner or
later, and, but for the great interruption in the
history of jurisprudence created by feudalism, it
is likely that all modern law would be distinctly
traceable to one or more of these fountain-heads.
But the point on which turned the history of
the race was, at what period, at what stage of
their social progress, they should have their
laws put into writing. In the Western world the
plebeian or popular element in each State successfully assailed the oligarchical monopoly, and
a code was nearly universally obtained early in
the history of the Commonwealth. But, in the
East, as I have before mentioned, the ruling

aristocracies tended to become religious rather than military or political, and gained, therefore, rather than lost in power; while in some instances the physical conformation of Asiatic countries had the effect of making individual communities larger and more numerous than in the West; and it is a known social law that the larger the space over which a particular set of institutions is diffused, the greater is its tenacity and vitality. From whatever cause, the codes obtained by Eastern societies were obtained, relatively, much later than by Western, and wore a very different character. The religious oligarchies of Asia, either for their own guidance, or for the relief of their memory, or for the instruction of their disciples, seem in all cases to have ultimately embodied their legal learning in a code; but the opportunity of increasing and consolidating their influence was probably too tempting to be resisted. Their complete monopoly of legal knowledge appears to have enabled them to put off on the world collections, not so much of the rules actually observed as of the rules which the priestly order considered proper to be observed. The Hindoo Code, called the Laws of Manu, which is certainly a Brahmin compilation, undoubtedly enshrines many genuine observances of the Hindoo race, but the opinion of the best contemporary orientalists is, that it does not, as a whole, represent a set of rules ever actually administered in Hindostan. It is, in great part, an ideal picture of that which, in the view of the Brahmins, *ought* to be the law. It is consistent with human nature and with the special motives of their authors.

that codes like that of Manu should pretend to
the highest antiquity and claim to have emanated
in their complete form from the Deity. Manu,
according to Hindoo mythology, is an emanation
from the supreme God; but the compilation
which bears his name, though its exact date is
not easily discovered, is, in point of the relative
progress of Hindoo jurisprudence, a recent pro-
duction.

Among the chief advantages which the Twelve
Tables and similar codes conferred on the societies
which obtained them, was the protection which
they afforded against the frauds of the privileged
oligarchy and also against the spontaneous deprava-
tion and debasement of the national institutions.
The Roman Code was merely an enunciation in
words of the existing customs of the Roman
people. Relatively to the progress of the Romans
in civilisation, it was a remarkably early code, and
it was published at a time when Roman society
had barely emerged from that intellectual condition in which civil obligation and religious duty
are inevitably confounded. Now a barbarous
society practising a body of customs, is exposed
to some especial dangers which may be absolutely
fatal to its progress in civilisation. The usages
which a particular community is found to have
adopted in its infancy and in its primitive seats
are generally those which are on the whole best
suited to promote its physical and moral well-
being; and, if they are retained in their integrity
until new social wants have taught new practices,
the upward march of society is almost certain.
But unhappily there is a law of development which

ever threatens to operate upon unwritten usage.
The customs are of course obeyed by multitudes
who are incapable of understanding the true
ground of their expediency, and who are therefore
left inevitably to invent superstitious reasons for
their permanence. A process then commences
which may be shortly described by saying that
usage which is reasonable generates usage which
is unreasonable. Analogy, the most valuable of
instruments in the maturity of jurisprudence, is
the most dangerous of snares in its infancy. Pro-
hibitions and ordinances, originally confined, for
good reasons, to a single description of acts, are
made to apply to all acts of the same class, because
a man menaced with the anger of the gods for
doing one thing, feels a natural terror in doing
any other thing which is remotely like it. After
one kind of food has been interdicted for sanitary
reasons, the prohibition is extended to all food
resembling it, though the resemblance occasionally
depends on analogies the most fanciful. So again,
a wise provision for insuring general cleanliness
dictates in time long routines of ceremonial
ablution ; and that division into classes which at
a particular crisis of social history is necessary
for the maintenance of the national existence
degenerates into the most disastrous and blighting
of all human institutions—Caste. The fate of the
Hindoo law is, in fact, the measure of the value of
the Roman Code. Ethnology shows us that the
Romans and the Hindoos sprang from the same
original stock, and there is indeed a striking resemblance between what appear to have been
their original customs. Even now, Hindoo juris-

prudence has a substratum of forethought and
sound judgment, but irrational imitation has
engrafted in it an immense apparatus of cruel
absurdities. From these corruptions the Romans
were protected by their code. It was compiled
while usage was still wholesome, and a hundred
years afterwards it might have been too late.
The Hindoo law has been to a great extent embodied in writing, but, ancient as in one sense are
the compendia which still exist in Sanskrit, they
contain ample evidence that they were drawn up
after the mischief had been done. We are not of
course entitled to say that if the Twelve Tables
had not been published the Romans would have
been condemned to a civilisation as feeble and
perverted as that of the Hindoos, but thus much
at least is certain, that *with* their code they were
exempt from the very chance of so unhappy a
destiny.

NOTE A

ANTIQUITY OF ROMAN LAW

THE description of Roman law, in the preface to the first
edition, as "bearing in its earlier portions the traces of the most
remote antiquity," is literally correct unless, contrary to the
usage of good authors, we press the superlative to its extreme
construction, as if it had been meant to exclude the possibility
that traces of still more remote antiquity may be found elsewhere.
Maine obviously did not mean to deny that Germanic and Hindu
law, for example, have at some points preserved more archaic
features than those of the earliest Roman law known to us;
much less to disparage the extremely modern character of classical
Roman law, which gives it most of its value for modern jurisprudence: compare the passage cited from "Early Law and
Custom" in Note F below. It may be still a natural temptation
for a student unacquainted with other legal antiquities to suppose

that the law of the Twelve Tables, or the law of the later Roman Republic as a whole, belongs to a more archaic type than it really does. Fifty years ago the temptation was almost inevitable; and we have to remember that Maine had been endeavouring, with indifferent success at the time, to revive the study of Roman law in a country where the educated public was in a state of absolute ignorance on the subject (as it probably still is), and the tradition of the civilians, confined, under the old division of jurisdictions and practice, to a small minority of the legal profession, was at least a century out of date. If Maine did use language tending to exaggerate the intrinsic merits and the practical importance of Roman jurisprudence, it was under those conditions a fault on the right side. But modern students must be warned not to assume that Roman law was in fact at any one time a perfect and symmetrical whole, or that its history can be deduced from any one formula. The Twelve Tables were no doubt regarded as an ultimate source of law for the field they covered, but they did not purport to include the whole of the recognised customary law. For the classical period of the Empire the most important and fruitful written embodiment of law was the Prætor's Edict, as almost every title of the Digest bears witness. Moreover, the Twelve Tables themselves were no mere consolidation, but a reforming code. It is certain that they incorporated Greek materials, and it is of very little importance whether the story of a special commission being sent to Greece is literally acceptable or not. In any case the means of information were at hand in the Greek cities of southern Italy, a region where the Greek language is not yet extinct. Borrowing of this kind from neighbours who have reached a more advanced stage is by no means abnormal in archaic legislation. Indeed, it is rather common for the lawgiver of the heroic age to be represented as a stranger, or as having learnt the wisdom of older and greater kingdoms; and even if the personal element of such a tradition is dubious, it is not likely to be a gratuitous invention. Ingenious paradoxical doubts have quite lately been cast on the antiquity of the Twelve Tables; but the hypothesis that they are really a compilation or fabrication of the second century B.C. has not met with a favourable reception: see Dr. A. H. J. Greenidge, "The Authenticity of the Twelve Tables," English Historical Review, January, 1905, and Professor Goudy in the Juridical Review, June, 1905. It is perhaps unnecessary to warn English students against implicit acceptance of the conjectural restorations of the Decemvirs' work essayed by various learned persons. The most elaborate of these, that of Voigt, is described by the no less learned M. Girard as containing "une restitution tout à fait inacceptable et un commentaire fort aventureux" (Manuel élémentaire du droit romain, 3ᵉ éd., 1901,

p. 23). Dr. Roby ("Roman Private Law in the Times of Cicero and of the Antonines," 1902, vol. i., p. x) calls it in even plainer terms a house of cards.

NOTE B

CUSTOMARY LAW IN HOMER

Maine's reference to the Homeric poems as some of our best evidence for the archaic forms of legal ideas in Indo-European communities is a brilliant example of his insight. As he points out, the poet or poets had no conscious theory of the matter at all, and this is our best warranty for the witness of the poems being true. They describe a society in which custom is understood if not always observed, positive duties are definable if not easily enforceable, and judgments are rendered with solemnity and regarded as binding, although we hear nothing of any standing authority such as could be called either legislative or executive in the modern sense. And Maine is clearly right in holding (p. 2) that the description is not wholly idealised—we might even say not much—and is of a state of society known to the writer. To all appearance the usages described are real, and those of the singer's own time. The deliberate archaism of modern fiction has no place in Homer; only the wealth and prowess of the heroic age are exaggerated. The Chanson de Roland endows Charlemagne and his peers with the arms and manners of the twelfth century, as the Arthurian cycle attributes those of the fourteenth to the knights of the Round Table; and we cannot believe that Homer did otherwise.

Maine gives a hint (p. 6) that the analysis of positive law laid down by Bentham and Austin (following Hobbes, though Bentham seems not to have been aware of it) cannot be made to fit archaic society. For in communities like those of the Homeric age, or of Iceland as described in the Sagas, there is no sovereign (in Hobbes's sense) to be found, nor any legislative command, nor any definite sanction; and yet in Iceland there were regularly constituted courts with a regular and even technical procedure, as the Njáls Saga tells us at large. Maine afterwards worked out this position in the lectures on Sovereignty in "The Early History of Institutions," which are the foundation of sound modern criticism on the Hobbist doctrine. In those classical pages he dealt rather tenderly with Bentham and Austin, whom to some extent he regarded as his masters, in spite of the wholly unhistorical character of their work; and, apart from any particular feeling in this case, it was not his habit to exhibit the full consequences of his ideas. Those who come after him are free to push the conclusion home, as Mr. Bryce has done ("Studies in History and

Jurisprudence," Essay X). As to the absence of executive sanction in archaic procedure, cp. "Early Law and Custom," p. 170.

With regard to the "Themistes" of the Homeric chiefs, the word appears to be not an anomalous plural of θέμις, but distinct, and to mean principles of law or justice; "Themis," the singular noun, being "right" in the abstract sense (E. C. Clark, "Practical Jurisprudence," pp. 42-9). Once it means "tribute," which does not offer much difficulty when compared with the constant use of *consuetudo* in medieval Latin. Some of the language used here by Maine seems to imply that the decisions called by this name were or might be arbitrary; but Maine himself added the desirable qualification in his chapter on "The King and Early Civil Justice." "The Homeric King is chiefly busy with fighting. But he is also a judge, and it is to be observed that he has no assessors. His sentences come directly into his mind by divine dictation from on high." That is, if the king is just; we read in the Iliad, though it occurs only in the course of a simile, of unjust kings who give crooked judgments, disregarding the voice of the gods:

> Ὡς δ' ὑπὸ λαίλαπι πᾶσα κελαίνη βέβριθε χθὼν
> ἤματ' ὀπωρινῷ, ὅτε λαβρότατον χέει ὕδωρ
> Ζεύς, ὅτε δή ῥ' ἀνδρεσσι κοτεσσάμενος χαλεπήνῃ,
> οἳ βίῃ εἰν ἀγορῇ σκολιὰς κρίνωσι θέμιστας,
> ἐκ δὲ δίκην ἐλάσωσι, θεῶν ὄπιν οὐκ ἀλέγοντες . . .
>
> Π. 384 sqq.

"These sentences, or θέμιστες—which is the same word with our "Teutonic word 'dooms'—*are doubtless drawn from pre-existing custom or usage*, but the notion is that they are conceived by the king spontaneously or through divine prompting. It is plainly a later development of the same view when the prompting comes from a learned lawyer, or from an authoritative law-book" ("Early Law and Custom," p. 163).

Custom, indeed, is so strong in Homer that the gods themselves are bound by it. Zeus is the greatest of chiefs, but he owes justice to his people, and justice implies the observance of rule. Power is not wanting, but a sense of duty moderates it. Thus in the Iliad Zeus is tempted to rescue Sarpedon from his fate, but dares not break his custom in the face of Hera's rebuke ("Do it if thou wilt: but the rest of the gods in no wise approve": Π. 443): and in the Odyssey the Sun-God threatens to go down and shine among the dead men if he is not to be avenged for the sacrilege of Odysseus' men who have killed and eaten his oxen :—

> Ζεῦ πάτερ ἠδ' ἄλλοι μάκαρες θεοὶ αἰὲν ἐόντες,
> τῖσαι δὴ ἑτάρους Λαερτιάδεω 'Οδυσῆος,
> οἳ μευ βοῦς ἔκτειναν ὑπέρβιον, ᾗσιν ἐγώ γε
> χαίρεσκον μὲν ἰὼν εἰς οὐρανὸν ἀστερόεντα,
> ἠδ' ὁπότ' ἂψ ἐπὶ γαῖαν ἀπ' οὐρανόθεν προτραποίμην.
> εἰ δέ μοι οὐ τίσουσι βοῶν ἐπιεικέ' ἀμοιβήν,
> δύσομαι εἰς 'Αΐδαο καὶ ἐν νεκύεσσι φαείνω.
>
> μ. 377 sqq.

NOTE C

EARLY FORMS OF LAW: "WRITTEN" AND "UNWRITTEN" LAW: EARLY CODES

It should be noted that the growth of institutions is much too complicated, even if we confine our attention to one society, to be represented as a simple series in order of time. We constantly speak of one rule or custom as belonging to a more advanced stage of ideas than another; but this does not mean that in every society where it is found it must have been preceded in fact by a less advanced institution belonging to the next lower grade of culture. Imitation of neighbours or conquerors, or peculiar local conditions, may materially shorten a given stage in the normal development, or even cut it out altogether. What we do mean is that the order is not found reversed. Chalk is not everywhere in England, nor red sandstone; but where red sandstone is, we know that chalk is not below it. Iron was known in Africa so early that Africa may be said not to have had a bronze age; but this does not make it more credible that any tribe should ever have abandoned iron for bronze. In like manner there may have been tribes that had lawgivers almost or quite as soon as they had judges. But no one has heard of a nation which, having acquired a body of legislation, reverted from it to pure customary law (cp. Kohler, "Zur Urgeschichte der Ehe," pp. 7–10).

A king's or chieftain's judicial dooms are very different from express laws promulgated for general observance; but it is noticeable that early traditions ascribe a divine origin to both. In the former case the judge enjoys, in some undefined way, the confidence of the gods; in the latter the human lawgiver is merely the scribe or reporter of a "Deity dictating an entire code or body of law," which, as Maine points out (above, p. 5), is a more artificial conception and belongs to a later stage. It appears, however, as early as anything that can be called legislation; and the tendency to refer the commandments of the law to a divine or semi-divine origin is quite regular. There is no reason, it may be added, why a lawgiver or recorder of divine law should not also be a speaker of dooms. A ruling ascribed to Moses, whom Sir Edward Coke claimed as the first law reporter, is at this day a practical decision, for it governs the civil law of succession in some Jewish communities (such as the Jews of Aden: Sir Courtenay Ilbert, "The Government of India," p. 397). Even if the Mosaic law has to admit the superior antiquity of King Hammurabi's code, we may safely say that the case of Zelophehad's daughters is the earliest recorded case which is still of authority.

When the king or chief ceases to bear all offices in his own person, and the political division of labour begins, those functions which had a sacred character naturally become attached to a priesthood or sacred tribe or family, and among them the custody and interpretation of the law. The distinction between religious and secular law is, one need hardly say, much later. Thus we find in both Germanic and Roman antiquity more than traces of priests, or nobles who claimed the priest's office as a birthright, being the first judges (Grimm, "D.R.A." 272, i. 378 in 4th ed.). In Iceland the rather vague but not ineffectual authority which was ascribed to the Speaker of the Law seems to have had a religious character. At any rate we read in the Njáls Saga that to him, and him alone, was left the momentous decision of the question, which had all but led to civil war, whether Christianity should be adopted (Dasent, "Burut Njal," ch. ci.). There seems to be no reason against accepting this incident as mainly historical. It is worth observing that Thorgeir would not make his award until both the Christian and the heathen party had given pledges to abide by it: a striking illustration of the voluntary and arbitral character of early jurisdiction. Edward I. of England, more than two centuries later, used similar precaution when he adjudicated on the claims to the crown of Scotland.

Whether a monopoly of legal knowledge is established in the hands of a privileged caste or order, or a tradition of learning is handed down in something like a school, or, without any profession of secrecy, certain persons enjoy for the time being the reputation of superior knowledge, appears to depend on the particular circumstances of each community. Besides the Speaker of the Law, we find in the Iceland of the Sagas a few specially wise men, Njál himself, and after his death one or two others, whose advice is eagerly sought by their neighbours, and whose deliberate opinion is almost conclusive; yet there is no possible distinction of race or rank in that singularly homogeneous republic. A like position is ascribed to Nestor. This kind of reputation is obviously not less but more important in a society where jurisdiction and judicial power have not yet become compulsory; for the chances that any judgment or award will be observed will, in such a society, depend largely on the respect in which the acting judge or daysman is held.

Maine adds that law preserved as a kind of trade secret by a privileged class is the only real unwritten law. This may be literally true. But our current professional use of the term is really a matter of literary convention. We find it useful to confine the term "written law" to an enactment or declaration which is authoritative not only in matter but in form, so that its very words not only contain but constitute the law. An exposition whose very words are not binding is "unwritten law," however great its authority may be in substance. Consider the case of a judge in England, or any other jurisdiction under the system of the Common Law, making a careful statement of some point of law in a book written and published by him. This is only a private learned opinion, and has, properly speaking, no authority at all. But the same or another judge may adopt the statement in a reported judgment. It then acquires authority as a judicial exposition of the law, but still its actual terms are not binding, and it counts as "unwritten law." Finally, the proposition may be embodied in a statute. It then becomes " written law," and the Courts will have for the future to treat not only the substance but every word of it as authentic. The distinction is quite real, and no better way of expressing it has been found. French usage, moreover, presents a close analogy. Under the old monarchy the provinces of written law (*pays de droit écrit*) were those where the texts of Roman law were received as having binding authority, while in the *pays de droit coutumier* they were cited only for example and illustration, on the merits of the reason embodied in them, as they may be and sometimes are in England. Thus the same text might be "written" law in one province and "unwritten" (though there is no corresponding French term) in another. A learned modern writer says of the antithesis between *ius scriptum* and *ius non scriptum*, after careful examination of the various meanings with which they occur in the writings of the classical Roman lawyers: "Its general practical use with them is as a distinction between customary law, on the one hand, and law drawn up and issued in any regular manner by any legislative authority, on the other. . . . The above is also the practical use of the distinction . . . by our English jurists, so far as they use it at all. . . . With modern Continental writers *written* and *unwritten* in general designate respectively *enacted* and *customary* law " (E. C. Clark, " Practical Jurisprudence," p. 272).

Maine's brief remarks on early codes (above, pp. 12-18) include a few sentences on Hindu law; these were written at a time when the existence of the books called by the names of Manu and Narada was hardly known outside Anglo-Indian official circles except to a few students of Sanskrit. In later years, after having been a member of the Government of India, he returned to the subject. The chapters in " Early Law and Custom " on " The Sacred Laws of the Hindus," " Religion in Law," and "Classifications of Legal Rules," should be read accordingly as a supplement; and the second and third lectures in " Village Communities " should also be consulted as to the general nature of archaic customary law, and the effect produced on it by contact with a modern system.

An entirely new light has been thrown on the early history of written law by the discovery of Hammurabi's Babylonian code; an extensive, practical, and mainly secular code which dates from considerably more than two thousand years before the Christian era, which seems to presuppose even earlier authentic dooms

committed to writing, and which refers to conveyancing documents
as in common use (English translation by C. H. W. Johns, Edinb.
1903). Less striking, but still of importance, are the Tables of
Gortyn in Crete, discovered in 1884. They are later than the Roman
Twelve Tables, but preserved in an authentic and not much muti-
lated inscription. See Dr. H. J. Roby thereon, with translation,
L.Q.R. ii. 135.

Timely codification of customs, as Maine observes (pp. 14, 15),
may prevent degradation; I must confess that the ascription of
such an effect to the Twelve Tables, though ingenious and pleasing
as a conjecture, appears to me to go beyond what is warranted
by our knowledge of the state and tendencies of Roman society
under the earlier Republic. It is certain that conversely the fixing
of law in a codified form at a later stage may arrest a normal and
scientific development. Such was the result of the Ordinance
which stereotyped the French law of negotiable instruments in 1673
(Chalmers, " Bills of Exchange," Introduction, p. lvi). It would seem,
indeed, that the Twelve Tables themselves went near to stereotype
an archaic and formalist procedure, and that the Romans of later
generations escaped from great inconvenience only by the devices
of legal fictions and equity which Maine considers in the following
chapter.

CHAPTER II

LEGAL FICTIONS

WHEN primitive law has once been embodied in a Code, there is an end to what may be called its spontaneous development. Henceforward the changes effected in it, if effected at all, are effected deliberately and from without. It is impossible to suppose that the customs of any race or tribe remained unaltered during the whole of the long —in some instances the immense—interval between their declaration by a patriarchal monarch and their publication in writing. It would be unsafe too to affirm that no part of the alteration was effected deliberately. But from the little we know of the progress of law during this period, we are justified in assuming that set purpose had the very smallest share in producing change. Such innovations on the earliest usages as disclose themselves appear to have been dictated by feelings and modes of thought which, under our present mental conditions, we are unable to comprehend. A new era begins, however, with the Codes. Wherever, after this epoch, we trace the course of legal modification, we are able to attribute it to the conscious desire of improvement, or at all events of compassing objects other than those which were aimed at in the primitive times.

It may seem at first sight that no general propositions worth trusting can be elicited from the history of legal systems subsequent to the codes. The field is too vast. We cannot be sure that we have included a sufficient number of phenomena in our observations, or that we accurately understand those which we have observed. But the undertaking will be seen to be more feasible, if we consider that after the epoch of codes the distinction between stationary and progressive societies begins to make itself felt. It is only with the progressive societies that we are concerned, and nothing is more remarkable than their extreme fewness. In spite of overwhelming evidence, it is most difficult for a citizen of Western Europe to bring thoroughly home to himself the truth that the civilisation which surrounds him is a rare exception in the history of the world. The tone of thought common among us, all our hopes, fears, and speculations, would be materially affected, if we had vividly before us the relation of the progressive races to the totality of human life. It is indisputable that much the greatest part of mankind has never shown a particle of desire that its civil institutions should be improved since the moment when external completeness was first given to them by their embodiment in some permanent record. One set of usages has occasionally been violently overthrown and superseded by another; here and there a primitive code, pretending to a supernatural origin, has been greatly extended, and distorted into the most surprising forms, by the perversity of sacerdotal commentators; but, except in a small section of the world, there has been nothing like the gradual amelioration of a legal system. There has been material civilisation, but, instead of the civilisation expanding the law, the law has limited the civilisation. The study of races in their primitive condition affords us some clue to the point at which the development of certain societies has stopped. We can see that Brahminical India has not passed beyond a stage which occurs in the history of all the families of mankind, the stage at which a rule of law is not yet discriminated from a rule of religion. The members of such a society consider that the transgression of a religious ordinance should be punished by civil penalties, and that the violation of a civil duty exposes the delinquent to divine correction. In China this point has been passed, but progress seems to have been there arrested, because the civil laws are co-extensive with all the ideas of which the race is capable. The difference between the stationary and progressive societies is, however, one of the great secrets which inquiry has yet to penetrate. Among partial explanations of it I venture to place the considerations urged at the end of the last chapter. It may further be remarked that no one is likely to succeed in the investigation who does not clearly realise that the stationary condition of the human race is the rule, the progressive the exception. And another indispensable condition of success is an accurate knowledge of Roman law in all its principal stages. The Roman jurisprudence has the longest known history of any set of human institutions. The character of all the changes which it underwent is tolerably well ascertained. From its commencement to its close, it was progressively modified for the better, or for what the authors of the modification conceived to be the better, and the course of improvement was continued through periods at which all the rest of human thought and action materially slackened its pace, and repeatedly threatened to settle down into stagnation.

I confine myself in what follows to the progressive societies. With respect to them it may be laid down that social necessities and social opinion are always more or less in advance of Law. We may come indefinitely near to the closing of the gap between them, but it has a perpetual tendency to reopen. Law is stable ; the societies we are speaking of are progressive. The greater or less happiness of a people depends on the degree of promptitude with which the gulf is narrowed.

A general proposition of some value may be advanced with respect to the agencies by which Law is brought into harmony with society. These instrumentalities seem to me to be three in number, Legal Fictions, Equity, and Legislation. Their historical order is that in which I have placed them. Sometimes two of them will be seen operating together, and there are legal systems which have escaped the influence of one or other of them. But I know of no instance in which the order of their appearance has been changed or inverted. The early history of one of them, Equity, is universally obscure, and hence it may be thought by some that certain isolated statutes, reformatory of the civil law, are older than any equitable jurisdiction. My own belief is that remedial Equity is everywhere older than remedial Legislation ; but, should this be not strictly true, it would only be necessary to limit the proposition respecting their order of sequence to the periods at which they exercised a sustained and substantial influence in transforming the original law.

I employ the word " fiction " in a sense considerably wider than that in which English lawyers are accustomed to use it, and with a meaning much more extensive than that which belonged to the Roman " fictiones." Fictio, in old Roman law, is properly a term of pleading, and signifies a false averment on the part of the plaintiff which the defendant was not allowed to traverse ; such, for example, as an averment that the plaintiff was a Roman citizen, when in truth he was a foreigner. The object of these " fictiones " was, of course, to give jurisdiction, and they therefore strongly resembled the allegations in the writs of the English Queen's Bench and Exchequer, by which those courts contrived to usurp the jurisdiction of the Common Pleas :—the allegation that the defendant was in custody of the king's marshal, or that the plaintiff was the king's debtor, and could not pay his debt by reason of the defendant's default. But now I employ the expression " Legal Fiction " to signify any assumption which conceals, or affects to conceal, the fact that a rule of law has undergone alteration its letter remaining unchanged, its operation being modified. The words, therefore, include the instances of fictions which I have cited from the English and Roman law, but they embrace much more, for I should speak both of the English Case-law and of the Roman Responsa Prudentium as resting on fictions. Both these examples will be examined presently. The *fact* is in both cases that the law has been wholly changed; the *fiction* is that it remains what it always was. It is not difficult to understand why fictions in all their forms are particularly congenial to the infancy of society. They satisfy the desire for improvement, which is not quite wanting, at the same time that they do not offend the superstitious disrelish for change which is always present. At a particular stage of social progress they are invaluable expedients for overcoming the rigidity of law, and, indeed, without one of them, the Fiction of Adoption which permits the family tie to be artificially created, it is difficult to understand how society would ever have escaped from its swaddling-clothes, and taken its first steps towards civilisation. We must, therefore, not suffer ourselves to be affected by the ridicule which Bentham pours on legal fictions wherever he meets them. To revile them as merely fraudulent is to betray ignorance of their peculiar office in the historical development of law. But at the same time it would be equally foolish to agree with those theorists who, discerning that fictions have had their uses, argue that they ought to be stereotyped in our system. There are several Fictions still exercising powerful influence on English jurisprudence which could not be discarded without a severe shock to the ideas, and considerable change in the language, of English practitioners ; but there can be no doubt of the general truth that it is unworthy of us to effect an admittedly beneficial object by so rude a device as a legal fiction. I cannot admit any anomaly to be innocent, which makes the law either more difficult to understand or harder to arrange in harmonious order. Now, among other disadvantages, legal fictions are the greatest of obstacles to symmetrical classification. The rule of law remains sticking in the system, but it is a mere shell. It has been long ago undermined, and a new rule hides itself under its cover. Hence there is at once a difficulty in knowing whether the rule which is actually operative should be classed in its true or in its apparent place, and minds of different casts will differ as to the branch of the alternative which ought to be selected. If the English law is ever to assume an orderly distribution, it will be necessary to prune away the legal fictions which, in spite of some recent legislative improvements, are still abundant in it.

The next instrumentality by which the adaptation of law to social wants is carried on I call Equity, meaning by that word any body of rules existing by the side of the original civil law, founded on distinct principles and claiming incidentally to supersede the civil law in virtue of a superior sanctity inherent in those principles. The Equity whether of the Roman Prætors or of the English Chancellors, differs from the Fictions which in each case preceded it, in that the inter-

ference with law is open and avowed. On the
other hand, it differs from Legislation, the agent
of legal improvement which comes after it, in
that its claim to authority is grounded, not on
the prerogative of any external person or body,
not even on that of the magistrate who enunciates
it, but on the special nature of its principles, to
which it is alleged that all law ought to conform.
The very conception of a set of principles, invested
with a higher sacredness than those of the original
law and demanding application independently
of the consent of any external body, belongs to
a much more advanced stage of thought than
that to which legal fictions originally suggested
themselves.

Legislation, the enactments of a legislature
which, whether it take the form of an autocratic
prince or of a parliamentary assembly, is the
assumed organ of the entire society, is the last of
the ameliorating instrumentalities. It differs from
Legal Fictions just as Equity differs from them,
and it is also distinguished from Equity, as
deriving its authority from an external body or
person. Its obligatory force is independent of
its principles. The legislature, whatever be the
actual restraints imposed on it by public opinion,
is in theory empowered to impose what obligations it pleases on the members of the community.
There is nothing to prevent its legislating in the
wantonness of caprice. Legislation may be dictated by equity, if that last word be used to
indicate some standard of right and wrong to
which its enactments happen to be adjusted;
but then these enactments are indebted for their

3

binding force to the authority of the legislature
and not to that of the principles on which the
legislature acted ; and thus they differ from rules
of Equity, in the technical sense of the word,
which pretend to a paramount sacredness entitling
them at once to the recognition of the courts even
without the concurrence of prince or parliamentary
assembly. It is the more necessary to note these
differences, because a student of Bentham would
be apt to confound Fictions, Equity, and Statute
Law under the single head of Legislation. They
all, he would say, involve *law-making* ; they
differ only in respect of the machinery by which
the new law is produced. That is perfectly true,
and we must never forget it ; but it furnishes no
reason why we should deprive ourselves of so
convenient a term as Legislation in the special
sense. Legislation and Equity are disjoined in
the popular mind and in the minds of most
lawyers ; and it will never do to neglect the
distinction between them, however conventional,
when important practical consequences follow
from it.

It would be easy to select from almost any
regularly developed body of rules examples of
legal fictions, which at once betray their true
character to the modern observer. In the two
instances which I proceed to consider, the nature
of the expedient employed is not so readily detected. The first authors of these fictions did not
perhaps intend to innovate, certainly did not wish
to be suspected of innovating. There are, moreover, and always have been, persons who refuse
to see any fiction in the process, and conventional

language bears out their refusal. No examples, therefore, can be better calculated to illustrate the wide diffusion of legal fictions, and the efficiency with which they perform their twofold office of transforming a system of laws and of concealing the transformation.

We in England are well accustomed to the extension, modification, and improvement of law by a machinery which, in theory, is incapable of altering one jot or one line of existing jurisprudence. The process by which this virtual legislation is effected is not so much insensible as unacknowledged. With respect to that great portion of our legal system which is enshrined in cases and recorded in law reports, we habitually employ a double language, and entertain, as it would appear, a double and inconsistent set of ideas. When a group of facts comes before an English Court for adjudication, the whole course of the discussion between the judge and the advocates assumes that no question is, or can be, raised which will call for the application of any principles but old ones, or of any distinctions but such as have long since been allowed. It is taken absolutely for granted that there is somewhere a rule of known law which will cover the facts of the dispute now litigated, and that, if such a rule be not discovered, it is only that the necessary patience, knowledge, or acumen is not forthcoming to detect it. Yet the moment the judgment had been rendered and reported, we slide unconsciously or unavowedly into a new language and a new train of thought. We now admit that the new decision *has* modified the law. The rules applicable have, to use the

very inaccurate expression sometimes employed,
become more elastic. In fact they have been
changed. A clear addition has been made to the
precedents, and the canon of law elicited by comparing the precedents is not the same with that
which would have been obtained if the series of
cases had been curtailed by a single example.
The fact that the old rule has been repealed, and
that a new one has replaced it, eludes us, because
we are not in the habit of throwing into precise
language the legal formulas which we derive from
the precedents, so that a change in their tenor is
not easily detected unless it is violent and glaring.
I shall not now pause to consider at length the
causes which have led English lawyers to acquiesce
in these curious anomalies. Probably it will be
found that originally it was the received doctrine
that somewhere, *in nubibus* or *in gremio magis-
tratuum*, there existed a complete, coherent, symmetrical body of English law, of an amplitude
sufficient to furnish principles which would apply
to any conceivable combination of circumstances.
The theory was at first much more thoroughly
believed in than it is now, and indeed it may have
had a better foundation. The judges of the
thirteenth century may have really had at their
command a mine of law unrevealed to the bar
and to the lay-public, for there is some reason for
suspecting that in secret they borrowed freely,
though not always wisely, from current compendia
of the Roman and Canon laws. But that store-
house was closed as soon as the points decided
at Westminster Hall became numerous enough
to supply a basis for a substantive system of

jurisprudence ; and now for centuries English practitioners have so expressed themselves as to convey the paradoxical proposition that, except by Equity and Statute law, nothing has been added to the basis since it was first constituted. We do not admit that our tribunals legislate ; we imply that they have never legislated ; and yet we maintain that the rules of the English common law, with some assistance from the Court of Chancery and from Parliament, are coextensive with the complicated interests of modern society.

A body of law bearing a very close and very instructive resemblance to our case-law in those particulars which I have noticed, was known to the Romans under the name of the Responsa Prudentium, the "answers of the learned in the law." The form of these Responses varied a good deal at different periods of the Roman jurisprudence, but throughout its whole course they consisted of explanatory glosses on authoritative written documents, and at first they were exclusively collections of opinions interpretative of the Twelve Tables. As with us, all legal language adjusted itself to the assumption that the text of the old Code remained unchanged. There was the express rule. It overrode all glosses and comments, and no one openly admitted that any interpretation of it, however eminent the interpreter, was safe from revision on appeal to the venerable texts. Yet in point of fact, Books of Responses bearing the names of leading jurisconsults obtained an authority at least equal to that of our reported cases, and constantly modified, extended, limited, or practically overruled the provisions of the Decemviral law. The authors of the new jurisprudence during the whole progress of its formation professed the most sedulous respect for the letter of the Code. They were merely explaining it, deciphering it, bringing out its full meaning ; but then, in the result, by piecing texts together, by adjusting the law to states of fact which actually presented themselves and by speculating on its possible application to others which might occur, by introducing principles of interpretation derived from the exegesis of other written documents which fell under their observation, they educed a vast variety of canons which had never been dreamed of by the compilers of the Twelve Tables and which were in truth rarely or never to be found there. All these treatises of the jurisconsults claimed respect on the ground of their assumed conformity with the Code, but their comparative authority depended on the reputation of the particular jurisconsults who gave them to the world. Any name of universally acknowledged greatness clothed a Book of Responses with a binding force hardly less than that which belonged to enactments of the legislature ; and such a book in its turn constituted a new foundation on which a further body of jurisprudence might rest. The responses of the early lawyers were not however published, in the modern sense, by their author. They were recorded and edited by his pupils, and were not therefore in all probability arranged according to any scheme of classification. The part of the students in these publications must be carefully noted, because the service they rendered to their teacher seems to have been generally repaid by his sedulous attention to the pupils' education. The educational treatises called Institutes or Commentaries, which are a later fruit of the duty then recognised, are among the most remarkable features of the Roman system. It was apparently in these Institutional works, and not in the books intended for trained lawyers, that the jurisconsults gave to the public their classifications and their proposals for modifying and improving the technical phraseology.

In comparing the Roman Responsa Prudentium with their nearest English counterpart, it must be carefully borne in mind that the authority by which this part of the Roman jurisprudence was expounded was not the *bench*, but the *bar*. The decision of a Roman tribunal, though conclusive in the particular case, had no ulterior authority except such as was given by the professional repute of the magistrate who happened to be in office for the time. Properly speaking, there was no institution at Rome during the republic analogous to the English Bench, the Chambers of Imperial Germany, or the Parliaments of Monarchical France. There were magistrates indeed, invested with momentous judicial functions in their several departments, but the tenure of the magistracies was but for a single year, so that they are much less aptly compared to a permanent judicature than to a cycle of offices briskly circulating among the leaders of the bar. Much might be said on the origin of a condition of things which looks to us like a startling anomaly, but which was in fact much more congenial than our own system to the spirit of ancient societies, tending, as they always did, to split into distinct orders which, however exclusive themselves, tolerated no professional hierarchy above them.

It is remarkable that this system did not produce certain effects which might on the whole have been expected from it. It did not, for example, *popularise* the Roman law,—it did not, as in some of the Greek republics, lessen the effort of intellect required for the mastery of science, although its diffusion and authoritative exposition were opposed by no artificial barriers. On the contrary, if it had not been for the operation of a separate set of causes, there were strong probabilities that the Roman jurisprudence would have become as minute, technical, and difficult as any system which has since prevailed. Again, a consequence which might still more naturally have been looked for, does not appear at any time to have exhibited itself. The jurisconsults, until the liberties of Rome were overthrown, formed a class which was quite undefined and must have fluctuated greatly in numbers ; nevertheless, there does not seem to have existed a doubt as to the particular individuals whose opinion, in their generation, was conclusive on the cases submitted to them. The vivid pictures of a leading jurisconsult's daily practice which abound in Latin literature—the clients from the country flocking to his antechamber in the early morning, and the students standing round with their note-books to record the great lawyer's replies—are seldom or never identified at any given period with more than one or two conspicuous names. Owing too to the direct contact of the client and the advocate, the Roman people itself seems to have been always alive to the rise and fall of professional reputation, and there is abundance of proof, more particularly in the well-known oration of Cicero, "Pro Muræna," that the reverence of the commons for forensic success was apt to be excessive rather than deficient.

We cannot doubt that the peculiarities which have been noted in the instrumentality by which the development of the Roman law was first effected, were the source of its characteristic excellence, its early wealth in principles. The growth and exuberance of principle was fostered, in part, by the competition among the expositors of the law, an influence wholly unknown where there exists a Bench, the depositaries intrusted by king or commonwealth with the prerogative of justice. But the chief agency, no doubt, was the uncontrolled multiplication of cases for legal decision. The state of facts which caused genuine perplexity to a country client was not a whit more entitled to form the basis of the jurisconsult's Response, or legal decision, than a set of hypothetical circumstances propounded by an ingenious pupil. All combinations of fact were on precisely the same footing, whether they were real or imaginary. It was nothing to the jurisconsult that his opinion was overruled for the moment by the magistrate who adjudicated on his client's case, unless that magistrate happened to rank above him in legal knowledge or the esteem of his profession. I do not, indeed, mean it to be inferred that he would wholly omit to consider his client's advantage, for the client was

in earlier times the great lawyer's constituent and
at a later period his paymaster, but the main road
to the rewards of ambition lay through the good
opinion of his order, and it is obvious that under
such a system as I have been describing this was
much more likely to be secured by viewing each
case as an illustration of a great principle, or an
exemplification of a broad rule, than by merely
shaping it for an insulated forensic triumph.   It
is evident that powerful influence must have been
exercised by the want of any distinct check on
the suggestion or invention of possible questions.
Where the data can be multiplied at pleasure, the
facilities for evolving a general rule are immensely
increased.   As the law is administered among
ourselves, the judge cannot travel out of the sets
of facts exhibited before him or before his predecessors.   Accordingly each group of circumstances which is adjudicated upon receives, to
employ a Gallicism, a sort of consecration.   It
acquires certain qualities which distinguish it
from every other case genuine or hypothetical.
But at Rome, as I have attempted to explain,
there was nothing resembling a Bench or Chamber
of judges ; and therefore no combination of facts
possessed any particular value more than another.
When a difficulty came for opinion before the
jurisconsult, there was nothing to prevent a person
endowed with a nice perception of analogy from
at once proceeding to adduce and consider an
entire class of supposed questions with which a
particular feature connected it.   Whatever were
the practical advice given to the client, the
responsum treasured up in the note-books of

listening pupils would doubtless contemplate the circumstances as governed by a great principle, or included in a sweeping rule. Nothing like this has ever been possible among ourselves, and it should be acknowledged that in many criticisms passed on the English law the manner in which it has been enunciated seems to have been lost sight of. The hesitation of our courts in declaring principles may be much more reasonably attributed to the comparative scantiness of our precedents, voluminous as they appear to him who is acquainted with no other system, than to the temper of our judges. It is true that in the wealth of legal principle we are considerably poorer than several modern European nations. But they, it must be remembered, took the Roman jurisprudence for the foundation of their civil institutions. They built the *débris* of the Roman law into their walls ; but in the materials and workmanship of the residue there is not much which distinguishes it favourably from the structure erected by the English judicature.

The period of Roman freedom was the period during which the stamp of a distinctive character was impressed on the Roman jurisprudence ; and through all the earlier part of it, it was by the Responses of the jurisconsults that the development of the law was mainly carried on. But as we approach the fall of the republic there are signs that the Responses are assuming a form which must have been fatal to their farther expansion. They are becoming systematised and reduced into compendia. Q. Mucius Scævola, the Pontifex, is said to have published a manual of the entire Civil Law, and there are traces in the writings of Cicero of growing disrelish for the old methods, as compared with the more active instruments of legal innovation. Other agencies had in fact by this time been brought to bear on the law. The Edict, or annual proclamation of the Prætor, had risen into credit as the principal engine of law reform, and L. Cornelius Sylla, by causing to be enacted the great group of statutes called the *Leges Corneliæ*, had shown what rapid and speedy improvements can be effected by direct legislation. The final blow to the Responses was dealt by Augustus, who limited to a few leading jurisconsults the right of giving binding opinions on cases submitted to them, a change which, though it brings us nearer the ideas of the modern world, must obviously have altered fundamentally the characteristics of the legal profession and the nature of its influence on Roman law. At a later period another school of jurisconsults arose, the great lights of jurisprudence for all time. But Ulpian and Paulus, Gaius and Papinian, were not authors of Responses. Their works were regular treatises on particular departments of the law, more especially on the Prætor's Edict.

The *Equity* of the Romans and the Prætorian Edict by which it was worked into their system, will be considered in the next chapter. Of the Statute Law it is only necessary to say that it was scanty during the republic, but became very voluminous under the empire. In the youth and infancy of a nation it is a rare thing for the legislature to be called into action for the general reform of private law. The cry of the people is not for change in the laws, which are usually valued above their real worth, but solely for their pure, complete, and easy administration; and recourse to the legislative body is generally directed to the removal of some great abuse, or the decision of some incurable quarrel between classes and dynasties. There seems in the minds of the Romans to have been some association between the enactment of a large body of statutes and the settlement of society after a great civil commotion. Sylla signalised his reconstitution of the republic by the Leges Corneliæ; Julius Cæsar contemplated vast additions to the Statute Law; Augustus caused to be passed the all-important group of Leges Juliæ; and among later emperors the most active promulgators of constitutions are princes who, like Constantine, have the concerns of the world to readjust. The true period of Roman Statute Law does not begin till the establishment of the empire. The enactments of the emperors, clothed at first in the pretence of popular sanction, but afterwards emanating undisguisedly from the imperial prerogative, extend in increasing massiveness from the consolidation of Augustus's power to the publication of the Code of Justinian. It will be seen that even in the reign of the second emperor a considerable approximation is made to that condition of the law and that mode of administering it with which we are all familiar. A statute law and a limited board of expositors have arisen into being; a permanent court of appeal and a collection of approved commentaries will very shortly be added; and thus we are brought close on the ideas of our own day.

NOTE D

ENGLISH CASE-LAW AND FICTION

ABOUT the middle of the nineteenth century, and somewhat later, the language currently used by text-writers was such as to warrant Maine's selection of the authority of decided cases in England as an example of legal fiction. But the twentieth-century reader, if he has taken to heart Maine's brilliant generalisation in the earlier part of the chapter, will hardly expect the ideas and formulas even of English lawyers to have remained stationary in the midst of a progressive society; and in fact, though probably no society has ever made progress at a uniform rate all along the line, and there may quite conceivably be stagnation or even falling back in some departments while there is advance in others, criticism of legal ideas has advanced a good deal in the English-speaking world. No intelligent lawyer would at this day pretend that the decisions of the Courts do not add to and alter the law. The Courts themselves, in the course of the reasons given for those decisions, constantly and freely use language admitting that they do. Certainly they do not claim legislative power; nor, with all respect for Maine, do they exercise it. For a legislator is not bound to conform to the known existing rules or principles of law; statutes may not only amend but reverse the rule, or they may introduce absolutely novel principles and remedies, like the Work-men's Compensation Act. Still less, if possible, is he bound to respect previous legislation. But English judges are bound to give their decisions in conformity with the settled general principles of English law, with any express legislation applicable to the matter in hand, and with the authority of their predecessors and their own former decisions. At the same time they are bound to find a decision for every case, however novel it may be; and that decision will be authority for other like cases in future; therefore it is part of their duty to lay down new rules if required. Perhaps this is really the first and greatest rule of our customary law: that, failing a specific rule already ascertained and fitting the case in hand, the King's judges must find and apply the most reasonable rule they can, so that it be not inconsistent with any established principle. They not only may but must develop the law in every direction except that of contradicting rules which authority has once fixed. Whoever denies this must deny that novel combinations of facts are brought before the Courts from time to time, which is a truth vouched by common experience and recognised in the forensic phrase describing such cases as " of the first impression "; or else he must refuse to accept the principle that the Court is bound to find a decision for every case, however novel. It is true that at many times the Courts have been over-anxious to avoid the appear ance of novelty; and the shifts to which they resorted to avoid it have encumbered the Common Law with several of the fictions which Maine denounces (p. 32) as almost hopeless obstacles to an orderly distribution of its contents.

Observe that the process of making case-law cannot properly be called legislation even with any qualifying epithet intended to mark it as an exercise of limited or subordinate power. Many law-making authorities in the world are not sovereign, being merely delegated, or otherwise restrained, but are still sources of enactments which are verbally and literally binding within their competence. But the judicial authority of precedents is not of that kind. Under our system the Court is bound to give judgments consistent with former judgments of higher or equal rank, so far as their effect has not been abrogated by legislation or overruled by still higher authority; but it is not bound to follow their very words. Only the principle is binding, and it must be collected from the decision as a whole, and not assumed to be completely expressed by this or that sentence in a reported judgment, however carefully framed.

Perhaps Maine's exposition hardly brings out the prevailing motive for introducing fictions, the desire of obtaining a speedier or more complete remedy than the strictly appropriate form of procedure affords. Among the regular though not invariable marks of fictions in modern English law is the use of the word "constructive" or the word "implied," as any careful student may note for himself. It would be rash to suppose that the age of legal fictions is wholly past. When "Ancient Law" was written, one example was quite recent in our Courts, the rule that a man who professes to contract as an agent is deemed to warrant that he has authority from his alleged principal. This is a fiction, but beneficent and elegant, and it is now fully accepted.

CHAPTER III

LAW OF NATURE AND EQUITY

THE theory of a set of legal principles entitled by their intrinsic superiority to supersede the older law, very early obtained currency both in the Roman State and in England. Such a body of principles, existing in any system, has in the foregoing chapters been denominated Equity, a term which, as will presently be seen, was one (though only one) of the designations by which this agent of legal change was known to the Roman jurisconsults. The jurisprudence of the Court of Chancery, which bears the name of Equity in England, could only be adequately discussed in a separate treatise. It is extremely complex in its texture, and derives its materials from several heterogeneous sources. The early ecclesiastical chancellors contributed to it, from the Canon Law, many of the principles which lie deepest in its structure. The Roman law, more fertile than the Canon Law in rules applicable to secular disputes, was not seldom resorted to by a later generation of Chancery judges, amid whose recorded dicta we often find entire texts from the *Corpus Juris Civilis* imbedded, with their terms unaltered, though their origin is never acknowledged. Still more recently, and particularly at the middle and during the latter half of the

eighteenth century, the mixed systems of jurisprudence and morals constructed by the publicists
of the Low Countries appear to have been much
studied by English lawyers, and from the chancellorship of Lord Talbot to the commencement
of Lord Eldon's chancellorship these works had
considerable effect on the rulings of the Court
of Chancery. The system, which obtained its
ingredients from these various quarters, was
greatly controlled in its growth by the necessity
imposed on it of conforming itself to the analogies
of the common law, but it has always answered
the description of a body of comparatively novel
legal principles claiming to override the older
jurisprudence of the country on the strength of
an intrinsic ethical superiority.

The Equity of Rome was a much simpler
structure, and its development from its first
appearance can be much more easily traced.
Both its character and its history deserve attentive
examination. It is the root of several conceptions which have exercised profound influence on
human thought, and through human thought have
seriously affected the destinies of mankind.

The Romans described their legal system as
consisting of two ingredients. " All nations,"
says the Institutional Treatise published under the
authority of the Emperor Justinian, " who are
ruled by laws and customs, are governed partly
by their own particular laws, and partly by those
laws which are common to all mankind. The
law which a people enacts is called the Civil Law
of that people, but that which natural reason
appoints for all mankind is called the Law of

4

Nations, because all nations use it." The part of the law "which natural reason appoints for all mankind" was the element which the Edict of the Prætor was supposed to have worked into Roman jurisprudence. Elsewhere it is styled more simply Jus Naturale, or the Law of Nature; and its ordinances are said to be dictated by Natural Equity (*naturalis æquitas*) as well as by natural reason. I shall attempt to discover the origin of these famous phrases, Law of Nations, Law of Nature, Equity, and to determine how the conceptions which they indicate are related to one another.

The most superficial student of Roman history must be struck by the extraordinary degree in which the fortunes of the republic were affected by the presence of foreigners, under different names, on her soil. The causes of this immigration are discernible enough at a later period, for we can readily understand why men of all races should flock to the mistress of the world; but the same phenomenon of a large population of foreigners and denizens meets us in the very earliest records of the Roman State. No doubt, the instability of society in ancient Italy, composed as it was in great measure of robber tribes, gave men considerable inducement to locate themselves in the territory of any community strong enough to protect itself and them from external attack, even though protection should be purchased at the cost of heavy taxation, political disfranchisement, and much social humiliation. It is probable, however, that this explanation is imperfect, and that it could only be completed by taking into account those active commercial relations which, though they are little reflected in the military traditions of the republic, Rome appears certainly to have had with Carthage and with the interior of Italy in pre-historic times. Whatever were the circumstances to which it was attributable, the foreign element in the commonwealth determined the whole course of its history, which, at all its stages, is little more than a narrative of conflicts between a stubborn nationality and an alien population. Nothing like this has been seen in modern times ; on the one hand, because modern European communities have seldom or never received any accession of foreign immigrants which was large enough to make itself felt by the bulk of the native citizens, and on the other, because modern states, being held together by allegiance to a king or political superior, absorb considerable bodies of immigrant settlers with a quickness unknown to the ancient world, where the original citizens of a commonwealth always believed themselves to be united by kinship in blood, and resented a claim to equality of privilege as a usurpation of their birthright. In the early Roman republic the principle of the absolute exclusion of foreigners pervaded the Civil Law no less than the constitution. The alien or denizen could have no share in any institution supposed to be coeval with the State. He could not have the benefit of Quiritarian law. He could not be a party to the *nexum* which was at once the conveyance and the contract of the primitive Romans. He could not sue by the Sacramental Action, a mode of litigation of which the origin mounts up to the very infancy

of civilisation. Still, neither the interest nor the
security of Rome permitted him to be quite
outlawed. All ancient communities ran the risk
of being overthrown by a very slight disturbance
of equilibrium, and the mere instinct of self-
preservation would force the Romans to devise
some method of adjusting the rights and duties
of foreigners, who might otherwise—and this was
a danger of real importance in the ancient world—
have decided their controversies by armed strife.
Moreover, at no period of Roman history was
foreign trade entirely neglected. It was therefore
probably half as a measure of police and half in
furtherance of commerce that jurisdiction was first
assumed in disputes to which the parties were
either foreigners or a native and a foreigner. The
assumption of such a jurisdiction brought with
it the immediate necessity of discovering some
principles on which the questions to be adjudicated
upon could be settled, and the principles applied
to this object by the Roman lawyers were emi-
nently characteristic of the time. They refused,
as I have said before, to decide the new cases by
pure Roman Civil Law. They refused, no doubt
because it seemed to involve some kind of degradation, to apply the law of the particular State from
which the foreign litigant came. The expedient
to which they resorted was that of selecting the
rules of law common to Rome and to the different
Italian communities in which the immigrants were
born. In other words, they set themselves to form
a system answering to the primitive and literal
meaning of Jus Gentium, that is, Law common to
all Nations. Jus Gentium was, in fact, the sum

of the common ingredients in the customs of the old Italian tribes, for they were *all the nations* whom the Romans had the means of observing, and who sent successive swarms of immigrants to Roman soil.   Whenever a particular usage was seen to be practised by a large number of separate races in common, it was set down as part of the Law common to all Nations, or Jus Gentium.   Thus, although the conveyance of property was certainly accompanied by very different forms in the different commonwealths surrounding Rome, the actual transfer, tradition, or delivery of the article intended to be conveyed was a part of the ceremonial in all of them.   It was, for instance, a part, though a subordinate part, in the Mancipation or conveyance peculiar to Rome.   Tradition, therefore, being in all probability the only common ingredient in the modes of conveyance which the jurisconsults had the means of observing, was set down as an institution Juris Gentium, or rule of the Law common to all Nations.   A vast number of other observances were scrutinised with the same result. Some common characteristic was discovered in all of them, which had a common object, and this characteristic was classed in the Jus Gentium. The Jus Gentium was accordingly a collection of rules and principles, determined by observation to be common to the institutions which prevailed among the various Italian tribes.

The circumstances of the origin of the Jus Gentium are probably a sufficient safeguard against the mistake of supposing that the Roman lawyers had any special respect for it.   It was the fruit in part of their disdain for all foreign law, and in part of their disinclination to give the foreigner the advantage of their own indigenous Jus Civile. It is true that we, at the present day, should probably take a very different view of the Jus Gentium, if we were performing the operation which was effected by the Roman jurisconsults. We should attach some vague superiority or precedence to the element which we had thus discerned underlying and pervading so great a variety of usage. We should have a sort of respect for rules and principles so universal. Perhaps we should speak of the common ingredient as being of the essence of the transaction into which it entered, and should stigmatise the remaining apparatus of ceremony, which varied in different communities, as adventitious and accidental. Or it may be, we should infer that the races which we were comparing once obeyed a great system of common institutions of which the Jus Gentium was the reproduction, and that the complicated usages of separate commonwealths were only corruptions and depravations of the simpler ordinances which had once regulated their primitive state. But the results to which modern ideas conduct the observer are, as nearly as possible, the reverse of those which were instinctively brought home to the primitive Roman. What we respect or admire, he disliked or regarded with jealous dread. The parts of jurisprudence which he looked upon with affection were exactly those which a modern theorist leaves out of consideration as accidental and transitory ; the solemn gestures of the mancipation ; the nicely adjusted questions and answers of the verbal contract ; the endless formalities of pleading and procedure. The Jus Gentium was merely a system forced on his attention by a political necessity. He loved it as little as he loved the foreigners from whose institutions it was derived and for whose benefit it was intended. A complete revolution in his ideas was required before it could challenge his respect, but so complete was it when it did occur, that the true reason why our modern estimate of the Jus Gentium differs from that which has just been described, is that both modern jurisprudence and modern philosophy have inherited the matured views of the later jurisconsults on this subject. There did come a time when, from an ignoble appendage of the Jus Civile, the Jus Gentium came to be considered a great though as yet imperfectly developed model to which all law ought as far as possible to conform. This crisis arrived when the Greek theory of a Law of Nature was applied to the practical Roman administration of the Law common to all Nations.

The Jus Naturale, or Law of Nature, is simply the Jus Gentium or Law of Nations seen in the light of a peculiar theory. An unfortunate attempt to discriminate them was made by the jurisconsult Ulpian, with the propensity to distinguish characteristic of a lawyer, but the language of Gaius, a much higher authority, and the passage quoted before from the Institutes, leave no room for doubt, that the expressions were practically convertible. The difference between them was entirely historical, and no distinction in essence could ever be established between them. It is almost unnecessary to add that the confusion

between Jus Gentium, or Law common to all
Nations, and *international law* is entirely modern.
The classical expression for international law is
Jus Feciale, or the law of negotiation and diplo-
macy. It is, however, unquestionable that indis-
tinct impressions as to the meaning of Jus Gentium
had considerable share in producing the modern
theory that the relations of independent states
are governed by the Law of Nature.

It becomes necessary to investigate the Greek
conceptions of Nature and her law. The word
φύσις which was rendered in the Latin *natura*
and our *nature*, denoted beyond all doubt originally
the material universe, but it was the material
universe contemplated under an aspect which—
such is our intellectual distance from those times
—it is not very easy to delineate in modern language. Nature signified the physical world regarded as the result of some primordial element
or law. The oldest Greek philosophers had been
accustomed to explain the fabric of creation
as the manifestation of some single principle
which they variously asserted to be movement,
fire, moisture, or generation. In its simplest
and most ancient sense, Nature is precisely the
physical universe looked upon in this way as
the manifestation of a principle. Afterwards, the
later Greek sects, returning to a path from which
the greatest intellects of Greece had meanwhile
strayed, added the *moral* to the *physical* world
in the conception of Nature. They extended
the term till it embraced not merely the visible
creation, but the thoughts, observances, and
aspirations of mankind. Still, as before, it was

not solely the moral phenomena of human society
which they understood by *Nature,* but these
phenomena considered as resolvable into some
general and simple laws.

Now, just as the oldest Greek theorists supposed that the sports of chance had changed
the material universe from its simple primitive
form into its present heterogeneous condition,
so their intellectual descendants imagined that
but for untoward accident the human race would
have conformed itself to simpler rules of conduct
and a less tempestuous life.   To live according to
nature came to be considered as the end for which
man was created, and which the best men were
bound to compass.   To live according to *nature*
was to rise above the disorderly habits and gross
indulgences of the vulgar to higher laws of action
which nothing but self-denial and self-command
would enable the aspirant to observe.   It is
notorious that this proposition—live according to
nature—was the sum of the tenets of the famous
Stoic philosophy.   Now on the subjugation of
Greece that philosophy made instantaneous progress in Roman society.   It possessed natural
fascinations for the powerful class who, in theory
at least, adhered to the simple habits of the
ancient Italian race, and disdained to surrender
themselves to the innovations of foreign fashions.
Such persons began immediately to affect the
Stoic precepts of life according to nature—an
affectation all the more grateful, and, I may add,
all the more noble, from its contrast with the
unbounded profligacy which was being diffused
through the imperial city by the pillage of the

world and by the example of its most luxurious races. In the front of the disciples of the new Greek school, we might be sure, even if we did not know it historically, that the Roman lawyers figured. We have abundant proof that, there being substantially but two professions in the Roman republic, the military men were generally identified with the party of movement, but the lawyers were universally at the head of the party of resistance.

The alliance of the lawyers with the Stoic philosophers lasted through many centuries. Some of the earliest names in the series of renowned jurisconsults are associated with Stoicism, and ultimately we have the golden age of Roman jurisprudence fixed by general consent as the era of the Antonine Cæsars, the most famous disciples to whom that philosophy has given a rule of life. The long diffusion of these doctrines among the members of a particular profession was sure to affect the art which they practised and influenced. Several positions which we find in the remains of the Roman jurisconsults are scarcely intelligible, unless we use the Stoic tenets as our key; but at the same time it is a serious, though a very common, error to measure the influence of Stoicism on Roman law by counting up the number of legal rules which can be confidently affiliated on Stoical dogmas. It has often been observed that the strength of Stoicism resided not in its canons of conduct, which were often repulsive or ridiculous, but in the great though vague principle which it inculcated of resistance to passion. Just in the same way the influence on jurisprudence of the Greek theories, which had their most distinct expression in Stoicism, consisted not in the number of specific positions which they contributed to Roman law, but in the single fundamental assumption which they lent to it. After Nature had become a household word in the mouths of the Romans, the belief gradually prevailed among the Roman lawyers that the old Jus Gentium was in fact the lost code of Nature, and that the Prætor in framing an Edictal jurisprudence on the principles of the Jus Gentium was gradually restoring a type from which law had only departed to deteriorate. The inference from this belief was immediate that it was the Prætor's duty to supersede the Civil Law as much as possible by the Edict, to revive as far as might be the institutions by which Nature had governed man in the primitive state. Of course there were many impediments to the amelioration of law by this agency. There may have been prejudices to overcome even in the legal profession itself, and Roman habits were far too tenacious to give way at once to mere philosophical theory. The indirect methods by which the Edict combated certain technical anomalies, show the caution which its authors were compelled to observe, and down to the very days of Justinian there was some part of the old law which had obstinately resisted its influence. But on the whole, the progress of the Romans in legal improvement was astonishingly rapid as soon as stimulus was applied to it by the theory of Natural Law. The ideas of simplification and generalisation had always been associated with the conception of Nature ; simplicity, symmetry, and intelligibility came therefore to be regarded as the characteristics of a good legal system, and the taste for involved language, multiplied ceremonials, and useless difficulties disappeared altogether. The strong will and unusual opportunities of Justinian were needed to bring the Roman law to its existing shape, but the ground-plan of the system had been sketched long before the imperial reforms were effected.

What was the exact point of contact between the old Jus Gentium and the Law of Nature ? I think that they touch and blend through Æquitas, or Equity in its original sense ; and here we seem to come to the first appearance in jurisprudence of this famous term Equity. In examining an expression which has so remote an origin and so long a history as this, it is always safest to penetrate, if possible, to the simple metaphor or figure which at first shadowed forth the conception. It has generally been supposed that Æquitas is the equivalent of the Greek ἰσότης, *i.e.*, the principle of equal or proportionate distribution. The equal division of numbers or physical magnitudes is doubtless closely entwined with our perceptions of justice ; there are few associations which keep their ground in the mind so stubbornly or are dismissed from it with such difficulty by the deepest thinkers. Yet in tracing the history of this association, it certainly does not seem to have suggested itself to very early thought, but is rather the offspring of a comparatively late philosophy. It is remarkable too that the " equality " of laws on which the Greek

democracies prided themselves—that equality
which, in the beautiful drinking song of Callis-
tratus, Harmodius and Aristogiton are said to
have given to Athens—had little in common with
the "equity" of the Romans. The first was an
equal administration of civil laws among the
citizens, however limited the class of citizens
might be; the last implied the applicability of
a law, which was not civil law, to a class which
did not necessarily consist of citizens. The first
excluded a despot; the last included foreigners,
and for some purposes slaves. On the whole,
I should be disposed to look in another direction
for the germ of the Roman "Equity." The
Latin word "æquus" carries with it more distinctly than the Greek "ἴσος" the sense of
levelling. Now its levelling tendency was exactly
the characteristic of the Jus Gentium, which
would be most striking to a primitive Roman.
The pure Quiritarian law recognised a multitude
of arbitrary distinctions between classes of men
and kinds of property: the Jus Gentium, generalised
from a comparison of various customs, neglected
the Quiritarian divisions. The old Roman law
established, for example, a fundamental difference
between "Agnatic" and "Cognatic" relationship, that is, between the Family considered as
based upon common subjection to patriarchal
authority and the Family considered (in conformity with modern ideas) as united through
the mere fact of a common descent. This distinction disappears in the "law common to all
nations," as also does the difference between the
archaic forms of property, Things "Mancipi"

and Things "nec Mancipi." The neglect of demarcations and boundaries seems to me, therefore, the feature of the Jus Gentium which was depicted in Æquitas. I imagine that the word was at first a mere description of that constant *levelling* or removal of irregularities which went on wherever the prætorian system was applied to the cases of foreign litigants. Probably no colour of ethical meaning belonged at first to the expression; nor is there any reason to believe that the process which it indicated was otherwise than extremely distasteful to the primitive Roman mind.

On the other hand, the feature of the Jus Gentium which was presented to the apprehension of a Roman by the word Equity, was exactly the first and most vividly realised characteristic of the hypothetical state of nature. Nature implied symmetrical order, first in the physical world, and next in the moral, and the earliest notion of order doubtless involved straight lines, even surfaces, and measured distances. The same sort of picture or figure would be unconsciously before the mind's eye, whether it strove to form the outlines of the supposed natural state, or whether it took in at a glance the actual administration of the "law common to all nations"; and all we know of primitive thought would lead us to conclude that this ideal similarity would do much to encourage the belief in an identity of the two conceptions. But then, while the Jus Gentium had little or no antecedent credit at Rome, the theory of a Law of Nature came in surrounded with all the prestige of philosophical

authority, and invested with the charms of
association with an elder and more blissful condition of the race. It is easy to understand how
the difference in the point of view would affect
the dignity of the term which at once described
the operation of the old principles and the results
of the new theory. Even to modern ears it is
not at all the same thing to describe a process as
one of " levelling " and to call it the " correction
of anomalies," though the metaphor is precisely
the same. Nor do I doubt that, when once
Æquitas was understood to convey an allusion
to the Greek theory, associations which grew
out of the Greek notion of ἰσότης began to cluster
round it. The language of Cicero renders it more
than likely that this was so, and it was the first
stage of a transmutation of the conception of
Equity, which almost every ethical system which
has appeared since those days has more or less
helped to carry on.

Something must be said of the formal instrumentality by which the principles and distinctions
associated, first with the Law common to all
nations, and afterwards with the Law of Nature,
were gradually incorporated with the Roman law.
At the crisis of primitive Roman history which is
marked by the expulsion of the Tarquins, a change
occurred which has its parallel in the early annals
of many ancient states, but which had little in
common with those passages of political affairs
which we now term revolutions. It may best be
described by saying that the monarchy was put
into commission. The powers heretofore accumulated in the hands of a single person were

parcelled out among a number of elective functionaries, the very name of the kingly office being
retained and imposed on a personage known
subsequently as the Rex Sacrorum or Rex Sacrificulus. As part of the change, the settled duties
of the supreme judicial office devolved on the
Prætor, at the time the first functionary in the
commonwealth, and together with these duties
was transferred the undefined supremacy over law
and legislation which always attached to ancient
sovereigns, and which is not obscurely related to
the patriarchal and heroic authority they had once
enjoyed. The circumstances of Rome gave great
importance to the more indefinite portion of the
functions thus transferred, as with the establishment of the republic began that series of recurrent
trials which overtook the state, in the difficulty
of dealing with a multitude of persons who, not
coming within the technical description of indigenous Romans, were nevertheless permanently
located within Roman jurisdiction. Controversies
between such persons, or between such persons and
native-born citizens, would have remained without
the pale of the remedies provided by Roman law,
if the Prætor had not undertaken to decide them,
and he must soon have addressed himself to the
more critical disputes which in the extension of
commerce arose between Roman subjects and
avowed foreigners. The great increase of such
cases in the Roman Courts about the period of the
first Punic War is marked by the appointment
of a special Prætor, known subsequently as the
Prætor Peregrinus, who gave them his undivided
attention. Meantime, one precaution of the

Roman people against the revival of oppression, had consisted in obliging every magistrate whose duties had any tendency to expand their sphere, to publish, on commencing his year of office, an Edict or proclamation in which he declared the manner in which he intended to administer his department. The Prætor fell under the rule with other magistrates ; but as it was necessarily impossible to construct each year a separate system of principles, he seems to have regularly republished his predecessor's Edict with such additions and changes as the exigency of the moment or his own views of the law compelled him to introduce. The Prætor's proclamation, thus lengthened by a new portion every year, obtained the name of the Edictum Perpetuum, that is the *continuous* or *unbroken* edict. The immense length to which it extended, together perhaps with some distaste for its necessarily disorderly texture, caused the practice of increasing it to be stopped in the year of Salvius Julianus, who occupied the magistracy in the reign of the Emperor Hadrian. The edict of that Prætor embraced therefore the whole body of equity jurisprudence, which it probably disposed in new and symmetrical order, and the perpetual edict is therefore often cited in Roman law merely as the Edict of Julianus.

Perhaps the first inquiry which occurs to an Englishman who considers the peculiar mechanism of the Edict is, what were the limitations by which these extensive powers of the Prætor were restrained ? How was authority so little definite to be reconciled with a settled condition of society and of law ? The answer can only be supplied by

5

careful observation of the conditions under which
our own English law is administered. The Prætor,
it should be recollected, was a jurisconsult himself,
or a person entirely in the hands of advisers who
were jurisconsults, and it is probable that every
Roman lawyer waited impatiently for the time
when he should fill or control the great judicial
magistracy. In the interval, his tastes, feelings,
prejudices, and degree of enlightenment were
inevitably those of his own order, and the qualifications which he ultimately brought to office were
those which he had acquired in the practice and
study of his profession. An English Chancellor
goes through precisely the same training, and
carries to the woolsack the same qualifications. It
is certain when he assumes office that he will have,
to. some extent, modified the law before he leaves
it ; but until he has quitted his seat, and the series
of his decisions in the Law Reports has been
completed, we cannot discover how far he has
elucidated or added to the principles which his
predecessors bequeathed to him. The influence
of the Prætor on Roman jurisprudence differed
only in respect of the period at which its amount
was ascertained. As was before stated, he was in
office but for a year, and his decisions rendered
during his year, though of course irreversible as
regarded the litigants, were of no ulterior value.
The most natural moment for declaring the changes
he proposed to effect, occurred therefore at his
entrance on the prætorship ; and hence, when
commencing his duties, he did openly and
avowedly that which in the end his English
representative does insensibly and sometimes

unconsciously. The checks on his apparent liberty
are precisely those imposed on an English judge.
Theoretically there seems to be hardly any limit
to the powers of either of them, but practically the
Roman Prætor, no less than the English Chancellor, was kept within the narrowest bounds by
the prepossessions imbibed from early training,
and by the strong restraints of professional opinion,
restraints of which the stringency can only be
appreciated by those who have personally experienced them. It may be added that the lines
within which movement is permitted, and beyond
which there is to be no travelling, were chalked
with as much distinctness in the one case as in the
other. In England the judge follows the analogies
of reported decisions on insulated groups of facts.
At Rome, as the intervention of the Prætor was at
first dictated by simple concern for the safety of
the state, it is likely that in the earliest times it was
proportioned to the difficulty which it attempted
to get rid of. Afterwards, when the taste for
principle had been diffused by the Responses, he
no doubt used the Edict as the means of giving a
wider application to those fundamental principles
which he and the other practising jurisconsults,
his contemporaries, believed themselves to have
detected underlying the law. Latterly he acted
wholly under the influence of Greek philosophical
theories, which at once tempted him to advance
and confined him to a particular course of progress.

The nature of the measures attributed to
Salvius Julianus has been much disputed. Whatever they were, their effects on the Edict are
sufficiently plain. It ceased to be extended by

annual additions, and henceforward the equity
jurisprudence of Rome was developed by the
labours of a succession of great jurisconsults who
fill with their writings the interval between the
reign of Hadrian and the reign of Alexander
Severus. A fragment of the wonderful system
which they built up survives in the Pandects of
Justinian, and supplies evidence that their works
took the form of treatises on all parts of Roman
law, but chiefly that of commentaries on the Edict.
Indeed, whatever be the immediate subject of a
jurisconsult of this epoch, he may always be called
an expositor of Equity.   The principles of the
Edict had, before the epoch of its cessation, made
their way into every part of Roman jurisprudence.
The Equity of Rome, it should be understood, even
when most distinct from the Civil Law, was always
administered by the same tribunals.   The Prætor
was the chief equity judge as well as the great
common law magistrate, and as soon as the Edict
had evolved an equitable rule the Prætor's court
began to apply it in place of or by the side of
the old rule of the Civil Law, which was thus
directly or indirectly repealed without any express
enactment of the legislature.   The result, of course,
fell considerably short of a complete fusion of law
and equity, which was not carried out till the
reforms of Justinian.   The technical severance of
the two elements of jurisprudence entailed some
confusion and some inconvenience, and there were
certain of the stubborner doctrines of the Civil
Law with which neither the authors nor the expositors of the Edict had ventured to interfere.
But at the same time there was no corner of the

field of jurisprudence which was not more or less swept over by the influence of Equity. It supplied the jurist with all his materials for generalisation, with all his methods of interpretation, with his elucidations of first principles, and with that great mass of limiting rules which are rarely interfered with by the legislator, but which seriously control the application of every legislative act.

The period of jurists ends with Alexander Severus. From Hadrian to that emperor the improvement of law was carried on, as it is at the present moment in most continental countries, partly by approved commentaries and partly by direct legislation. But in the reign of Alexander Severus the power of growth in Roman Equity seems to be exhausted, and the succession of jurisconsults comes to a close The remaining history of the Roman law is the history of the imperial constitutions, and, at the last, of attempts to codify what had now become the unwieldy body of Roman jurisprudence. We have the latest and most celebrated experiment of this kind in the *Corpus Juris* of Justinian.

It would be wearisome to enter on a detailed comparison or contrast of English and Roman Equity ; but it may be worth while to mention two features which they have in common. The first may be stated as follows. Each of them tended, and all such systems tend, to exactly the same state in which the old common law was when Equity first interfered with it. A time always comes at which the moral principles originally adopted have been carried out to all their legitimate consequences, and then the system founded on them becomes as rigid, as unexpansive, and as liable to fall behind moral progress as the sternest code of rules avowedly legal. Such an epoch was reached at Rome in the reign of Alexander Severus; after which, though the whole Roman world was undergoing a moral revolution, the Equity of Rome ceased to expand. The same point of legal history was attained in England under the chancellorship of Lord Eldon, the first of our equity judges who, instead of enlarging the jurisprudence of his court by indirect legislation, devoted himself through life to explaining and harmonising it. If the philosophy of legal history were better understood in England, Lord Eldon's services would be less exaggerated on the one hand and better appreciated on the other than they appear to be among contemporary lawyers. Other misapprehensions, too, which bear some practical fruit, would perhaps be avoided. It is easily seen by English lawyers that English Equity is a system founded on moral rules; but it is forgotten that these rules are the morality of past centuries—not of the present—that they have received nearly as much application as they are capable of, and that, though of course they do not differ largely from the ethical creed of our own day, they are not necessarily on a level with it. The imperfect theories of the subject which are commonly adopted have generated errors of opposite sorts. Many writers of treatises on Equity, struck with the completeness of the system in its present state, commit themselves expressly or implicitly to the paradoxical assertion that the founders of the chancery jurisprudence contemplated its present fixity of form when they were settling its first basis. Others, again, complain—and this is a grievance frequently observed upon in forensic arguments—that the moral rules enforced by the Court of Chancery fall short of the ethical standard of the present day. They would have each Lord Chancellor perform precisely the same office for the jurisprudence which he finds ready to his hand, which was performed for the old common law by the fathers of English equity. But this is to invert the order of the agencies by which the improvement of the law is carried on. Equity has its place and its time; but I have pointed out that another instrumentality is ready to succeed it when its energies are spent.

Another remarkable characteristic of both English and Roman Equity is the falsehood of the assumptions upon which the claim of the equitable to superiority over the legal rule is originally defended. Nothing is more distasteful to men, either as individuals or as masses, than the admission of their moral progress as a substantive reality. This unwillingness shows itself, as regards individuals, in the exaggerated respect which is ordinarily paid to the doubtful virtue of consistency. The movement of the collective opinion of a whole society is too palpable to be ignored, and is generally too visibly for the better to be decried; but there is the greatest disinclination to accept it as a primary phenomenon, and it is commonly explained as the recovery of a lost perfection—the gradual return to a state from which the race has lapsed. This tendency to

look backward instead of forward for the goal
of moral progress produced anciently, as we have
seen, on Roman jurisprudence effects the most
serious and permanent. The Roman jurisconsults, in order to account for the improvement
of their jurisprudence by the Prætor, borrowed
from Greece the doctrine of a Natural state of
man—a Natural society—anterior to the organisation of commonwealths governed by positive
laws. In England, on the other hand, a range
of ideas especially congenial to Englishmen of
that day, explained the claim of Equity to override the common law by supposing a general right
to superintend the administration of justice which
was assumed to be vested in the king as a natural
result of his paternal authority. The same view
appears in a different and a quainter form in the
old doctrine that Equity flowed from the king's
conscience—the improvement which had in fact
taken place in the moral standard of the community being thus referred to an inherent elevation
in the moral sense of the sovereign. The growth
of the English constitution rendered such a theory
unpalatable after a time ; but as the jurisdiction
of the Chancery was then firmly established, it
was not worth while to devise any formal substitute for it. The theories found in modern
manuals of Equity are very various, but all are
alike in their untenability. Most of them are
modifications of the Roman doctrine of a natural
law, which is indeed adopted in terms by those
writers who begin a discussion of the jurisdiction
of the Court of Chancery by laying down a distinction between natural justice and civil.

NOTE E

THE LAW OF NATURE AND "IUS GENTIUM"

MAINE'S third and fourth chapters need more supplemental criticism than any other part of "Ancient Law." The medieval doctrine of the Law of Nature, and its continuity with the classical Roman doctrine, had been forgotten or misunderstood in England for quite two centuries at the time when these chapters were written; and even many years later there was no obvious way for an English scholar to get back to the right historical lines. I owe my own guidance mainly to a somewhat belated acquaintance with Dr. Gierke's exhaustive treatment of the controversies which occupied the publicists of the Middle Ages and "the Renaissance" ("Johannes Althusius und die Entwicklung der naturrechtlichen Staatstheorien," Breslau, 1880; "Political Theories of the Middle Age," transl. with introduction by F. W. Maitland, Cambridge, 1900, from "Die Staats- und Korporationslehre," etc., Berlin, 1881; Pollock, "The History of the Law of Nature," Journ. Soc. Comp. Legisl., 1900, p. 418). Mr. Bryce's recent essay on the Law of Nature ("Studies in History and Jurisprudence," Oxford, 1901, ii. 112) should be read and considered by all students of legal history. The latest considerable publication touching the subject in this country is A. J. Carlyle's "History of Mediaeval Political Theory in the West," 1903 (only vol. 1 yet published): and see Dr. H. Rashdall thereon, L.Q.R. xx. 322.

Maine was not a medievalist or a canonist, and shared the general ignorance of English lawyers and scholars of his time. Accordingly his statement practically neglects the Middle Ages, and suggests, though it does not assert in terms, that the law of nature as understood by the publicists of the seventeenth and eighteenth centuries was derived exclusively from the classical Roman lawyers; that the influence of Greek philosophy was only indirect and through Roman law; and that the conception of a primeval and innocent "state of nature" was an integral part of the doctrine. Not one of these inferences would be correct. The theory of Grotius is continuous with that of the canonists and schoolmen; the medieval doctrine is founded on Aristotle and Cicero, no less than on the Corpus Iuris; and the "state of nature" of eighteenth-century writers is an exaggerated perversion of what, in the traditional system, is a quite subordinate point.

Political justice is divided, according to Aristotle ("Eth. Nic." V. vii.; this is one of the books not written by Aristotle himself, but the substance is admitted to represent his teaching) into natural (τὸ μὲν φυσικόν, *naturale*) and conventional (τὸ δὲ νομικόν, *legale*). The Latin equivalents are from the current medieval translation directed by St. Thomas Aquinas. The rules of natural

justice are those which all civilized men recognise. Those of
conventional justice deal with matters indifferent in themselves
or otherwise capable of being settled only by positive authority.
Natural justice may tell me not to drive recklessly, but cannot tell
me which is the right side of the road, a question which conventional justice answers one way in these kingdoms and the
other in America and most, though not all, European Continental
countries Rules involving number and measure, again, cannot be
fixed by natural justice alone. It is to be observed that Aristotle's
conception of Nature implies rational design, and this was more
fully worked out by the later Greek schools, and especially the
Stoics Maine, though he was an excellent classical scholar, omits
all mention of Aristotle; but Aristotle is not prominent in the
later literature of the subject which he almost exclusively made
use of.

The Greek philosophical doctrine acquired an elegant Latin
form in Cicero's hands at the very time when thoughtful Roman
lawyers were in need of a theoretical foundation for the addition
of the *ius gentium* to the old strict and archaic rules. Now *ius
gentium*, in its original meaning, has nothing to do with distinct
nations or tribes (which is not the meaning of *gentes*), but signifies
the rules accepted as binding by all people (Nettleship, " Contributions to Latin Lexicography," *s. v.*; cp. E. C. Clark, " Practical
Jurisprudence," p. 354). Towards the end of the republican period,
it would seem not before Cicero's time, it became the special name
of the rules administered by Roman magistrates in causes where
Roman law proper was inapplicable, by reason of the parties not
being both Roman citizens or allies, or otherwise. The personal
and religious laws of one community are incapable, in archaic
society, of being used by members of another; and such is still
the universal custom of India, broken only, so far as it is broken,
by the introduction of cosmopolitan ideas and habits from Europe.
Many Roman legal formulas involved a religious element, and
for that reason, we may be pretty sure, were available for Romans
only : we know that in one case, that of the words *Dari spondes ?
spondeo*, such a restriction was still in force under the Empire.
Similarly two strangers living under different laws of their own
could not both be judged by either of those laws any more than
by Roman law. There is no necessary question of one law being
thought better in itself than another, or of " disdain for all
foreign law"; still less of the Romans having refused requests
for the application of Roman law which are most unlikely to
have ever been made (above, pp. 53, 54). What we find, at any
rate, in the conflict of personal laws in the early Middle Ages
is that every man wants to be judged by his own law. This being
out of the question, the needs of business called for some practical
solution in a jurisdiction into which the growing power of Rome

brought merchants and traders from all parts of the Mediterranean. It is hard to believe that there was not already some kind of general custom among those merchants for matters of common occurrence, or that the Roman Praetor did not find it easier to adopt any such custom, if satisfied of its existence, than to frame a new rule by deliberate selection from the elements common to the domestic law of Rome and other Italian States. The recognition of the Law Merchant in England by the Common Law seems a nearer modern parallel than the development of the rules of Equity. Maine himself pointed out, in a later work, that the *ius gentium* was in part originally a market law, and grew out of commercial exigencies ("Village Communities," pp. 193-4). It is significant in this connexion that in the later Middle Ages and down to the seventeenth century English books regularly treat the Law Merchant of Western Christendom as equivalent to the law of nature, or a branch of it (Pollock, Journ. Soc. Comp. Legisl., 1900, p. 431; "The Expansion of the Common Law," p. 117).

However this may be, the actual *ius gentium* agreed well enough with the rules of natural justice or natural law in the sense of the Greek philosophers, so far as these could be observed in practice. Accordingly the Roman lawyers, probably working on Greek materials now lost, identified *ius gentium* for most practical purposes with *ius naturale*: they regarded it as the sum of rules which were evident to natural reason, and received by all men because they were reasonable; "quod vero naturalis ratio inter omnes homines constituit, id apud omnes populos peraeque custoditur vocaturque ius gentium, quasi quo iure omnes gentes utuntur" (Gai. i. § 1). But this or any similar statement leaves it an open question whether *ius gentium* really coincides with *ius naturale*. There may possibly be rules that deserve to be recognised by all mankind, but in fact are not; and there may be universal or very widely prevailing usages which natural reason will not justify. Slavery was a recognised institution, part of the general customs of the Roman Empire if anything was; but the enlightened age of the Antonines could find no warrant for it in philosophy, and the incongruity pressed on at least one or two of the classical Roman jurists. Modern specialists in Roman law have not been able to agree what was exactly their doctrine as to the relation of the ideal to the actual usage of mankind, or whether there was any one accepted doctrine at all in the law schools of the empire. There is no apparent reason why there should have been any official or settled opinion on such a speculative point. Perhaps we should not be far from the truth if we said, in the language familiar to our own system, that *ius gentium* was presumed to follow *ius naturale* if the contrary did not appear. At the outset of Justinian's Institutes (I. ii. § 2) we read

that by the law of nature all men were born free, but capture and
slavery, things contrary to the law of nature, were introduced by
necessity as consequences of war, and are therefore part of the
ius gentium. This imperial dictum, though it can hardly be said
to solve the ethical or social problem, settled the terminology for
the medieval publicists of whom we shall have to say a word later
(Note G below). Similarly in tit. 5 pr. it is said that slavery was
unknown in the law of nature, and whereas by nature there was
only one name of man, the law of nations has distinguished free
men, slaves, and freed men who have ceased to be slaves.

As for the celebrated passage of Ulpian which defines the law
of nature as common to man and other animals, "quod natura
omnia animalia docuit," and distinguishes it on this ground from
ius gentium, the rule confined to men, "solis hominibus inter
se commune," we are not bound to believe that it was current
among Roman lawyers in Ulpian's own time, or anything but
a conceit borrowed from some forgotten Greek rhetorician. It
stands alone in the classical texts, but its conspicuous adoption
at the beginning of both the Digest and the Institutes of Justinian
was the cause of endless trouble to the medieval commentators,
for whom every word in the Corpus Iuris was of equal authority.
Maine assumes the invention to have been Ulpian's own, and
ascribes it to "the propensity to distinguish characteristic of a
lawyer"; I can only say that it does not look to me like a working
lawyer's point.[1] A modern Italian scholar has proposed to understand "ius quod natura omnia animalia docuit" as meaning the
instincts common to man and other animals which both morality
and law postulate as existing in fact (Del Rosso, Ann. Ist. di storia
di diritto Romano, Catania 1905-6). This appears as plausible an
explanation as, failing the discovery of Ulpian's ultimate authority,
we are likely to obtain.

Maine's suggestions, beginning at p. 60, as to "the exact point
of contact between the old *ius gentium* and the law of nature"
being given by a conjectured special sense of *aequitas* are
ingenious, but hardly seem required. The general coincidence
between *ius gentium* and the φυσικὸν δίκαιον of Greek philosophy
was obvious enough to jurists in search of a theory without being
emphasized by any one special point of contact. *Aequitas* appears,
in classical Latin usage, to come very near "reasonableness"; and
in fact the word *reason* and its derivatives are the proper terms

---

[1] The suggestion that it is the nature of lawyers to distinguish where there
is no difference may possibly have been inspired by Hobbes's censure of Coke
in his Dialogue of the Common Laws of England :—" Sir Edw. Coke does
seldom well distinguish when there are two divers Names for one and the same
thing; though one contain the other, he makes them always different, as if
it could not be that one and the same Man should be both an Enemy, and a
Traytor."

in the Common Law for conveying the ideas, or some of them, which are at the bottom of the law of nature, as St. German pointed out nearly four centuries ago in "Doctor and Student.' Maine appears to have assumed that the Roman doctrine included the historical acceptance of a golden age : "the belief gradually prevailed among the Roman lawyers that the old *jus gentium* was in fact the lost code of nature," p. 59. I am bound to say that I do not know of any evidence that such was the belief of either lawyers or philosophers. Certainly no Greek philosopher would have admitted that the law of nature was lost, nor would Cicero ; and as to the supposition that *ius gentium* was the law of the golden age in the opinion of the philosophic lawyers, "so far were they from such a delusion," says Mr. Bryce, ' that they ascribe to *ius gentium* war, captivity, slavery, and all the consequences of these facts, while in the golden age, the *Saturnia regna* of the poets, all men were free and war was unknown." *Ius gentium* is the common law or custom of mankind, actual not ideal custom. Just as little is there any traceable connection between the fables of a golden age and the fundamental conception of natural law, namely, that general rules of human conduct are at all times discoverable by human reason as being reasonable. The doctrine of the Roman jurists does not involve any historical assumption at all, neither, in itself, does that of the medieval doctors and commentators, although these, as good Catholics, accepted the Fall of Man and could give theological reasons for the law of nature not being sufficient in practice. Moreover, it is not probable that *ius gentium*, as a term of art, is much or at all older than *ius naturale* or *naturae*. The hypothesis of a "state of nature" antecedent to positive law, much more the suggestion that it was a golden age of ideal natural law, does not seem to occur before the sixteenth century. Where such a state is mentioned, down to the latter part of the fifteenth century, it is treated as barbarous ; before they founded commonwealths, it is said, men lived like beasts (Aen. Silv. de ortu imp. Rom.).

NOTE F

EQUITY

A peculiar historical development has given this word a technical meaning among English-speaking lawyers. "Reasonableness," as mentioned in the last note, appears to be the primary and general idea. This conception, when embodied for practical use as an appeal to the common sense of right-minded men, is closely akin to that of natural justice, and further resembles it in being traceable to Aristotle. It is of the utmost importance in many branches of our modern law ; but we have specialised the name of Equity for one application of it, namely that administration of extraordinary justice by the king with the advice of his Chancellor and Council, and afterwards through the Chancellor alone, which produced the Court of Chancery. Maine, when he wrote "Ancient Law," seems to have doubted the historical truth of "the king's general right to superintend the administration of justice" (p. 71); but in "Early Law and Custom" (ch. vi., "The King and Early Civil Justice," p. 164), it is fully recognised. The king was held to retain a "pre-eminence of jurisdiction . . . as well for amendment as for supply of the Common Law," though he could not alter a regular jurisdiction once established; this "supplementary or residuary jurisdiction," as Maine aptly calls it, was exercised to form the Court of Chancery, and in due time it was held, as was inevitable, that this also had become an established Court, that the king's power to do equity as well as strict legal justice had been completely delegated, and that accordingly he could not create any new equitable jurisdiction. It was no less inevitable that after this Equity should become a technical system (cp. Pollock, "The Expansion of the Common Law," pp. 67-73).

Maine pointed out (E. L. and C., p. 166) that the early Roman law, "a stiff system of technical and ceremonious law," "underwent a transformation through this very residuary or supplementary royal authority," which under the Roman Republic was vested in the Praetor. "What has descended to so large a part of the modern world is not the coarse Roman law, but the Roman law distilled through the jurisdiction of the Praetor, and by him gradually bent into supposed accordance with the law of nature."

As to the relation of our Court of Chancery to the law of nature, I endeavoured to sum it up in a course of lectures given in America in 1903 : "The early Chancellors did not disclose the sources of their inspiration; probably they had as good grounds of expediency for not talking about the law of nature as the common lawyers." The law of nature was intimately associated with the canon law, and for English lay people in the Middle Ages canon law signified obnoxious meddling of foreign ecclesiastics with English benefices and revenues, besides the vexatious and inquisitorial jurisdiction of bishops' and archdeacons' courts. "Certainly [the Chancellors] intended and endeavoured to follow the dictate of natural reason ; and if their version of natural justice was somewhat artificial in its details, and bore a decided civilian or canonical stamp, this was only to be expected. Some centuries later, when British judicial officers in India were instructed to decide, in the absence of any native law applicable to both parties, according to "justice, equity, and good conscience," the results bore, even more manifestly, the stamp of the Common Law" ("The Expansion of the Common Law," p. 114).

CHAPTER IV

IT will be inferred from what has been said that the theory which transformed the Roman jurisprudence had no claim to philosophical precision. It involved, in fact, one of those " mixed modes of thought " which are now acknowledged to have characterised all but the highest minds during the infancy of speculation, and which are far from undiscoverable even in the mental efforts of our own day. The Law of Nature confused the Past and the Present. Logically, it implied a state of Nature which had once been regulated by natural law ; yet the jurisconsults do not speak clearly or confidently of the existence of such a state, which indeed is little noticed by the ancients except where it finds a poetical expression in the fancy of a golden age. Natural law, for all practical purposes, was something belonging to the present, something entwined with existing institutions, something which could be distinguished from them by a competent observer. The test which separated the ordinances of Nature from the gross ingredients with which they were mingled was a sense of simplicity and harmony ; yet it was not on account of their simplicity and harmony that these finer elements were primarily respected, but on the score of their descent from the aboriginal reign of Nature. This confusion has not been successfully explained away by the modern disciples of the jurisconsults, and in truth modern speculations on the Law of Nature betray much more indistinctness of perception and are vitiated by much more hopeless ambiguity of language than the Roman lawyers can be justly charged with. There are some writers on the subject who attempt to evade the fundamental difficulty by contending that the code of Nature exists in the future and is the goal to which all civil laws are moving, but this is to reverse the assumptions on which the old theory rested, or rather perhaps to mix together two inconsistent theories. The tendency to look not to the past but to the future for types of perfection was brought into the world by Christianity. Ancient literature gives few or no hints of a belief that the progress of society is necessarily from worse to better.

But the importance of this theory to mankind has been very much greater than its philosophical deficiencies would lead us to expect. Indeed, it is not easy to say what turn the history of thought, and therefore of the human race, would have taken, if the belief in a law natural had not become universal in the ancient world.

There are two special dangers to which law, and society which is held together by law, appear to be liable in their infancy. One of them is that law may be too rapidly developed. This occurred with the codes of the more progressive Greek communities, which disembarrassed themselves with astonishing facility from cumbrous forms of procedure and needless terms of art, and soon

ceased to attach any superstitious value to rigid
rules and prescriptions. It was not for the ultimate advantage of mankind that they did so,
though the immediate benefit conferred on their
citizens may have been considerable. One of the
rarest qualities of national character is the capacity
for applying and working out the law, as such,
at the cost of constant miscarriages of abstract
justice, without at the same time losing the hope
or the wish that law may be conformed to a higher
ideal. The Greek intellect, with all its mobility
and elasticity, was quite unable to confine itself
within the strait waistcoat of a legal formula ;
and, if we may judge them by the popular courts
of Athens, of whose working we possess accurate
knowledge, the Greek tribunals exhibited the
strongest tendency to confound law and fact.
The remains of the Orators and the forensic commonplaces preserved by Aristotle in his Treatise
on Rhetoric, show that questions of pure law
were constantly argued on every consideration
which could possibly influence the mind of the
judges. No durable system of jurisprudence could
be produced in this way. A community which
never hesitated to relax rules of written law
whenever they stood in the way of an ideally
perfect decision on the facts of particular cases,
would only, if it bequeathed any body of judicial
principles to posterity, bequeath one consisting
of the ideas of right and wrong which happened
to be prevalent at the time. Such a jurisprudence
would contain no framework to which the more
advanced conceptions of subsequent ages could be
fitted. It would amount at best to a philosophy,

6

marked with the imperfections of the civilisation under which it grew up.

Few national societies have had their jurisprudence menaced by this peculiar danger of precocious maturity and untimely disintegration. It is certainly doubtful whether the Romans were ever seriously threatened by it, but at any rate they had adequate protection in their theory of Natural Law. For the Natural Law of the jurisconsults was distinctly conceived by them as a system which ought gradually to absorb civil laws, without superseding them so long as they remained unrepealed. There was no such impression of its sanctity abroad, that an appeal to it would be likely to overpower the mind of a judge who was charged with the superintendence of a particular litigation. The value and serviceableness of the conception arose from its keeping before the mental vision a type of perfect law, and from its inspiring the hope of an indefinite approximation to it, at the same time that it never tempted the practitioner or the citizen to deny the obligation of existing laws which had not yet been adjusted to the theory. It is important too to observe that this model system, unlike many of those which have mocked men's hopes in later days, was not entirely the product of imagination. It was never thought of as founded on quite untested principles. The notion was that it underlay existing law and must be looked for through it. Its functions were in short remedial, not revolutionary or anarchical. And this, unfortunately, is the exact point at which the modern view of a

Law of Nature has often ceased to resemble the ancient.

The other liability to which the infancy of society is exposed has prevented or arrested the progress of far the greater part of mankind. The rigidity of primitive law, arising chiefly from its early association and identification with religion, has chained down the mass of the human race to those views of life and conduct which they entertained at the time when their usages were first consolidated into a systematic form. There were one or two races exempted by a marvellous fate from this calamity, and grafts from these stocks have fertilised a few modern societies ; but it is still true that, over the larger part of the world, the perfection of law has always been considered as consisting in adherence to the ground-plan supposed to have been marked out by the original legislator. If intellect has in such cases been exercised on jurisprudence, it has uniformly prided itself on the subtle perversity of the conclusions it could build on ancient texts, without discoverable departure from their literal tenor. I know no reason why the law of the Romans should be superior to the laws of the Hindoos, unless the theory of Natural Law had given it a type of excellence different from the usual one. In this one exceptional instance, simplicity and symmetry were kept before the eyes of a society whose influence on mankind was destined to be prodigious from other causes, as the characteristics of an ideal and absolutely perfect law. It is impossible to overrate the importance to a nation or profession of having a

distinct object to aim at in the pursuit of improvement. The secret of Bentham's immense influence
in England during the past thirty years is his
success in placing such an object before the
country. He gave us a clear rule of reform.
English lawyers of the last century were probably
too acute to be blinded by the paradoxical commonplace that English law was the perfection of
human reason, but they acted as if they believed
it for want of any other principle to proceed upon.
Bentham made the good of the community take
precedence of every other object, and thus gave
escape to a current which had long been trying
to find its way outwards.

It is not an altogether fanciful comparison if
we call the assumptions we have been describing
the ancient counterpart of Benthamism. The
Roman theory guided men's efforts in the same
direction as the theory put into shape by the
Englishman ; its practical results were not widely
different from those which would have been
attained by a sect of law-reformers who maintained a steady pursuit of the general good of
the community. It would be a mistake, however,
to suppose it a conscious anticipation of Bentham's
principles. The happiness of mankind is, no
doubt, sometimes assigned, both in the popular
and in the legal literature of the Romans, as the
proper object of remedial legislation, but it is
very remarkable how few and faint are the
testimonies to this principle compared with the
tributes which are constantly offered to the overshadowing claims of the Law of Nature. It was
not to anything resembling philanthropy but to

their sense of simplicity and harmony—of what they significantly termed " elegance "—that the Roman jurisconsults freely surrendered themselves. The coincidence of their labours with those which a more precise philosophy would have counselled has been part of the good fortune of mankind

Turning to the modern history of the law of nature, we find it easier to convince ourselves of the vastness of its influence than to pronounce confidently whether that influence has been exerted for good or for evil. The doctrines and institutions which may be attributed to it are the material of some of the most violent controversies debated in our time, as will be seen when it is stated that the theory of Natural Law is the source of almost all the special ideas as to law, politics, and society which France during the last hundred years has been the instrument of diffusing over the western world. The part played by jurists in French history, and the sphere of jural conceptions in French thought, have always been remarkably large. It was not indeed in France, but in Italy, that the juridical science of modern Europe took its rise, but of the schools founded by emissaries of the Italian universities in all parts of the Continent, and attempted (though vainly) to be set up in our island, that established in France produced the greatest effect on the fortunes of the country. The lawyers of France immediately formed a strict alliance with the kings of the houses of Capet and Valois, and it was as much through their assertions of royal prerogative, and through their interpretations of the rules of feudal succession, as by the power of the sword that the French monarchy at last grew together out of the agglomeration of provinces and dependencies. The enormous advantage which their understanding with the lawyers conferred on the French kings in the prosecution of their struggle with the great feudatories, the aristocracy and the Church, can only be appreciated if we take into account the ideas which prevailed in Europe far down into the middle ages. There was, in the first place, a great enthusiasm for generalisation and a curious admiration for all general propositions, and consequently, in the field of law, an involuntary reverence for every general formula which seemed to embrace and sum up a number of the insulated rules which were practised as usages in various localities. Such general formulas it was, of course, not difficult for practitioners familiar with the Corpus Juris or the Glosses to supply in almost any quantity. There was, however, another cause which added yet more considerably to the lawyers' power. At the period of which we are speaking, there was universal vagueness of ideas as to the degree and nature of the authority residing in written texts of law. For the most part the peremptory preface, *Ita scriptum est*, seems to have been sufficient to silence all objections. Where a mind of our own day would jealously scrutinise the formula which had been quoted, would inquire its source, and would (if necessary) deny that the body of law to which it belonged had any authority to supersede local customs, the elder jurist would not probably have ventured to do more than question the applicability of the rule, or at best cite some counter-proposition from the Pandects or the Canon Law. It is extremely necessary to bear in mind the uncertainty of men's notions on this most important side of juridical controversies, not only because it helps to explain the weight which the lawyers threw into the monarchical scale, but on account of the light which it sheds on several curious historical problems. The motives of the author of the Forged Decretals and his extraordinary success are rendered more intelligible by it. And to take a phenomenon of smaller interest, it assists us, though only partially, to understand the plagiarisms of Bracton. That an English writer of the time of Henry III. should have been able to put off on his countrymen as a compendium of pure English law a treatise of which the entire form and a third of the contents were directly borrowed from the Corpus Juris, and that he should have ventured on this experiment in a country where the systematic study of the Roman Law was formally proscribed, will always be among the most hopeless enigmas in the history of jurisprudence; but still it is something to lessen our surprise when we comprehend the state of opinion at the period as to the obligatory force of written texts, apart from all consideration of the source whence they were derived.

When the kings of France had brought their long struggle for supremacy to a successful close, an epoch which may be placed roughly at the accession of the branch of Valois-Angoulême to

the throne, the situation of the French jurists
was peculiar, and continued to be so down to the
outbreak of the Revolution. On the one hand,
they formed the best instructed and nearly the
most powerful class in the nation. They had
made good their footing as a privileged order by
the side of the feudal aristocracy, and they had
assured their influence by an organisation which
distributed their profession over France in great
chartered corporations possessing large defined
powers and still larger indefinite claims. In all
the qualities of the advocate, the judge, and the
legislator, they far excelled their compeers throughout Europe. Their judicial tact, their ease of
expression, their fine sense of analogy and harmony,
and (if they may be judged by the highest names
among them) their passionate devotion to their
conceptions of justice, were as remarkable as
the singular variety of talent which they included,
a variety covering the whole ground between the
opposite poles of Cujas and Montesquieu, of
D'Aguesseau and Dumoulin. But, on the other
hand, the system of laws which they had to
administer stood in striking contrast with the
habits of mind which they had cultivated. The
France which had been in great part constituted
by their efforts was smitten with the curse of an
anomalous and dissonant jurisprudence beyond
every other country in Europe. One great division
ran through the country and separated it into
Pays de Droit Écrit and *Pays de Droit Coutumier*,
the first acknowledging the written Roman law
as the basis of their jurisprudence, the last admitting it only so far as it supplied general forms

of expression, and courses of juridical reasoning, which were reconcilable with the local usages. The sections thus formed were again variously subdivided. In the *Pays de Droit Coutumier* province differed from province, county from county, municipality from municipality, in the nature of its customs. In the *Pays de Droit Écrit* the stratum of feudal rules which overlay the Roman law was of the most miscellaneous composition. No such confusion as this ever existed in England. In Germany it did exist, but was too much in harmony with the deep political and religious divisions of the country to be lamented or even felt. It was the special peculiarity of France that an extraordinary diversity of laws continued without sensible alteration while the central authority of the monarchy was constantly strengthening itself, while rapid approaches were being made to complete administrative unity, and while a fervid national spirit had been developed among the people. The contrast was one which fructified in many serious results, and among them we must rank the effect which it produced on the minds of the French lawyers. Their speculative opinions and their intellectual bias were in the strongest opposition to their interests and professional habits. With the keenest sense and the fullest recognition of those perfections of jurisprudence which consist in simplicity and uniformity, they believed, or seemed to believe, that the vices which actually invested French law were ineradicable ; and in practice they often resisted the reformation of abuses with an obstinacy which was not shown by many among their less enlightened countrymen. But there was a way to reconcile these contradictions. They became passionate enthusiasts for Natural Law. The Law of Nature overleapt all provincial and municipal boundaries; it disregarded all distinctions between noble and burgess, between burgess and peasant; it gave the most exalted place to lucidity, simplicity, and system; but it committed its devotees to no specific improvement, and did not directly threaten any venerable or lucrative technicality. Natural law may be said to have become the common law of France, or, at all events, the admission of its dignity and claims was the one tenet which all French practitioners alike subscribed to. The language of the præ-revolutionary jurists in its eulogy is singularly unqualified, and it is remarkable that the writers on the Customs, who often made it their duty to speak disparagingly of the pure Roman law, speak even more fervidly of Nature and her rules than the civilians who professed an exclusive respect for the Digest and the Code. Dumoulin, the highest of all authorities on old French Customary Law, has some extravagant passages on the Law of Nature; and his panegyrics have a peculiar rhetorical turn which indicates a considerable departure·from the caution of the Roman jurisconsults. The hypothesis of a Natural Law had become not so much a theory guiding practice as an article of speculative faith, and accordingly we shall find that, in the transformation which it more recently underwent, its weakest parts rose to the level of its strongest in the esteem of its supporters.

The eighteenth century was half over when
the most critical period in the history of Natural
Law was reached. Had the discussion of the
theory and of its consequences continued to be
exclusively the employment of the legal profession,
there would possibly have been an abatement
of the respect which it commanded ; for by this
time the *Esprit des Lois* had appeared. Bearing
in some exaggerations the marks of the excessive
violence with which its author's mind had recoiled
from assumptions usually suffered to pass without
scrutiny, yet showing in some ambiguities the
traces of a desire to compromise with existing
prejudice, the book of Montesquieu, with all
its defects, still proceeded on that Historical
Method before which the Law of Nature has never
maintained its footing for an instant. Its influence
on thought ought to have been as great as its
general popularity ; but, in fact, it was never
allowed time to put it forth, for the counter-
hypothesis which it seemed destined to destroy
passed suddenly from the forum to the street,
and became the key-note of controversies far
more exciting than are ever agitated in the courts
or the schools. The person who launched it on
its new career was that remarkable man who,
without learning, with few virtues, and with no
strength of character, has nevertheless stamped
himself ineffaceably on history by the force of a
vivid imagination, and by the help of a genuine
and burning love for his fellow-men, for which
much will always have to be forgiven him. We
have never seen in our own generation—indeed
the world has not seen more than once or twice

in all the course of history—a literature which
has exercised such prodigious influence over the
minds of men, over every cast and shade of
intellect, as that which emanated from Rousseau
between 1749 and 1762. It was the first attempt
to re-erect the edifice of human belief after the
purely iconoclastic efforts commenced by Bayle,
and in part by our own Locke, and consummated
by Voltaire ; and besides the superiority which
every constructive effort will always enjoy over
one that is merely destructive, it possessed the
immense advantage of appearing amid an all
but universal scepticism as to the soundness of
all foregone knowledge in matters speculative.
Now, in all the speculations of Rousseau, the
central figure, whether arrayed in an English
dress as the signatary of a social compact, or
simply stripped naked of all historical qualities,
is uniformly Man, in a supposed state of nature.
Every law or institution which would misbeseem
this imaginary being under these ideal circumstances is to be condemned as having lapsed
from an original perfection ; every transformation
of society which would give it a closer resemblance
to the world over which the creature of Nature
reigned, is admirable and worthy to be effected
at any apparent cost. The theory is still that of
the Roman lawyers, for in the phantasmagoria
with which the Natural Condition is peopled,
every feature and characteristic eludes the mind
except the simplicity and harmony which possessed
such charms for the jurisconsult ; but the theory
is, as it were, turned upside down. It is not
the Law of Nature, but the State of Nature, which

is now the primary subject of contemplation. The Roman had conceived that by careful observation of existing institutions parts of them could be singled out which either exhibited already, or could by judicious purification be made to exhibit, the vestiges of that reign of nature whose reality he faintly affirmed. Rousseau's belief was that a perfect social order could be evolved from the unassisted consideration of the natural state, a social order wholly irrespective of the actual condition of the world and wholly unlike it. The great difference between the views is that one bitterly and broadly condemns the present for its unlikeness to the ideal past ; while the other, assuming the present to be as necessary as the past, does not affect to disregard or censure it.   It is not worth our while to analyse with any particularity that philosophy of politics, art, education, ethics, and social relations which was constructed on the basis of a state of nature. It still possesses singular fascination for the looser thinkers of every country, and is no doubt the parent, more or less remote, of almost all the prepossessions which impede the employment of the Historical Method of inquiry, but its discredit with the higher minds of our day is deep enough to astonish those who are familiar with the extraordinary vitality of speculative error.   Perhaps the question most frequently asked nowadays is not what is the value of these opinions, but what were the causes which gave them such overshadowing prominence a hundred years ago. The answer is, I conceive, a simple one.   The study which in the last century would best have corrected the misapprehensions into which an exclusive attention to legal antiquities is apt to betray was the study of religion. But Greek religion, as then understood, was dissipated in imaginative myths. The Oriental religions, if noticed at all, appeared to be lost in vain cosmogonies. There was but one body of primitive records which was worth studying—the early history of the Jews. But resort to this was prevented by the prejudices of the time. One of the few characteristics which the school of Rousseau had in common with the school of Voltaire was an utter disdain of all religious antiquities ; and, more than all, of those of the Hebrew race. It is well known that it was a point of honour with the reasoners of that day to assume not merely that the institutions called after Moses were not divinely dictated, nor even that they were codified at a later date than that attributed to them, but that they and the entire Pentateuch were a gratuitous forgery, executed after the return from the Captivity. Debarred, therefore, from one chief security against speculative delusion, the philosophers of France, in their eagerness to escape from what they deemed a superstition of the priests, flung themselves headlong into a superstition of the lawyers.

But though the philosophy founded on the hypothesis of a state of nature has fallen low in general esteem, in so far as it is looked upon under its coarser and more palpable aspect, it does not follow that in its subtler disguises it has lost plausibility, popularity, or power. I believe, as I have said, that it is still the great antagonist of the Historical Method ; and whenever (religious objections apart) any mind is seen to resist or contemn that mode of investigation, it will generally be found under the influence of a prejudice or vicious bias traceable to a conscious or unconscious reliance on a non-historic, natural condition of society or the individual. It is chiefly, however, by allying themselves with political and social tendencies that the doctrines of Nature and her law have preserved their energy. Some of these tendencies they have stimulated, others they have actually created, to a great number they have given expression and form. They visibly enter largely into the ideas which constantly radiate from France over the civilised world, and thus become part of the general body of thought by which its civilisation is modified. The value of the influence which they thus exercise over the fortunes of the race is of course one of the points which our age debates most warmly, and it is beside the purpose of this treatise to discuss it. Looking back, however, to the period at which the theory of the state of nature acquired the maximum of political importance, there are few who will deny that it helped most powerfully to bring about the grosser disappointments of which the first French Revolution was fertile. It gave birth, or intense stimulus, to the vices of mental habit all but universal at the time, disdain of positive law, impatience of experience, and the preference of à priori to all other reasoning. In proportion too as this philosophy fixes its grasp on minds which have thought less than others and fortified

themselves with smaller observation, its tendency
it to become distinctly anarchical. It is surprising
to note how many of the *Sophismes Anarchiques*
which Dumont published for Bentham, and which
embody Bentham's exposure of errors distinctively
French, are derived from the Roman hypothesis
in its French transformation, and are unintelligible
unless referred to it. On this point too it is a
curious exercise to consult the *Moniteur* during
the principal eras of the Revolution. The appeals
to the Law and State of Nature become thicker
as the times grow darker.

There is a single example which very strikingly
illustrates the effects of the theory of natural law
on modern society, and indicates how very far are
those effects from being exhausted. There cannot,
I conceive, be any question that to the assumption
of a Law Natural we owe the doctrine of the
fundamental equality of human beings. That " all
men are equal " is one of a large number of legal
propositions which in progress of time have
become political. The Roman jurisconsults of
the Antonine era lay down that " omnes homines
naturâ æquales sunt," but in their eyes this is a
strictly juridical axiom. They intend to affirm
that, under the hypothetical Law of Nature, and
in so far as positive law approximates to it, the
arbitrary distinctions which the Roman Civil Law
maintained between classes of persons cease to
have a legal existence. The rule was one of considerable importance to the Roman practitioner,
who required to be reminded that, wherever
Roman jurisprudence was assumed to conform
itself exactly to the code of Nature, there was no

difference in the contemplation of the Roman tribunals between citizen and foreigner, between freeman and slave, between Agnate and Cognate. The jurisconsults who thus expressed themselves most certainly never intended to censure the social arrangements under which civil law fell somewhat short of its speculative type ; nor did they apparently believe that the world would ever see human society completely assimilated to the economy of nature.   But when the doctrine of human equality makes its appearance in a modern dress it has evidently clothed itself with a new shade of meaning. Where the Roman jurisconsult had written " æquales sunt," meaning exactly what he said, the modern civilian wrote " all men are equal " in the sense of " all men ought to be equal." The peculiar Roman idea that natural law coexisted with civil law and gradually absorbed it, had evidently been lost sight of, or had become unintelligible, and the words which had at most conveyed a theory concerning the origin, composition, and development of human institutions, were beginning to express the sense of a great standing wrong suffered by mankind. As early as the beginning of the fourteenth century, the current language concerning the birth-state of men, though visibly intended to be identical with that of Ulpian and his contemporaries, has assumed an altogether different form and meaning. The preamble to the celebrated ordinance of King Louis Hutin, enfranchising the serfs of the royal domains, would have sounded strangely to Roman ears.   " Whereas, according to natural law, everybody ought to be born free ; and by some usages

7

and customs which, from long antiquity, have
been introduced and kept until now in our realm,
and peradventure by reason of the misdeeds of
their predecessors, many persons of our common
people have fallen into servitude, therefore, We,"
etc. This is the enunciation not of a legal rule but
of a political dogma; and from this time the
equality of men is spoken of by the French lawyers
just as if it were a political truth which happened
to have been preserved among the archives of
their science. Like all other deductions from the
hypothesis of a Law Natural, and like the belief
itself in a Law of Nature, it was languidly assented
to and suffered to have little influence on opinion
and practice until it passed out of the possession
of the lawyers into that of the literary men of the
eighteenth century and of the public which sat
at their feet. With them it became the most
distinct tenet of their creed, and was even regarded
as a summary of all the others. It is probable,
however, that the power which it ultimately acquired over the events of 1789 was not entirely
owing to its popularity in France, for in the middle
of the century it passed over to America. The
American lawyers of the time, and particularly
those of Virginia, appear to have possessed a stock
of knowledge which differed chiefly from that of
their English contemporaries in including much
which could only have been derived from the legal
literature of continental Europe. A very few
glances at the writings of Jefferson will show how
strongly his mind was affected by the semi-juri-
dical, semi-popular opinions which were fashionable
in France, and we cannot doubt that it was

sympathy with the peculiar ideas of the French
jurists which led him and the other colonial
lawyers who guided the course of events in America
to join the specially French assumption that " all
men are born equal " with the assumption, more
familiar to Englishmen, that all men are born
free, in the very first lines of their Declaration of
Independence. The passage was one of great
importance to the history of the doctrine before
us. The American lawyers, in thus prominently
and emphatically affirming the fundamental equality of human beings, gave an impulse to political
movements in their own country, and in a less
degree in Great Britain, which is far from having
yet spent itself; but besides this they returned
the dogma they had adopted to its home in France,
endowed with vastly greater energy and enjoying
much greater claims on general reception and
respect. Even the more cautious politicians of
the first Constituent Assembly repeated Ulpian's
proposition as if it at once commended itself to the
instincts and intuitions of mankind; and of all
the " principles of 1789 " it is the one which has
been least strenuously assailed, which has most
thoroughly leavened modern opinion, and which
promises to modify most deeply the constitution
of societies and the politics of states.

The greatest function of the Law of Nature was
discharged in giving birth to modern International
Law and to the modern Law of War, but this part
of its effects must here be dismissed with consideration very unequal to its importance.

Among the postulates which form the foundation of International Law, or of so much of it

as retains the figure which it received from its
original architects, there are two or three of pre-
eminent importance. The first of all is expressed
in the position that there is a determinable Law
of Nature. Grotius and his successors took the
assumption directly from the Romans, but they
differed widely from the Roman jurisconsults and
from each other in their ideas as to the mode of
determination. The ambition of almost every
Publicist who has flourished since the revival of
letters has been to provide new and more manage-
able definitions of Nature and of her law, and it
is indisputable that the conception in passing
through the long series of writers on Public Law
has gathered round it a large accretion, consisting
of fragments of ideas derived from nearly every
theory of ethics which has in its turn taken
possession of the schools. Yet it is a remarkable
proof of the essentially historical character of the
conception that, after all the efforts which have
been made to evolve the code of Nature from the
necessary characteristics of the natural state, so
much of the result is just what it would have been
if men had been satisfied to adopt the dicta of the
Roman lawyers without questioning or reviewing
them. Setting aside the Conventional or Treaty
Law of Nations, it is surprising how large a part
of the system is made up of pure Roman law.
Wherever there is a doctrine of the jurisconsults
affirmed by them to be in harmony with the Jus
Gentium, the Publicists have found a reason for
borrowing it, however plainly it may bear the
marks of a distinctively Roman origin. We may
observe too that the derivative theories are afflicted

with the weakness of the primary notion. In the majority of the Publicists, the mode of thought is still "mixed." In studying these writers, the great difficulty is always to discover whether they are discussing law or morality—whether the state of international relations they describe is actual or ideal—whether they lay down that which is, or that which, in their opinion, ought to be.

The assumption that Natural Law is binding on states *inter se* is the next in rank of those which underlie International Law. A series of assertions or admissions of this principle may be traced up to the very infancy of modern juridical science, and at first sight it seems a direct inference from the teaching of the Romans. The civil condition of society being distinguished from the natural by the fact that in the first there is a distinct author of law, while in the last there is none, it appears as if the moment a number of *units* were acknowledged to obey no common sovereign or political superior they were thrown back on the ulterior behests of the Law Natural. States are such units ; the hypothesis of their independence excludes the notion of a common lawgiver, and draws with it, therefore, according to a certain range of ideas, the notion of subjection to the primeval order of nature. The alternative is to consider independent communities as not related to each other .by any law, but this condition of lawlessness is exactly the vacuum which the Nature of the jurisconsults abhorred. There is certainly apparent reason for thinking that if the mind of a Roman lawyer rested on any sphere from which civil law was banished, it would

instantly fill the void with the ordinances of
Nature. It is never safe, however, to assume that
conclusions, however certain and.immediate in our
own eyes, were actually drawn at any period of
history. No passage has ever been adduced from
the remains of Roman law which, in my judgment,
proves the jurisconsults to have believed natural
law to have obligatory force between independent
commonwealths ; and we cannot but see that to
citizens of the Roman empire, who regarded their
sovereign's dominions as conterminous with civilisation, the equal subjection of states to the Law
of Nature, if contemplated at all, must have
seemed at most an extreme result of curious
speculation. The truth appears to be that modern
International Law, undoubted as is its descent
from Roman law, is only connected with it by an
irregular filiation. The early modern interpreters
of the jurisprudence of Rome, misconceiving the
meaning of Jus Gentium, assumed without hesitation that the Romans had bequeathed to them a
system of rules for the adjustment of international
transactions. This " Law of Nations " was at first
an authority which had formidable competitors
to strive with, and the condition of Europe was
long such as to preclude its universal reception.
Gradually, however, the western world arranged
itself in a form more favourable to the theory of
the civilians ; circumstances destroyed the credit
of rival doctrines ; and at last, at a peculiarly
felicitous conjuncture, Ayala and Grotius were
able to obtain for it the enthusiastic assent of
Europe, an assent which has been over and over
again renewed in every variety of solemn engage-

ment. The great men to whom its triumph is chiefly owing attempted, it need scarcely be said, to place it on an entirely new basis, and it is unquestionable that in the course of this displacement they altered much of its structure, though far less of it than is commonly supposed. Having adopted from the Antonine jurisconsults the position that the Jus Gentium and the Jus Naturæ were identical, Grotius, with his immediate predecessors and his immediate successors, attributed to the Law of Nature an authority which would never perhaps have been claimed for it, if " Law of Nations " had not in that age been an ambiguous expression. They laid down unreservedly that Natural Law is the code of states, and thus put in operation a process which has continued almost down to our own day, the process of engrafting on the international system rules which are supposed to have been evolved from the unassisted contemplation of the conception of Nature. There is, too, one consequence of immense practical importance to mankind which, though not unknown during the early modern history of Europe, was never clearly or universally acknowledged till the doctrines of the Grotian school had prevailed. If the society of nations is governed by Natural Law, the atoms which compose it must be absolutely equal. Men under the sceptre of Nature are all equal, and accordingly commonwealths are equal if the international state be one of nature. The proposition that independent communities, however different in size and power, are all equal in the view of the law of nations, has largely contributed to the happiness of mankind, though

it is constantly threatened by the political tendencies of each successive age. It is a doctrine
which probably would never have obtained a
secure footing at all if International Law had not
been entirely derived from the majestic claims of
Nature by the Publicists who wrote after the
revival of letters.

On the whole, however, it is astonishing, as I
have observed before, how small a proportion the
additions made to International Law since Grotius's day bear to the ingredients which have been
simply taken from the most ancient stratum of
the Roman Jus Gentium. Acquisition of territory
has always been the great spur of national ambition, and the rules which govern this acquisition,
together with the rules which moderate the wars
in which it too frequently results, are merely
transcribed from the part of the Roman Law
which treats of the modes of acquiring property
jure gentium. These modes of acquisition were
obtained by the elder jurisconsults, as I have
attempted to explain, by abstracting a common
ingredient from the usages observed to prevail
among the various tribes surrounding Rome ; and,
having been classed on account of their origin
in the " law common to all nations," they were
thought by the later lawyers to fit in, on the score
of their simplicity, with the more recent conception
of a Law Natural. They thus made their way
into the modern Law of Nations, and the result
is that those parts of the international system
which refer to *dominion*, its nature, its limitations,
the modes of acquiring and securing it, are pure
Roman Property Law—so much, that is to say,

of the Roman Law of Property as the Antonine
jurisconsults imagined to exhibit a certain con-
gruity with the natural state.   In order that these
chapters of International Law may be capable of
application, it is necessary that sovereigns should
be related to each other like the members of a
group of Roman proprietors.   This is another of
the postulates which lie at the threshold of the
International Code, and it is also one which could
not possibly have been subscribed to during the
first centuries of modern European history.   It is
resolvable into the double proposition that " sovereignty is territorial," *i.e.*, that it is always associated with the proprietorship of a limited portion
of the earth's surface, and that " sovereigns *inter
se* are to be deemed not *paramount*, but *absolute*,
owners of the state's territory."

Many contemporary writers on International
Law tacitly assume that the doctrines of their
system, founded on principles of equity and
common sense, were capable of being readily
reasoned out in every stage of modern civilisation.
But this assumption, while it conceals some real
defects of the international theory, is altogether
untenable so far as regards a large part of modern
history.   It is not true that the authority of the
Jus Gentium in the concerns of nations was
always uncontradicted ; on the contrary, it had
to struggle long against the claims of several
competing systems.   It is again not true that the
territorial character of sovereignty was always
recognised, for long after the dissolution of the
Roman dominion the minds of men were under
the empire of ideas irreconcilable with such a

conception. An old order of things, and of views
founded on it, had to decay—a new Europe, and
an apparatus of new notions congenial to it, had
to spring up—before two of the chiefest postulates
of International Law could be universally conceded.

It is a consideration well worthy to be kept in
view, that during a large part of what we usually
term modern history no such conception was
entertained as that of "*territorial sovereignty*."
Sovereignty was not associated with dominion
over a portion or subdivision of the earth. The
world had lain for so many centuries under the
shadow of Imperial Rome as to have forgotten that
distribution of the vast spaces comprised in the
Empire which had once parcelled them out into
a number of independent commonwealths, claiming
immunity from extrinsic interference, and pretending to equality of national rights. After the
subsidence of the barbarian irruptions, the notion
of sovereignty that prevailed seems to have been
twofold. On the one hand it assumed the form
of what may be called "*tribe*-sovereignty." The
Franks, the Burgundians, the Vandals, the Lom-
bards, and Visigoths were masters, of course, of
the territories which they occupied, and to which
some of them have given a geographical appellation ; but they based no claim of right upon the
fact of territorial possession, and indeed attached
no importance to it whatever. They appear to
have retained the traditions which they brought
with them from the forest and the steppe, and to
have still been in their own view a patriarchal
society, a nomad horde, merely encamped for the

time upon the soil which afforded them sustenance.
Part of Transalpine Gaul, with part of Germany,
had now become the country *de facto* occupied by
the Franks—it was France ; but the Merovingian
line of chieftains, the descendants of Clovis, were
not Kings of France, they were Kings of the
Franks.   Territorial titles were not unknown, but
they seem at first to have come into use only as a
convenient mode of designating the ruler of a *portion* of the tribe's possessions ; the king of a *whole*
tribe was king of his people, not of his people's
lands.   The alternative to this peculiar notion of
sovereignty appears to have been—and this is the
important point—the idea of universal dominion.
When a monarch departed from the special
relation of chief to clansmen, and became solicitous,
for purposes of his own, to invest himself with a
novel form of sovereignty, the precedent which
suggested itself for his adoption was the domination of the Emperors of Rome.   To parody a
common quotation, he became " *aut Cæsar aut
nullus.*"   Either he pretended to the full prerogative of the Byzantine Emperor, or he had no
political status.   In our own age, when a new
dynasty is desirous of obliterating the prescriptive
title of a deposed line of sovereigns, it takes its
designation from the *people*, instead of the *territory*.
Thus we have Emperors and Kings of the French,
and a King of the Belgians.   At the period of
which we have been speaking, under similar
circumstances, a different alternative presented
itself.   The Chieftain who would no longer call
himself King of the tribe must claim to be Emperor
of the world.   Thus, when the hereditary Mayors

of the Palace had ceased to compromise with the monarchs they had long since virtually dethroned, they soon became unwilling to call themselves merely Kings of the Franks, a title which belonged to the displaced Merovings ; but they could not style themselves Kings of France, for such a designation, though apparently not unknown, was not a title of dignity. Accordingly they came forward as aspirants to universal empire. Their motive has been greatly misapprehended. It has been taken for granted by recent French writers that Charlemagne was far before his age, quite as much in the character of his designs as in the energy with which he prosecuted them. Whether it be true or not that anybody is at any time before his age, it is certainly true that Charlemagne, in aiming at an unlimited dominion, was emphatically taking the only course which the characteristic ideas of his age permitted him to follow. Of his intellectual eminence there cannot be a question, but it is proved by his acts and not by his theory.

The speculative universality of sovereignty long continued to be associated with the Imperial throne, and indeed was never thoroughly dissociated from it so long as the empire of Germany lasted. Territorial sovereignty—the view which connects sovereignty with the possession of a limited portion of the earth's surface—was distinctly an offshoot, though a tardy one, of *feudalism*. This might have been expected *à priori*, for it was feudalism which for the first time linked personal duties, and by consequence personal rights, to the ownership of land. Whatever be

the proper view of its origin and legal nature, the
best mode of vividly picturing to ourselves the
feudal organisation is to begin with the basis ;
to consider the relation of the tenant to the patch
of soil which created and limited his services—and
then to mount up, through narrowing circles of
super-feudation, till we approximate to the apex
of the system.   Where that summit exactly was
during the later portion of the dark ages it is not
easy to decide.   Probably, wherever the conception of tribe sovereignty had really decayed, the
topmost point was always assigned to the supposed
successor of the Cæsars of the West.   But before
long, when the actual sphere of Imperial authority
had immensely contracted, and when the emperors
had concentrated the scanty remains of their
power upon Germany and North Italy, the highest
feudal superiors in all the outlying portions of
the former Carlovingian empire found themselves
practically without a supreme head.   Gradually
they habituated themselves to the new situation,
and the fact of immunity put at last out of sight
the theory of dependence ; but there are many
symptoms that this change was not quite easily
accomplished; and, indeed, to the impression that
in the nature of things there must necessarily be
a culminating domination somewhere, we may,
no doubt, refer the increasing tendency to attribute
secular superiority to the See of Rome.   The
completion of the first stage in the revolution of
opinion is marked, of course, by the accession of
the Capetian dynasty in France.   Before that
epoch arrived, several of the holders of the great
territorial fiefs into which the Carlovingian empire

was now split up, had begun to call themselves
Kings, instead of Dukes or Counts; but the
important change occurred when the feudal prince
of a limited territory surrounding Paris, usurped
from the earlier house their dynastic title of *Kings
of the French*. Hugues Capet and his descendants
were kings in quite a new sense, sovereigns standing
in the same relation to the soil of France as the
baron to his estate, the tenant to his freehold;
and the old tribal appellation, though long retained
in the official Latin style of the reigning house,
passed rapidly, in the vernacular, into *Kings of
France*. The form of the monarchy in France
had visible effects in hastening changes which
were elsewhere proceeding in the same direction.
The kingship of our Anglo-Saxon regal houses was
midway between the chieftainship of a tribe and
a territorial supremacy; but the superiority of
the Norman monarchs, imitated from that of the
King of France, was distinctly a territorial sovereignty. Every subsequent dominion which was
established or consolidated was formed on the
later model. Spain, Naples, and the principalities
founded on the ruins of municipal freedom in
Italy, were all under rulers whose sovereignty
was territorial. Few things, I may add, are
more curious than the gradual lapse of the
Venetians from one view to the other. At the
commencement of its foreign conquests, the republic regarded itself as an antitype of the
Roman commonwealth, governing a number of
subject provinces. Move a century onwards,
and you find that it wishes to be looked upon
as a corporate sovereign, claiming the rights of

a feudal suzerain over its possessions in Italy and the Ægean.

During the period through which the popular ideas on the subject of sovereignty were undergoing this remarkable change, the system which stood in the place of what we now call International Law was heterogeneous in form and inconsistent in the principles to which it appealed. Over so much of Europe as was comprised in the Romano-German empire, the connection of the confederate states was regulated by the complex and as yet incomplete mechanism of the Imperial constitution ; and, surprising as it may seem to us, it was a favourite notion of German lawyers that the relations of commonwealths, whether inside or outside the empire, ought to be regulated not by the *Jus Gentium*, but by the pure Roman jurisprudence of which Cæsar was still the centre. This doctrine was less confidently repudiated in the outlying countries than we might have supposed antecedently ; but substantially, through the rest of Europe feudal subordinations furnished a substitute for a public law ; and when those were undetermined or ambiguous, there lay behind, in theory at least, a supreme regulating force in the authority of the head of the Church. It is certain, however, that both feudal and ecclesiastical influences were rapidly decaying during the fifteenth and even the fourteenth century ; and if we closely examine the current pretexts of wars, and the avowed motives of alliances, it will be seen that, step by step with the displacement of the old principles, the views afterwards harmonised and consolidated by Ayala and Grotius were

making considerable progress, though it was silent
and but slow. Whether the fusion of all the
sources of authority would ultimately have evolved
a system of international relations, and whether
that system would have exhibited material differences from the fabric of Grotius, is not now possible
to decide, for as a matter of fact the Reformation
annihilated all its potential elements except one.
Beginning in Germany, it divided the princes of
the empire by a gulf too broad to be bridged over
by the Imperial supremacy, even if the Imperial
superior had stood neutral. He, however, was
forced to take colour with the Church against the
reformers; the Pope was, as a matter of course,
in the same predicament; and thus the two
authorities to whom belonged the office of media-
tion between combatants became themselves the
chiefs of one great faction in the schism of the
nations. Feudalism, already enfeebled and discredited as a principle of public relations, furnished
no bond whatever which was stable enough to
countervail the alliances of religion. In a condition, therefore, of public law which was little less
than chaotic, those views of a state system to
which the Roman jurisconsults were supposed to
have given their sanction alone remained standing.
The shape, the symmetry, and the prominence
which they assumed in the hands of Grotius are
known to every educated man; but the great
marvel of the treatise " De Jure Belli et Pacis,"
was its rapid, complete, and universal success.
The horrors of the Thirty Years' War, the boundless terror and pity which the unbridled licence
of the soldiery was exciting, must, no doubt, be

taken to explain that success in some measure, but they do not wholly account for it. Very little penetration into the ideas of that age is required to convince one that, if the ground-plan of the international edifice which was sketched in the great book of Grotius had not appeared to be theoretically perfect, it would have been discarded by jurists and neglected by statesmen and soldiers.

It is obvious that the speculative perfection of the Grotian system is intimately connected with that conception of territorial sovereignty which we have been discussing. The theory of International Law assumes that commonwealths are, relatively to each other, in a state of nature ; but the component atoms of a natural society must, by the fundamental assumption, be insulated and independent of each other. If there be a higher power connecting them, however slightly and occasionally, by the claim of common supremacy, the very conception of a common superior introduces the notion of positive Law, and excludes the idea of a law natural. It follows, therefore, that if the universal suzerainty of an Imperial head had been admitted even in bare theory, the labours of Grotius would have been idle. Nor is this the only point of junction between modern public law and those views of sovereignty of which I have endeavoured to describe the development. I have said that there are entire departments of international jurisprudence which consist of the Roman Law of Property. What then is the inference ? It is, that if there had been no such change as I have described in the estimate of

8

sovereignty—if sovereignty had not been associated with the proprietorship of a limited portion of the earth, had not, in other words, become territorial—three parts of the Grotian theory would have been incapable of application.

NOTE G

MEDIEVAL AND MODERN TREATMENT OF THE LAW OF NATURE: BRACTON: FRENCH PUBLICISTS

MUCH that has been written about the law of nature in modern times is, as Maine says, extremely confused. This may be due to several causes, but one cause which would alone be sufficient is the neglect of the scholastic tradition, amounting to practical oblivion, which followed on the Reformation controversies. Hooker was the latest English writer who possessed the tradition, and accordingly stated a consistent and intelligible doctrine. What the canonists and schoolmen added to the classical Roman theory was the identification of the law of nature with the law of God revealed in human reason: in this way they reconciled the temporal authority of the Corpus Iuris and the moral authority of the philosophers (for Aristotle and Cicero, though heathens, had become almost sacred by orthodox commendations) with the spiritual authority of the Church. The natural revelation through reason and the supernatural revelation committed to the Church are equally divine, and cannot contradict one another; and the law of nature is no less paramount to any positive rule or custom of human origin than express revelation itself. The risk of this doctrine being turned against the Church or the Pope was, no doubt, serious, as later events proved; but it had to be taken. Hence the scholastic theory of the law of nature, though attempts were made to use it for the most opposite purposes, was on the whole rationalist and progressive. Indeed, it had several points of affinity with the utilitarian doctrine of our own times, although the founders of that school, who may be said to have neglected history on principle, were unaware of the fact. Natural justice had been identified by Epicurus with an agreement among men for their common advantage to abstain from harming one another (see Bryce, "Studies," ii. 127). In the fourteenth century we actually find *communis utilitas* a current term with William of Ockham and others, and it is used to denote a criterion for ascertaining what the law of nature prescribes; and this was only the development of a tendency already visible in St. Thomas

Aquinas. Maine perceived the analogy, and suggested that it might not be too fanciful to call natural law the ancient counterpart of Benthamism (p. 84).

Beyond the fundamental principles of natural justice, we may deduce by natural reason various rules which may or might be convenient in the absence of competent jurisdiction, but, as they are in matter of convenience and not of absolute right, may be modified by the law of the land. Rules of this kind were said to be secondary; and the so-called "state of nature" is, from the point of view of the schoolmen, merely human society conceived as governed by the "secondary law of nature" in default of positive ordinance, or any human society so far as it is actually found in that condition. Thus during a great part of the Middle Ages most of what we know as the law of contract was left to the law of nature, which was supposed to be the ultimate authority for the custom of merchants. Nothing can more strongly illustrate the confusion which resulted from neglecting this distinction than the modern belief that natural law as a whole depends on the "state of nature," or assumes it to be better than civilization. The scholastic habit of mind was alien from ours in many ways; but at any rate the schoolmen took some pains to know what they were talking about.

Hooker's statement of the first principles, as understood down to the sixteenth century, is quite accurate, and perhaps the most profitable for English readers. The law of nature is a law of reason. Its rules "are investigable by Reason, without the help of Revelation supernatural and divine . . . the knowledge of them is general, the world hath always been acquainted with them. . . . It is not agreed upon by one, or two, or few, but by all. Which we may not so understand, as if every particular man in the whole world did know and confess whatsoever the law of reason doth contain; but this law is such that being proposed no man can reject it as unreasonable and unjust. Again, there is nothing in it but any man (having natural perfection of wit and ripeness of judgment) may by labour and travail find out." But the law of nature does not include all binding laws: "we restrain it to those only duties, which all men by force of natural wit either do or might understand to be such duties as concern all men" ("Eccl. Pol." I. viii. 10). A strange contrast to Hooker's clear apprehension and intelligent use of the medieval tradition is presented by the loose talk about the law of nature and the law of reason (apparently supposed to be different things) in Sir Henry Finch's "Discourse of Law," published in 1613. Before the middle of the eighteenth century the conception of "the aboriginal reign of nature" had gained a footing, and the confusion was complete. No less a man than Montesquieu thought natural law could be defined merely as the rules that would have been appropriate for men living before the

formation of civil society ("Esprit des Lois," I. ii.). The vitality of
the old doctrine had in truth passed into the new science built on
its foundations by Grotius and his successors ; and such ornamental
references to the law of nature as occur in Blackstone and other
English writers of his time are echoes of contemporary or recent
Continental publicists whose real subject-matter was the law of
nations in its modern sense. In later Continental and especially
German usage natural law is taken, by a considerable but legitimate extension, to denote all speculative construction in jurisprudence and politics as contrasted with the purely historical or
comparative study of institutions : in the terms most familiar to
English readers, it covers the whole ground of general jurisprudence
and the theory of legislation. Herbert Spencer's volume on Justice
and the essays of the Fabian Society would alike be classed as
books of *Naturrecht*. Writers of the historical school who consider the law of nature obsolete include British utilitarian doctrine
in their condemnation as a matter of course, as being a mere
branch of it.

There are some incidental statements of Maine's in this connexion which need comment. What is said about the unquestion-
ing respect paid in the Middle Ages to written texts is undoubtedly
true, and is indeed rather understated. Reverence for any plausible
show of authority was not confined to theology or law, and it was
not necessary that the text quoted should purport to have any
obligatory force, or that the sense in which it was quoted should be
the natural one. Aristotle was nearly as good authority as the
Bible, though not quite ; Cicero was only second to Aristotle ; and
the Corpus Iuris was " written reason " even in jurisdictions where
it was not binding. But in default of the Vulgate or the Philosopher,
learned writers were glad enough to quote Virgil or Ovid or Lucan,
though without any intention of putting them on a level with
Scripture. Maine's particular illustration from "the plagiarisms
of Bracton" is unfortunate. I do not know on what book or man
having a pretended knowledge of Bracton he relied ; certainly there
were very few men living forty-five years ago who had studied
Bracton to such purpose as to be qualified to inform him, and
certainly he had not then made any critical examination of his own ;
but the solution of the historical enigma which Maine, with great
reason, found in Bracton's alleged wholesale borrowing from Roman
law is simply that the fact is not so. Not one-thirtieth of Bracton's
matter, instead of a third as affirmed by Maine's unknown authority,
is taken from the Corpus Iuris (Maitland, " Bracton and Azo,"
Selden Soc. 1895, p. xiv, which see on the whole matter). Bracton
used Roman law, chiefly through Azo's famous gloss, partly as a
systematic framework and partly as a store of written reason to
fill up gaps in English learning. He had no thought of putting
it off on his countrymen as "pure English law," any more than

a lawyer at Paris would have sought to put it off as pure Parisian custom; there is no concealment of its origin. When actual English custom was contrary to Roman law, Henry of Bratton (for such, it is now known, was his real name) did not hesitate to deny the Roman propositions.

Further, it is at least misleading to say that "the systematic study of the Roman law was formerly proscribed" in England. The only prohibition of which there is any evidence was confined to London; it is doubtful whether its purpose was to hold clerks in orders to their proper study of the canon as distinguished from the civil law, or to prevent London teachers from competing with the civilians of Oxford (Pollock and Maitland, "H.E.L.," i. 102). The earlier story of Stephen prohibiting Vacarius is ambiguous; it does not show whether he objected to the doctrines of Roman law or to the person of Vacarius, or whether his objection was founded on any permanent reason. All we know is that John of Salisbury thought Stephen's action, whatever it was, unreasonable; as indeed it is quite likely to have been. It may have been a mere caprice. Roman law was not only taught at Oxford and Cambridge without interruption, but sometimes, though not often, cited, at least in a general way, in the King's Courts (Selden ad Fletam, pp. 528-530).[1] There is no reason whatever to suppose that any one thought it needful or expedient to protect the Common Law against a Roman invasion. Blackstone (" Comm.," i. 20-22) contrived, by accumulating mistakes, to draw an imaginary picture of English aversion and contempt for the civil law. In the case cited by him, Y. B. 22 Ed. III. 14 (not 24), what really happened was this. Counsel said, by way of preliminary objection, that the Court had no judicial knowledge of what the civilian—or rather, in the case in hand, canonist—process of *inhibitio novi operis* was: to which Justice Shardelowe replied in effect: " That is only what they call restitution in their law, so we think nothing of your point; you must answer to the merits "; and the argument proceeded accordingly. Nothing here shows very gross ignorance, although the language might not satisfy a learned civilian; the Court, so far from treating Roman words of art as nonsense, professed to understand them quite enough for the purpose in hand; and the only contempt in question was that of an abbot who was charged with having cited a prior to the Pope's Court at Avignon and persisted in disregard of the king's prohibition. But in the nineteenth century an over-zealous Romanizing lawyer

[1] Selden speaks of two cases in a certain Inner Temple MS. of Year Books of Ed. II., where Roman texts are even cited with precise reference in the accustomed form of civilians. But this MS. is not now to be found, and, such references being otherwise unknown in other extant Year Books, it is safer to think that they were added by a specially learned scribe. See Maitland's Introduction to Y.B. 3 Ed. II., Seld. Soc. 1905, p. xx.

called Shardelowe an old savage on the strength of Blackstone's misunderstanding. What is really curious in the matter is that Blackstone appears to have been misled by Selden (ad Fletam, p. 533), who cites this to prove that Roman law had become unknown in the King's Courts in the reign of Edward III., though he does not use anything like Blackstone's rhetorical language about contempt and aversion. With all respect for Selden, I see no room for doubt that he did misunderstand the case; perhaps he was nodding a little, for he calls Shardelowe J. "Shardus." His general thesis that knowledge of Roman law in England, except among professed canonists, declined rapidly after the reign of Edward II., is doubtless correct. But there was no question of hostility. Not the fourteenth or thirteenth, but the sixteenth century was the time of recrimination between common lawyers and civilians, and perhaps of some real danger to the Common Law (Maitland, "English Law and the Renaissance"; Pollock, "The Expansion of the Common Law," p. 88).

Maine's remarks on the enthusiasm of French lawyers for natural law (p. 88 sqq.) seems rather to ignore its general reception by Continental publicists; though the centralization of the French monarchy no doubt made it easier for them to have something like uniform official doctrine. The enfranchising ordinance of Louis Hutin cited at p. 97, which asserts that all men ought to be free by natural law, repeats an earlier one issued by Philip the Fair in 1311 ("Journ. Soc. Comp. Legisl.," 1900, pp. 426-7). It is not very clear that the framers of this ordinance were thinking of the Roman maxim, "omnes homines natura aequales sunt" (or rather "quod ad ius naturale attinet omnes homines aequales sunt ": Ulpian in D. *de div. reg.* 50, 17, 32); for the general tone is decidedly more religious than secular, and the Church had always favoured manumission as a pious work. If they had wanted to vouch the authority of the Digest or the Institutes that slavery was not recognised by the law of nature, they might easily have made the reference more pointed. That Ulpian did not mean to preach an ethical or political creed of equality is, as Maine says, plain enough; his assertion is that slavery (like other inequalities of condition) is justified only by positive law. At the same time no medieval publicist who desired to use the passage for his own purposes would have troubled himself about the author's original intention. In Justinian's authoritative declaration on the subject, already referred to in Note E, there is an ethical element which Maine seems to me to have underrated; and this is the passage of the Corpus Iuris, if any, which was present to the mind of King Philip's counsellors.

At p. 90 there is a statement about Dumoulin's opinions which I have not been able to verify. Charles Dumoulin (properly Du Molin, latinized as Molinaeus, 1500-1566) was a profound jurist and a famous champion of Gallican liberties against the Papal claims. He was for some time a Calvinist, and afterwards a Lutheran, but his biographer Julien Brodeau, whose book[1] seems to be the ultimate authority, was anxious to make it clear that he died a Catholic; which from the Gallican point of view was only natural. His life was wandering and troubled, and is a striking example of the general disturbance into which the world of letters as well as of action was thrown by the Reformation controversies; twice he fled from Paris, and twice his house was sacked under colour of zeal for Roman orthodoxy. The standard edition of his works was printed at Paris in 1681 in five volumes, folio, and is copiously indexed. I have not found in them anything about the law of nature except one depreciatory remark in a note on the Decretum of Gratian (Annotationes ad ius canonicum, in vol. 4): "politia externa regitur iure naturali et politico, sed utrumque subest divino quod altius est naturali." This directly contradicts the received theory, which put the law of nature (principles of right revealed in human reason) before the Law of God (interpretation of specific precepts communicated by external revelation). I suspect that Du Molin, writing at that time as a Protestant, took the Law of God to be the text of Scripture, and meant that the text was to be preferred to the reasonings of the schools: compare the so-called Protestant declaration formerly in use on the admission of Fellows at Trinity College, Cambridge, "verbum Dei iudiciis hominum praepositurum." Whatever the exact significance may be, Du Molin's observation is the reverse of a panegyric on the law of nature. One can only suppose that the rhetorical passages of which Maine appears to have had a pretty distinct recollection occur in some other French jurist of the time, and that the introduction of Du Molin's name was due to a slip of memory or to some accidental dislocation or misreading of manuscript notes

It has already been pointed out that Maine greatly exaggerated the place of the "state of nature" in the doctrines of natural law. This comes out again in a startling manner in his remarks on Rousseau (p. 92).[2] Whatever Rousseau may have said elsewhere, we shall not find anything about the original perfection of mankind in the "Contrat Social," to which Maine apparently meant to refer. Rousseau believed, certainly, in natural law, and to some extent in the virtues of the "natural man" as an individual; but his "state of nature" is not much better than Hobbes's; it is

---

[1] La vie de Maistre Charles Du Molin, advocat au Parlement de Paris . . . et sa mort chrestienne et catholique. Par M⁰ Julien Brodeau, advocat au mesme Parlement. Paris 1654, 4°.

[2] "Nothing that Rousseau had to say about the state of nature was seriously meant for scientific exposition, any more than the Sermon on the Mount was meant for political economy" (John Morley, "Rousseau," i. 183).

unstable and becomes intolerable, and the social contract is dictated by the need of self-preservation (liv. i. ch. vi.); justice, which did not exist in the state of nature, is due to the establishment of political society (ch. viii.).   This is not the place to speak at large of Rousseau's influence on the founders of American independence and the leaders of the French Revolution ; but the careful research of American scholars has lately shown that the Principles of 1789 owed more to the American Declaration of Independence and the earlier Bills of Rights of several States than we used to suppose, and less to Rousseau, and that the language of the American constitutional instruments proceeded from the school not of Rousseau but of Locke (Scherger, " The Evolution of Modern Liberty," New York, 1904).

NOTE H

THE ORIGINS OF THE MODERN LAW OF NATIONS

Maine's statement (p. 100) seems to ignore the continuity of Grotius and his immediate precursors with the scholastic doctrine. It is true that the spread of the New Learning, and still more the Reformation, did largely increase the weight of the classical and diminish that of the medieval elements ; but it is also true that Grotius did not rely exclusively on Roman or on legal authorities. That Grotius and his contemporaries misunderstood the classical *ius gentium*, or supposed the modern rules of conduct between sovereign states to be contained in it, I am unable, with great respect for any suggestion of Maine's, to believe.   The term had become less common than its practical synonym *ius naturale* in the Middle Ages, but came into fashion again with the Renaissance. Grotius, like Alberico Gentili, takes *ius gentium* as the rule of natural reason attested by general agreement, and makes it the starting-point of a new development.   He may or may not have known that in its classical meaning it could, and sometimes did, include, among other rules of conduct sanctioned by general usage, whatever rules are reasonable and customary as between sovereign states.   But as a scholar he must have known that *gentes* is not the plural of *civitas* or *populus*, which are the only apt words in classical Latin for a state or nation in its political capacity.   At the same time Suarez had spoken of *iura gentium* with an approach to the modern " law of nations," and Hooker had used the English term in a fully international sense (" Eccl. Pol." I. x. § 12).   There was no reason for Grotius to refuse the assistance of a verbal ambiguity, so far as it existed and could further his purposes (cp. L.Q.R. xviii. 425-8).   The modern law of nations embodies certain distinctly legal conceptions.   These are Roman and purely Roman. Inasmuch as, from the sixteenth century onwards, Roman law was generally received throughout Western Christendom, with the one material exception of England, as a kind of universal law, there is nothing surprising in this fact, and indeed nothing else could have happened. Maine's following observations (p. 105 sqq.) as to the application of Roman ideas in the modern law of nations, and especially the treatment of every independent State, with regard to its territory, as if it were an owner or claimant of ownership under Roman law, and the relatively modern character of purely territorial dominion, show the author at his best. The theoretical equality of independent States naturally follows from their recognition as analogous to free persons, who must have full and equal rights in the absence of any definite reason for inequality. This indeed is all that the maxim of men's equality before the law of nature declares or involves according to its classical meaning (p. 118 above).

It is interesting in connexion with Maine's thesis to observe how in our time the usual rules of international law cease to be applicable, or fail to give an adequate solution of difficulties, just in proportion as the fact of territorial sovereignty is not complete and definite. This is now of frequent occurrence in cases of "spheres of influence" in unsettled parts of the world, of protectorates, and of what are called semi-sovereign States dependent in various degrees on other and more powerful ones. In the last-named class we may notice a certain reversion to feudal conceptions. It would have been much easier to express the relations of Great Britain to the late South African Republic in medieval than in classical Latin. As to the Anglo-Saxon kingship, it should be remembered that the English kings never owed or rendered any temporal allegiance to the Empire or any other power, and that the assumption of the imperial title "Basileus" involved a pretty strong claim to temporal supremacy within approximately certain territorial limits. In this respect the situation of England was peculiar. Modern national sovereignty may be regarded, in a general way, as a reaction against both the feudal and the imperial conceptions. Rulers of the Middle Ages, as and when they felt strong enough, expressly or tacitly renounced both homage to any overlord and submission to the Emperor. A German electoral prince or grand duke in the decadence of the Holy Roman Empire, say the Elector of Brandenburg, is from the strictly feudal point of view an overgrown tenant of the Emperor who has added one "immunity" to another till he has strained the tie of fealty to the breaking point. From the strictly imperial point of view, if it had been maintained to any practical purpose, he would or might be a rebel. Feudal tenure, however, probably led to the notion of the territory ruled by a sovereign prince being really—not by mere analogy to ownership in private law—his property. For, so long as overlordship was a reality, every principality, short of the Empire and the few monarchies which did not acknowledge the

Emperor as superior, was in theory a "tenement"; and in the feudal system a tenement is indistinguishable from property; for absolute property is not recognised save in the supreme overlord, as is the strict theory of English and Scottish law to this day. This ultimate and now shadowy feudal superiority has nothing to do with the modern and purely political conception of Eminent Domain, though more than once they have been confused by able writers.

It must not be supposed, however, that medieval lawyers were incapable of distinguishing between territorial sovereignty and feudal overlordship. The distinction was clearly made in 1284 by the framers of Edward I.'s Statute of Wales. In its preamble the king is made to acknowledge the bounty of Providence whereby the land of Wales, formerly subject to him as a fief, has been wholly reduced into his lordship in possession and annexed to his crown as part of the body of the kingdom.

"Divina Providentia . . inter alia dispensacionis sue munera quibus nos et regnum nostrum Anglie decorare dignata est terram Wallie cum incolis suis prius nobis iure feodali subiectam iam sui [*sic*] gratia in proprietatis nostre dominium . . . totaliter et cum integritate convertit et corone Regni predicti tanquam partem corporis eiusdem annexuit et univit" ("Statutes of the Realm," i. 55).

CHAPTER V

PRIMITIVE SOCIETY AND ANCIENT LAW

THE necessity of submitting the subject of jurisprudence to scientific treatment has never been
entirely lost sight of in modern times, and the
essays which the consciousness of this necessity
has produced have proceeded from minds of very
various calibre, but there is not much presumption,
I think, in asserting that what has hitherto stood
in the place of science has for the most part been
a set of guesses, those very guesses of the Roman
lawyers which were examined in the two preceding
chapters. A series of explicit statements, recog-
nising and adopting these conjectural theories of
a natural state, and of a system of principles
congenial to it, has been continued with but brief
interruption from the days of their inventors to
our own. They appear in the annotations of the
Glossators who founded modern jurisprudence,
and in the writings of the scholastic jurists who
succeeded them. They are visible in the dogmas
of the canonists. They are thrust into prominence
by those civilians of marvellous erudition, who
flourished at the revival of ancient letters. Grotius
and his successors invested them not more with
brilliancy and plausibility than with practical
importance. They may be read in the intro-
ductory chapters of our own Blackstone, who has

transcribed them textually from Burlamaqui, and wherever the manuals published in the present day for the guidance of the student or the practitioner begin with any discussion of the first principles of law, it always resolves itself into a restatement of the Roman hypothesis. It is however from the disguises with which these conjectures sometimes clothe themselves, quite as much as from their native form, that we gain an adequate idea of the subtlety with which they mix themselves in human thought. The Lockeian theory of the origin of Law in a Social Compact scarcely conceals its Roman derivation, and indeed is only the dress by which the ancient views were rendered more attractive to a particular generation of the moderns; but on the other hand the theory of Hobbes on the same subject was purposely devised to repudiate the reality of a law of nature as conceived by the Romans and their disciples. Yet these two theories, which long divided the reflecting politicians of England into hostile camps, resemble each other strictly in their fundamental assumption of a non-historic, unverifiable condition of the race. Their authors differed as to the characteristics of the præ-social state, and as to the nature of the abnormal action by which men lifted themselves out of it into that social organisation with which alone we are acquainted, but they agreed in thinking that a great chasm separated man in his primitive condition from man in society, and this notion we cannot doubt that they borrowed, consciously or unconsciously, from the Romans. If indeed the phenomena of law be regarded in the way in which these theorists regarded them—that is, as one vast complex whole—it is not surprising that the mind should often evade the task it has set to itself by falling back on some ingenious conjecture which (plausibly interpreted) will seem to reconcile everything, or else that it should sometimes abjure in despair the labour of systematisation.

From the theories of jurisprudence which have the same speculative basis as the Roman doctrine two of much celebrity must be excepted. The first of them is that associated with the great name of Montesquieu. Though there are some ambiguous expressions in the early part of the *Esprit des Lois,* which seem to show its writer's unwillingness to break quite openly with the views hitherto popular, the general drift of the book is certainly to indicate a very different conception of its subject from any which had been entertained before. It has often been noticed that, amidst the vast variety of examples which, in its immense width of survey, it sweeps together from supposed systems of jurisprudence, there is an evident anxiety to thrust into especial prominence those manners and institutions which astonish the civilised reader by their uncouthness, strangeness, or indecency. The inference constantly suggested is, that laws are the creatures of climate, local situation, accident, or imposture—the fruit of any causes except those which appear to operate with tolerable constancy. Montesquieu seems, in fact, to have looked on the nature of man as entirely plastic, as passively reproducing the impressions, and submitting implicitly to the impulses, which it receives from without. And here no doubt lies the error which vitiates his system as a system. He greatly underrates the stability of human nature. He pays little or no regard to the inherited qualities of the race, those qualities which each generation receives from its predecessors, and transmits but slightly altered to the generation which follows it. It is quite true, indeed, that no complete account can be given of social phenomena, and consequently of laws, till due allowance has been made for those modifying causes which are noticed in the *Esprit des Lois* ; but their number and their force appear to have been over-estimated by Montesquieu. Many of the anomalies which he parades have since been shown to rest on false report or erroneous construction, and of those which remain not a few prove the permanence rather than the variableness of man's nature, since they are relics of older stages of the race which have obstinately defied the influences that have elsewhere had effect. The truth is that the stable part of our mental, moral, and physical constitution is the largest part of it, and the resistance it opposes to change is such that, though the variations of human society in a portion of the world are plain enough, they are neither so rapid nor so extensive that their amount, character, and general direction cannot be ascertained. An approximation to truth may be all that is attainable with our present knowledge, but there is no reason for thinking that it is so remote, or (what is the same thing) that it requires so much future correction, as to be entirely useless and uninstructive.

The other theory which has been adverted to

is, the historical theory of Bentham.   This theory
which is obscurely (and, it might even be said,
timidly) propounded in several parts of Bentham's
works is quite distinct from that analysis of the
conception of law which he commenced in the
" Fragment on Government," and which was more
recently completed by Mr. John Austin.   The
resolution of a law into a command of a particular
nature, imposed under special conditions, does not
affect to do more than protect us against a difficulty—a most formidable one certainly—of language.   The whole question remains open as to
the motives of societies in imposing these commands on themselves, as to the connection of these
commands with each other, and the nature of
their dependence on those which preceded them,
and which they have superseded.   Bentham suggests the answer that societies modify, and have
always modified, their laws according to modifications of their views of general expediency.   It is
difficult to say that this proposition is false, but
it certainly appears to be unfruitful.   For that
which seems expedient to a society, or rather to
the governing part of it, when it alters a rule of
law, is surely the same thing as the object,
whatever it may be, which it has in view when it
makes the change.   Expediency and the greatest
good are nothing more than different names for
the impulse which prompts the modification ; and
when we lay down expediency as the rule of change
in law or opinion, all we get by the proposition is
the substitution of an express term for a term
which is necessarily implied when we say that a
change takes place.

There is such wide-spread dissatisfaction with existing theories of jurisprudence, and so general a conviction that they do not really solve the questions they pretend to dispose of, as to justify the suspicion that some line of inquiry, necessary to a perfect result, has been incompletely followed or altogether omitted by their authors. And indeed there is one remarkable omission with which all these speculations are chargeable, except perhaps those of Montesquieu. They take no account of what law has actually been at epochs remote from the particular period at which they made their appearance. Their originators carefully observed the institutions of their own age and civilisation, and those of other ages and civilisations with which they had some degree of intellectual sympathy, but, when they turned their attention to archaic states of society which exhibited much superficial difference from their own, they uniformly ceased to observe and began guessing. The mistake which they committed is therefore analogous to the error of one who, in investigating the laws of the material universe, should commence by contemplating the existing physical world as a whole, instead of beginning with the particles which are its simplest ingredients. One does not certainly see why such a scientific solecism should be more defensible in jurisprudence than in any other region of thought. It would seem antecedently that we ought to commence with the simplest social forms in a state as near as possible to their rudimentary condition. In other words, if we followed the course usual in such inquiries, we should penetrate as far up as we could in the history of primitive societies. The phenomena which early societies present us with are not easy at first to understand, but the difficulty of grappling with them bears no proportion to the perplexities which beset us in considering the baffling entanglement of modern social organisation. It is a difficulty arising from their strangeness and uncouthness, not from their number and complexity. One does not readily get over the surprise which they occasion when looked at from a modern point of view ; but when that is surmounted they are few enough and simple enough. But, even if they gave more trouble than they do, no pains would be wasted in ascertaining the germs out of which has assuredly been unfolded every form of moral restraint which controls our actions and shapes our conduct at the present moment.

The rudiments of the social state, so far as they are known to us at all, are known through testimony of three sorts—accounts by contemporary observers of civilisations less advanced than their own, the records which particular races have preserved concerning their primitive history, and ancient law. The first kind of evidence is the best we could have expected. As societies do not advance concurrently, but at different rates of progress, there have been epochs at which men trained to habits of methodical observation have really been in a position to watch and describe the infancy of mankind. Tacitus made the most of such an opportunity ; but the *Germany*, unlike most celebrated classical books, has not induced others to follow the excellent example set by its

9

author, and the amount of this sort of testimony
which we possess is exceedingly small. The lofty
contempt which a civilised people entertains for
barbarous neighbours has caused a remarkable
negligence in observing them, and this carelessness
has been aggravated at times by fear, by religious
prejudice, and even by the use of these very terms
—civilisation and barbarism—which convey to
most persons the impression of a difference not
merely in degree but in kind. Even the *Germany*
has been suspected by some critics of sacrificing
fidelity to poignancy of contrast and picturesque-
ness of narrative. Other histories, too, which
have been handed down to us among the archives
of the people to whose infancy they relate have
been thought distorted by the pride of race or
by the religious sentiment of a newer age. It is
important then to observe that these suspicions,
whether groundless or rational, do not attach to
a great deal of archaic law. Much of the old law
which has descended to us was preserved merely
because it was old. Those who practised and
obeyed it did not pretend to understand it ; and
in some cases they even ridiculed and despised it.
They offered no account of it except that it had
come down to them from their ancestors. If we
confine our attention, then, to those fragments of
ancient institutions which cannot reasonably be
supposed to have been tampered with, we are able
to gain a clear conception of certain great characteristics of the society to which they originally
belonged. Advancing a step further, we can
apply our knowledge to systems of law which,
like the Code of Manu, are as a whole of suspicious

authenticity ; and using the key we have obtained, we are in a position to discriminate those portions of them which are truly archaic from those which have been affected by the prejudices, interests, or ignorance of the compiler. It will at least be acknowledged that, if the materials for this process are sufficient, and if the comparisons be accurately executed, the methods followed are as little objectionable as those which have led to such surprising results in comparative philology.

The effect of the evidence derived from comparative jurisprudence is to establish that view of the primæval condition of the human race which is known as the Patriarchal Theory. There is no doubt, of course, that this theory was originally based on the Scriptural history of the Hebrew patriarchs in Lower Asia ; but, as has been explained already, its connection with Scripture rather militated than otherwise against its reception as a complete theory, since the majority of the inquirers who till recently addressed themselves with most earnestness to the colligation of social phenomena, were either influenced by the strongest prejudice against Hebrew antiquities or by the strongest desire to construct their system without the assistance of religious records. Even now there is perhaps a disposition to undervalue these accounts, or rather to decline generalising from them, as forming part of the traditions of a Semitic people. It is to be noted, however, that the legal testimony comes nearly exclusively from the institutions of societies belonging to the Indo-European stock, the Romans, Hindoos, and Sclavonians supplying the greater part of it ; and indeed the difficulty, at the present stage of the inquiry, is to know where to stop, to say of what races of men it is *not* allowable to lay down that the society in which they are united was originally organised on the patriarchal model.   The chief lineaments of such a society, as collected from the early chapters in Genesis, I need not attempt to depict with any minuteness, both because they are familiar to most of us from our earliest childhood, and because, from the interest once attaching to the controversy which takes its name from the debate between Locke and Filmer, they fill a whole chapter, though not a very profitable one, in English literature.   The points which lie on the surface of the history are these :—The eldest male parent— the eldest ascendant—is absolutely supreme in his household.   His dominion extends to life and death, and is as unqualified over his children and their houses as over his slaves ; indeed, the relations of sonship and serfdom appear to differ in little beyond the higher capacity which the child in blood possesses of becoming one day the head of a family himself.   The flocks and herds of the children are the flocks and herds of the father, and the possessions of the parent, which he holds in a representative rather than in a proprietary character, are equally divided at his death among his descendants in the first degree, the eldest son sometimes receiving a double share under the name of birthright, but more generally endowed with no hereditary advantage beyond an honorary precedence.   A less obvious inference from the Scriptural accounts is that they seem to plant us on the traces of the breach which is first effected

in the empire of the parent.   The families of Jacob
and Esau separate and form two nations ; but
the families of Jacob's children hold together and
become a people.   This looks like the immature
germ of a state or commonwealth, and of an order
of rights superior to the claims of family relation.

If I were attempting, for the more special purposes of the jurist, to express compendiously the
characteristics of the situation in which mankind
disclose themselves at the dawn of their history,
I should be satisfied to quote a few verses from the
Odyssey of Homer ·

$$\text{τοῖσιν δ' οὔτ' ἀγοραὶ βουληφόροι οὔτε θέμιστες,}$$
$$\text{θεμιστεύει δὲ ἕκαστος}$$
$$\text{παίδων ἠδ' ἀλόχων, οὐδ' ἀλλήλων ἀλέγουσιν.}$$

" They have neither assemblies for consultation
nor *themistes*, but every one exercises jurisdiction
over his wives and his children, and they pay no
regard to one another."   These lines are applied
to the Cyclops, and it may not perhaps be an
altogether fanciful idea when I suggest that the
Cyclops is Homer's type of an alien and less
advanced civilisation ; for the almost physical
loathing which a primitive community feels for
men of widely different manners from its own
usually expresses itself by describing them as
monsters, such as giants, or even (which is almost
always the case in Oriental mythology) as demons.
However that may be, the verses condense in
themselves the sum of the hints which are given
us by legal antiquities.   Men are first seen distributed in perfectly insulated groups, held together by obedience to the parent.   Law is the

parent's word, but it is not yet in the condition of those *themistes* which were analysed in the first chapter of this work. When we go forward to the state of society in which these early legal conceptions show themselves as formed, we find that they still partake of the mystery and spontaneity which must have seemed to characterise a despotic father's commands, but that at the same time, inasmuch as they proceed from a sovereign, they presuppose a union of family groups in some wider organisation. The next question is, what is the nature of this union and the degree of intimacy which it involves ? It is just here that archaic law renders us one of the greatest of its services, and fills up a gap which otherwise could only have been bridged by conjecture. It is full, in all its provinces, of the clearest indications that society in primitive times was not what it is assumed to be at present, a collection of *individuals*. In fact, and in the view of the men who composed it, it was *an aggregation of families*. The contrast may be most forcibly expressed by saying that the *unit* of an ancient society was the Family, of a modern society the individual. We must be prepared to find in ancient law all the consequences of this difference. It is so framed as to be adjusted to a system of small independent corporations. It is therefore scanty, because it is supplemented by the despotic commands of the heads of households. It is ceremonious, because the transactions to which it pays regard resemble international concerns much more than the quick play of intercourse between individuals. Above all, it has a peculiarity of which the full importance cannot be shown at present. It takes a view of *life* wholly unlike any which appears in developed jurisprudence. Corporations *never die*, and accordingly primitive law considers the entities with which it deals, *i.e.*, the patriarchal or family groups, as perpetual and inextinguishable. This view is closely allied to the peculiar aspect under which, in very ancient times, moral attributes present themselves. The moral elevation and moral debasement of the individual appear to be confounded with, or postponed to, the merits and offences of the group to which the individual belongs. If the community sins, its guilt is much more than the sum of the offences committed by its members; the crime is a corporate act, and extends in its consequences to many more persons than have shared in its actual perpetration. If, on the other hand, the individual is conspicuously guilty, it is his children, his kinsfolk, his tribesmen, or his fellow-citizens who suffer with him, and sometimes for him. It thus happens that the ideas of moral responsibility and retribution often seem to be more clearly realised at very ancient than at more advanced periods, for, as the family group is immortal, and its liability to punishment indefinite, the primitive mind is not perplexed by the questions which become troublesome as soon as the individual is conceived as altogether separate from the group. One step in the transition from the ancient and simple view of the matter to the theological or metaphysical explanations of later days is marked by the early Greek notion of an inherited curse. The bequest

received by his posterity from the original criminal
was not a liability to punishment, but a liability
to the commission of fresh offences which drew
with them a condign retribution ; and thus the
responsibility of the family was reconciled with
the newer phase of thought which limited the
consequences of crime to the person of the actual
delinquent.

It would be a very simple explanation of the
origin of society if we could base a general conclusion on the hint furnished us by the Scriptural
example already adverted to, and could suppose
that communities began to exist wherever a family
held together instead of separating at the death
of its patriarchal chieftain. In most of the Greek
states and in Rome there long remained the
vestiges of an ascending series of groups out of
which the State was at first constituted. The
Family, House, and Tribe of the Romans may be
taken as the type of them, and they are so described
to us that we can scarcely help conceiving them
as a system of concentric circles which have
gradually expanded from the same point. The
elementary group is the Family, connected by
common subjection to the highest male descendant.
The aggregation of Families forms the Gens or
House. The aggregation of Houses makes the
Tribe. The aggregation of Tribes constitutes the
commonwealth. Are we at liberty to follow these
indications, and to lay down that the commonwealth is a collection of persons united by common
descent from the progenitor of an original family ?
Of this we may at least be certain, that all ancient
societies regarded themselves as having proceeded

from one original stock, and even laboured under an incapacity for comprehending any reason except this for their holding together in political union. The history of political ideas begins, in fact, with the assumption that kinship in blood is the sole possible ground of community in political functions ; nor is there any of those subversions of feeling, which we term emphatically revolutions, so startling and so complete as the change which is accomplished when some other principle—such as that, for instance, of *local contiguity*—establishes itself for the first time as the basis of common political action. It may be affirmed, then, of early commonwealths that their citizens considered all the groups in which they claimed membership to be founded on common lineage. What was obviously true of the Family was believed to be true first of the House, next of the Tribe, lastly of the State. And yet we find that along with this belief, or, if we may use the word, this theory, each community preserved records or traditions which distinctly showed that the fundamental assumption was false. Whether we look to the Greek States, or to Rome, or to the Teutonic aristocracies in Ditmarsh which furnished Niebuhr with so many valuable illustrations, or to the Celtic clan associations, or to that strange social organisation of the Sclavonic Russians and Poles which has only lately attracted notice, everywhere we discover traces of passages in their history when men of alien descent were admitted to, and amalgamated with, the original brotherhood. Adverting to Rome singly, we perceive that the primary group, the Family, was being constantly adulterated by the practice of adoption, while stories seem to have been always current respecting the exotic extraction of one of the original Tribes, and concerning a large addition to the Houses made by one of the early kings. The composition of the state uniformly assumed to be natural was nevertheless known to be in great measure artificial. This conflict between belief or theory and notorious fact is at first sight extremely perplexing; but what it really illustrates is the efficiency with which Legal Fictions do their work in the infancy of society. The earliest and most extensively employed of legal fictions was that which permitted family relations to be created artificially, and there is none to which I conceive mankind to be more deeply indebted. If it had never existed, I do not see how any one of the primitive groups, whatever were their nature, could have absorbed another, or on what terms any two of them could have combined, except those of absolute superiority on one side and absolute subjection on the other. No doubt, when with our modern ideas we contemplate the union of independent communities, we can suggest a hundred modes of carrying it out, the simplest of all being that the individuals comprised in the coalescing groups shall vote or act together according to local propinquity; but the idea that a number of persons should exercise political rights in common simply because they happened to live within the same topographical limits was utterly strange and monstrous to primitive antiquity. The expedient which in those times commanded favour was that the incoming population should

feign themselves to be descended from the same
stock as the people on whom they were engrafted ;
and it is precisely the good faith of this fiction, and
the closeness with which it seemed to imitate
reality, that we cannot now hope to understand.
One circumstance, however, which it is important
to recollect, is that the men who formed the various
political groups were certainly in the habit of
meeting together periodically for the purpose of
acknowledging and consecrating their association
by common sacrifices. Strangers amalgamated
with the brotherhood were doubtless admitted to
these sacrifices ; and when that was once done,
we can believe that it seemed equally easy, or not
more difficult, to conceive them as sharing in the
common lineage. The conclusion, then, which
is suggested by the evidence is, not that all early
societies were formed by descent from the same
ancestor, but that all of them which had any
permanence and solidity either were so descended
or assumed that they were. An indefinite number
of causes may have shattered the primitive groups,
but wherever their ingredients recombined, it was
on the model or principle of an association of
kindred. Whatever were the facts, all thought,
language, and law adjusted themselves to the
assumption. But though all this seems to me to
be established with reference to the communities
with whose records we are acquainted, the re-
mainder of their history sustains the position
before laid down as to the essentially transient and
terminable influence of the most powerful Legal
Fictions. At some point of time—probably as
soon as they felt themselves strong enough to

resist extrinsic pressure—all these states ceased
to recruit themselves by factitious extensions
of consanguinity. They necessarily, therefore,
became Aristocracies, in all cases where a fresh
population from any cause collected around them
which could put in no claim to community of
origin. Their sternness in maintaining the central
principle of a system under which political rights
were attainable on no terms whatever except
connection in blood, real or artificial, taught their
inferiors another principle, which proved to be
endowed with a far higher measure of vitality.
This was the principle of *local contiguity*, now
recognised everywhere as the condition of community in political functions. A new set of
political ideas came at once into existence, which,
being those of ourselves, our contemporaries, and
in great measure of our ancestors, rather obscure
our perception of the older theory which they
vanquished and dethroned.

The family, then, is the type of an archaic
society in all the modifications which it was
capable of assuming ; but the family here spoken
of is not exactly the family as understood by a
modern. In order to reach the ancient conception
we must give to our modern ideas an important
extension and an important limitation. We must
look on the family as constantly enlarged by the
absorption of strangers within its circle, and we
must try to regard the fiction of adoption as so
closely simulating the reality of kinship that
neither law nor opinion makes the slightest difference between a real and an adoptive connection.
On the other hand, the persons theoretically

amalgamated into a family by their common descent are practically held together by common obedience to their highest living ascendant, the father, grandfather, or great-grandfather. The patriarchal authority of a chieftain is as necessary an ingredient in the notion of the family group as the fact (or assumed fact) of its having sprung from his loins ; and hence we must understand that if there be any persons who, however truly included in the brotherhood by virtue of their blood-relationship, have nevertheless *de facto* withdrawn themselves from the empire of its ruler, they are always, in the beginnings of law, considered as lost to the family. It is this patriarchal aggregate—the modern family thus cut down on one side and extended on the other—which meets us on the threshold of primitive jurisprudence. Older, probably, than the State, the Tribe, and the House, it left traces of itself on private law long after the House and the Tribe had been forgotten, and long after consanguinity had ceased to be associated with the composition of States. It will be found to have stamped itself on all the great departments of jurisprudence, and may be detected, I think, as the true source of many of their most important and most durable characteristics. At the outset, the peculiarities of law in its most ancient state lead us irresistibly to the conclusion that it took precisely the same view of the family group which is taken of individual men by the systems of rights and duties now prevalent throughout Europe. There are societies open to our observation at this very moment whose laws and usages can scarcely be explained unless they are supposed never to have emerged from this primitive condition ; but in communities more fortunately circumstanced the fabric of jurisprudence fell gradually to pieces, and if we carefully observe the disintegration we shall perceive that it took place principally in those portions of each system which were most deeply affected by the primitive conception of the family. In one all-important instance, that of the Roman law, the change was effected so slowly, that from epoch to epoch we can observe the line and direction which it followed, and can even give some idea of the ultimate result to which it was tending. And in pursuing this last inquiry we need not suffer ourselves to be stopped by the imaginary barrier which separates the modern from the ancient world. For one effect of that mixture of refined Roman law with primitive barbaric usage, which is known to us by the deceptive name of feudalism, was to revive many features of archaic jurisprudence which had died out of the Roman world, so that the decomposition which had seemed to be over commenced again, and to some extent is still proceeding.

On a few systems of law the family organisation of the earliest society has left a plain and broad mark in the life-long authority of the Father or other ancestor over the person and property of his descendants, an authority which we may conveniently call by its later Roman name of Patria Potestas. No feature of the rudimentary associations of mankind is deposed to by a greater amount of evidence than this, and yet none seems to have disappeared so generally and so rapidly from the usages of advancing communities. Gaius, writing under the Antonines, describes the institution as distinctively Roman. It is true that, had he glanced across the Rhine or the Danube to those tribes of barbarians which were exciting the curiosity of some among his contemporaries, he would have seen examples of patriarchal power in its crudest form ; and in the far East a branch of the same ethnical stock from which the Romans sprang was repeating their Patria Potestas in some of its most technical incidents. But among the races understood to be comprised within the Roman Empire, Gaius could find none which exhibited an institution resembling the Roman " Power of the Father," except only the Asiatic Galatæ. There are reasons, indeed, as it seems to me, why the direct authority of the ancestor should, in the greater number of progressive societies, very shortly assume humbler proportions than belonged to it in their earliest state. The implicit obedience of rude men to their parent is doubtless a primary fact, which it would be absurd to explain away altogether by attributing to them any calculation of its advantages ; but, at the same time, if it is natural in the sons to obey the father, it is equally natural that they should look to him for superior strength or superior wisdom. Hence, when societies are placed under circumstances which cause an especial value to be attached to bodily and mental vigour, there is an influence at work which tends to confine the Patria Potestas to the cases where its possessor is actually skilful and strong. When we obtain our first glimpse of organised Hellenic society, it seems as if super-eminent wisdom would keep alive the father's power in persons whose bodily strength had decayed; but the relations of Ulysses and Laertes in the *Odyssey* appear to show that, where extraordinary valour and sagacity were united in the son, the father in the decrepitude of age was deposed from the headship of the family. In the mature Greek jurisprudence, the rule advances a few steps on the practice hinted at in the Homeric literature; and though very many traces of stringent family obligation remain, the direct authority of the parent is limited, as in European codes, to the nonage or minority of the children, or, in other words, to the period during which their mental and physical inferiority may always be presumed. The Roman law, however, with its remarkable tendency to innovate on ancient usage only just so far as the exigency of the commonwealth may require, preserves both the primeval institution and the natural limitation to which I conceive it to have been subject. In every relation of life in which the collective community might have occasion to avail itself of his wisdom and strength, for all purposes of counsel or of war, the Filius Familias, or Son under Power, was as free as his father. It was a maxim of Roman jurisprudence that the Patria Potestas did not extend to the Jus Publicum. Father and son voted together in the city, and fought side by side in the field; indeed, the son, as general, might happen to command the father, or, as magistrate, decide on his contracts and punish his delinquencies. But in all the relations created by Private Law, the son lived under a domestic despotism which, considering the severity it retained to the last, and the number of centuries through which it endured, constitutes one of the strangest problems in legal history.

The Patria Potestas of the Romans, which is necessarily our type of the primeval paternal authority, is equally difficult to understand as an institution of civilised life, whether we consider its incidence on the person or its effects on property. It is to be regretted that a chasm which exists in its history cannot be more completely filled. So far as regards the person, the parent, when our information commences, has over his children the *jus vitæ necisque*, the power of life and death, and *à fortiori* of uncontrolled corporal chastisement ; he can modify their personal condition at pleasure ; he can give a wife to his son ; he can give his daughter in marriage ; he can divorce his children of either sex ; he can transfer them to another family by adoption ; and he can sell them. Late in the Imperial period we find vestiges of all these powers, but they are reduced within very narrow limits. The unqualified right of domestic chastisement has become a right of bringing domestic offences under the cognisance of the civil magistrate ; the privilege of dictating marriage has declined into a conditional veto ; the liberty of selling has been virtually abolished, and adoption itself, destined to lose almost all its ancient importance in the reformed system of Justinian, can no longer be effected without the assent of the child transferred to the adoptive parentage. In short, we are brought very close to the verge of the ideas which have at length prevailed in the modern world. But between these widely distant

10

epochs there is an interval of obscurity, and we can only guess at the causes which permitted the Patria Potestas to last as long as it did by rendering it more tolerable than it appears. The active discharge of the most important among the duties which the son owed to the state must have tempered the authority of his parent, if they did not annul it. We can readily persuade ourselves that the paternal despotism could not be brought into play, without great scandal, against a man of full age occupying a high civil office. During the earlier history, however, such cases of practical emancipation would be rare compared with those which must have been created by the constant wars of the Roman republic. The military tribune and the private soldier, who were in the field three-quarters of a year during the earlier contests, at a later period the proconsul in charge of a province, and the legionaries who occupied it, cannot have had practical reason to regard themselves as the slaves of a despotic master ; and all these avenues of escape tended constantly to multiply themselves. Victories led to conquests, conquests to occupations ; the mode of occupation by colonies was exchanged for the system of occupying provinces by standing armies. Each step in advance was a call for the expatriation of more Roman citizens, and a fresh draft on the blood of the failing Latin race. We may infer, I think, that a strong sentiment in favour of the relaxation of the Patria Potestas had become fixed by the time that the pacification of the world commenced on the establishment of the Empire. The first serious blows at the ancient institution

are attributed to the earlier Cæsars, and some
isolated interferences of Trajan and Hadrian seem
to have prepared the ground for a series of express
enactments which, though we cannot always determine their dates, we know to have limited the
father's powers on the one hand, and on the other
to have multiplied facilities for their voluntary
surrender. The older.mode of getting rid of the
Potestas, by effecting a triple sale of the son's
person, is evidence, I may remark, of a very early
feeling against the unnecessary prolongation of
the powers. The rule which declared that the
son should be free after having been three times
sold by his father seems to have been originally
meant to entail penal consequences on a practice
which revolted even the imperfect morality of the
primitive Roman. But even before the publication of the Twelve Tables, it had been turned, by
the ingenuity of the jurisconsults, into an expedient
for destroying the parental authority wherever the
father desired that it should cease.

Many of the causes which helped to mitigate
the stringency of the father's power over the
persons of his children are doubtless among those
which do not lie upon the face of history. We
cannot tell how far public opinion may have
paralysed an authority which the law conferred ;
or how far natural affection may have rendered
it endurable. But though the powers over the
person may have been latterly nominal, the whole
tenour of the extant Roman jurisprudence suggests
that the father's rights over the son's *property*
were always exercised without scruple to the full
extent to which they were sanctioned by law.

There is nothing to astonish us in the latitude of
these rights when they first show themselves.
The ancient law of Rome forbade the Children
under Power to hold property apart from their
parent, or (we should rather say) never contemplated the possibility of their claiming a separate
ownership. The father was entitled to take the
whole of the son's acquisitions, and to enjoy the
benefit of his contracts, without being entangled
in any compensating liability. So much as this
we should expect from the constitution of the
earliest Roman society ; for we can hardly form
a notion of the primitive family group unless we
suppose that its members brought their earnings
of all kinds into the common stock, while they
were unable to bind it by improvident individual
engagements. The true enigma of the Patria
Potestas does not reside here, but in the slowness
with which these proprietary privileges of the
parent were curtailed, and in the circumstance
that, before they were seriously diminished, the
whole civilised world was brought within their
sphere. No innovation of any kind was attempted
till the first years of the Empire, when the acquisitions of soldiers on service were withdrawn from
the operation of the Patria Potestas, doubtless
as part of the reward of the armies which had
overthrown the free commonwealth. Three centuries afterwards the same immunity was extended
to the earnings of persons who were in the civil
employment of the state. Both changes were
obviously limited in their application, and they
were so contrived in technical form as to interfere
as little as possible with the principle of Patria

Potestas. A certain qualified and dependent ownership had always been recognised by the Roman law in the perquisites and savings which slaves and sons under power were not compelled to include in the household accounts, and the special name of this permissive property, Peculium, was applied to the acquisitions newly relieved from Patria Potestas, which were called in the case of soldiers Castrense Peculium, and Quasi-castrense Peculium in the case of civil servants. Other modifications of the parental privileges followed, which showed a less studious outward respect for the ancient principle. Shortly after the introduction of the Quasi-castrense Peculium, Constantine the Great took away the father's absolute control over property which his children had inherited from their mother, and reduced it to a *usufruct*, or life-interest. A few more changes of slight importance followed in the Western Empire, but the furthest point reached was in the East, under Justinian, who enacted that unless the acquisitions of the child were derived from the parent's own property, the parent's right over them should not extend beyond enjoying their produce for the period of his life. Even this, the utmost relaxation of the Roman Patria Potestas, left it far ampler and severer than any analogous institution of the modern world. The earliest modern writers on jurisprudence remark that it was only the fiercer and ruder of the conquerors of the Empire, and notably the nations of Sclavonic origin, which exhibited a Patria Potestas at all resembling that which was described in the Pandects and the Code. All the Germanic immigrants seem to have recognised a corporate union of the family under the *mund*, or authority of a patriarchal chief; but his powers are obviously only the relics of a decayed Patria Potestas, and fell far short of those enjoyed by the Roman father. The Franks are particularly mentioned as not having the Roman Institution, and accordingly the old French lawyers, even when most busily engaged in filling the interstices of barbarous customs with rules of Roman law, were obliged to protect themselves against the intrusion of the Potestas by the express maxim, *Puyssance de père en France n'a lieu.* The tenacity of the Romans in maintaining this relic of their most ancient condition is in itself remarkable, but it is less remarkable than the diffusion of the Potestas over the whole of a civilisation from which it had once disappeared. While the Castrense Peculium constituted as yet the sole exception to the father's power over property, and while his power over his children's persons was still extensive, the Roman citizenship, and with it the Patria Potestas, were spreading into every corner of the Empire. Every African or Spaniard, every Gaul, Briton, or Jew, who received this honour by gift, purchase, or inheritance, placed himself under the Roman Law of Persons, and, though our authorities intimate that children born before the acquisition of citizenship could not be brought under Power against their will, children born after it and all ulterior descendants were on the ordinary footing of a Roman *filius familias.* It does not fall within the province of this treatise to examine the mechanism of the later Roman society, but I may be permitted to remark that there is little

foundation for the opinion which represents the
constitution of Antoninus Caracalla conferring
Roman citizenship on the whole of his subjects
as a measure of small importance. However we
may interpret it, it must have enormously enlarged
the sphere of the Patria Potestas, and it seems to
me that the tightening of family relations which
it effected is an agency which ought to be kept in
view more than it has been, in accounting for the
great moral revolution which was transforming
the world.

Before this branch of our subject is dismissed,
it should be observed that the Paterfamilias was
answerable for the delicts (or *torts*) of his Sons
under Power. He was similarly liable for the
torts of his slaves ; but in both cases he originally
possessed the singular privilege of tendering the
delinquent's person in full satisfaction of the
damage. The responsibility thus incurred on
behalf of sons, coupled with the mutual incapacity
of Parent and Child under Power to sue one
another, has seemed to some jurists to be best
explained by the assumption of a " unity of
person " between the Paterfamilias and the Filius-
familias. In the Chapter on Successions I shall
attempt to show in what sense, and to what extent,
this " unity " can be accepted as a reality. I can
only say at present that these responsibilities of
the Paterfamilias, and other legal phenomena
which will be discussed hereafter, appear to me to
point at certain *duties* of the primitive Patriarchal
chieftain which balanced his *rights*. I conceive
that, if he disposed absolutely of the persons
and fortunes of his clansmen, this representative

ownership was coextensive with a liability to provide for all members of the brotherhood out of
the common fund. The difficulty is to throw ourselves out of our habitual associations sufficiently
for conceiving the nature of his obligation. It was
not a legal duty, for law had not yet penetrated
into the precinct of the Family. To call it *moral*
is perhaps to anticipate the ideas belonging to a
later stage of mental development; but the expression " moral obligation " is significant enough
for our purpose, if we understand by it a duty
semi-consciously followed and enforced rather by
instinct and habit than by definite sanctions.

The Patria Potestas, in its normal shape, has
not been, and, as it seems to me, could not have
been, a generally durable institution. The proof
of its former universality is therefore incomplete
so long as we consider it by itself; but the demonstration may be carried much further by examining
other departments of ancient law which depend
on it ultimately, but not by a thread of connection
visible in all its parts or to all eyes. Let us turn
for example to Kinship, or in other words, to the
scale on which the proximity of relatives to each
other is calculated in archaic jurisprudence. Here
again it will be convenient to employ the Roman
terms, Agnatic and Cognatic relationship. *Cognatic* relationship is simply the conception of
kinship familiar to modern ideas : it is the relationship arising through common descent from the
same pair of married persons, whether the descent
be traced through males or females. *Agnatic*
relationship is something very different: it excludes a number of persons whom we in our day

should certainly consider of kin to ourselves, and it includes many more whom we should never reckon among our kindred. It is in truth the connection existing between the members of the Family, conceived as it was in the most ancient times. The limits of this connection are far from conterminous with those of modern relationship.

Cognates then are all those persons who can trace their blood to a single ancestor and ancestress ; or if we take the strict technical meaning of the word in Roman law, they are all who trace their blood to the legitimate marriage of a common pair. " Cognation " is therefore a relative term, and the degree of connection in blood which it indicates depends on the particular marriage which is selected as the commencement of the calculation. If we begin with the marriage of father and mother, Cognation will only express the relationship of brothers and sisters ; if we take that of the grandfather and grandmother, then uncles, aunts, and their descendants will also be included in the notion of Cognation, and following the same process a larger number of Cognates may be continually obtained by choosing the starting point higher and higher up in the line of ascent. All this is easily understood by a modern ; but who are the Agnates ? In the first place, they are all the Cognates who trace their connection exclusively through males. A table of Cognates is, of course, formed by taking each lineal ancestor in turn and including all his descendants of both sexes in the tabular view ; if then, in tracing the various branches of such a genealogical table or tree, we stop whenever we come to the name of a female and pursue that particular branch or ramification no further, all who remain after the descendants of women have been excluded are Agnates, and their connection together is Agnatic Relationship. I dwell a little on the process which is practically followed in separating them from the Cognates, because it explains a memorable legal maxim, " Mulier est finis familiæ "—a woman is the terminus of the family. A female name closes the branch or twig of the genealogy in which it occurs. None of the descendants of a female are included in the primitive notion of family relationship.

If the system of archaic law at which we are looking be one which admits Adoption, we must add to the Agnates thus obtained all persons, male or female, who have been brought into the family by the artificial extension of its boundaries. But the descendants of such persons will only be Agnates, if they satisfy the conditions which have just been described.

What then is the reason of this arbitrary inclusion and exclusion ? Why should a conception of Kinship so elastic as to include strangers brought into the family by adoption, be nevertheless so narrow as to shut out the descendants of a female member ? To solve these questions we must recur to the Patria Potestas. The foundation of Agnation is not the marriage of Father and Mother, but the authority of the Father. All persons are Agnatically connected together who are under the same Paternal Power, or who have been under it, or who might have been under it if their lineal

ancestor had lived long enough to exercise his
empire.   In truth, in the primitive view, Relationship is exactly limited by Patria Potestas.   Where
the Potestas begins, Kinship begins ; and therefore adoptive relatives are among the kindred.
Where the Potestas ends, Kinship ends ; so that
a son emancipated by his father loses all rights
of Agnation.   And here we have the reason why
the descendants of females are outside the limits
of archaic kinship.   If a woman died unmarried,
she could have no legitimate descendants.   If she
married, her children fell under the Patria Potestas,
not of her Father, but of her Husband, and thus
were lost to her own family.   It is obvious that
the organisation of primitive societies would have
been confounded, if men had called themselves
relatives of their mother's relatives.   The inference would have been that a person might be
subject to two distinct Patriæ Potestates ; but
distinct Patriæ Potestates implied distinct jurisdictions, so that anybody amenable to two of
them at the same time would have lived under
two different dispensations.   As long as the
Family was an imperium in imperio, a community
within the commonwealth governed by its own
institutions of which the parent was the source,
the limitation of relationship to the Agnates was
a necessary security against a conflict of laws in
the domestic forum.

The Paternal Powers proper are extinguished
by the death of the Parent, but Agnation is as it
were a mould which retains their imprint after they
have ceased to exist.   Hence comes the interest
of Agnation for the inquirer into the history of

jurisprudence. The powers themselves are discernible in comparatively few monuments of ancient law, but Agnatic Relationship, which implies their former existence, is discoverable almost everywhere. There are few indigenous bodies of law belonging to communities of the Indo-European stock, which do not exhibit peculiarities in the most ancient part of their structure which are clearly referable to Agnation. In Hindoo law, for example, which is saturated with the primitive notions of family dependency, kinship is entirely Agnatic, and I am informed that in Hindoo genealogies the names of women are generally omitted altogether. The same view of relationship pervades so much of the laws of the races who overran the Roman Empire as appears to have really formed part of their primitive usage, and we may suspect that it would have perpetuated itself even more than it has in modern European jurisprudence, if it had not been for the vast influence of the later Roman law on modern thought. The Prætors early laid hold on Cognation as the *natural* form of kinship, and spared no pains in purifying their system from the older conception. Their ideas have descended to us, but still traces of Agnation are to be seen in many of the modern rules of succession after death. The exclusion of females and their children from governmental functions, commonly attributed to the usage of the Salian Franks, has certainly an agnatic origin, being descended from the ancient German rule of succession to allodial property. In Agnation too is to be sought the explanation of that extraordinary rule of English

Law, only recently repealed, which prohibited brothers of the half-blood from succeeding to one another's lands. In the Customs of Normandy, the rule applies to *uterine* brothers only, that is, to brothers by the same mother but not by the same father ; and, limited in this way, it is a strict deduction from the system of Agnation, under which uterine brothers are no relations at all to one another. When it was transplanted to England, the English judges, who had no clue to its principle, interpreted it as a general prohibition against the succession of the half-blood, and extended it to *consanguineous* brothers, that is to sons of the same father by different wives. In all the literature whch enshrines the pretended philosophy of law, there is nothing more curious than the pages of elaborate sophistry in which Blackstone attempts to explain and justify the exclusion of the half-blood.

It may be shown, I think, that the Family, as held together by the Patria Potestas, is the nidus out of which the entire Law of Persons has germinated. Of all the chapters of that Law the most important is that which is concerned with the status of Females. It has just been stated that Primitive Jurisprudence, though it does not allow a Woman to communicate any rights of Agnation to her descendants, includes herself nevertheless in the Agnatic bond. Indeed, the relation of a female to the family in which she was born is much stricter, closer, and more durable than that which unites her male kinsmen. We have several times laid down that early law takes notice of Families only ; this is the same thing as saying that it only takes notice of persons exercising Patria Potestas, and accordingly the only principle on which it enfranchises a son or grandson at the death of his Parent, is a consideration of the capacity inherent in such son or grandson to become himself the head of a new family and the root of a new set of Parental Powers. But a woman, of course, has no capacity of the kind, and no title accordingly to the liberation which it confers. There is therefore a peculiar contrivance of archaic jurisprudence for retaining her in the bondage of the Family for life. This is the institution known to the oldest Roman law as the Perpetual Tutelage of Women, under which a Female, though relieved from her Parent's authority by his decease, continues subject through life to her nearest male relations, or to her father's nominees, as her Guardians. Perpetual Guardianship is obviously neither more nor less than an artificial prolongation of the Patria Potestas, when for other purposes it has been dissolved. In India, the system survives in absolute completeness, and its operation is so strict that a Hindoo Mother frequently becomes the ward of her own sons. Even in Europe, the laws of the Scandinavian nations respecting women preserved it until quite recently. The invaders of the Western Empire had it universally among their indigenous usages, and indeed their ideas on the subject of Guardianship, in all its forms, were among the most retrogressive of those which they introduced into the Western world. But from the mature Roman jurisprudence it had entirely disappeared. We should know almost nothing about it, if we had only the com-

pilations of Justinian to consult ; but the discovery
of the manuscript of Gaius discloses it to us at a
most interesting epoch, just when it had fallen
into complete discredit and was verging on
extinction. The great jurisconsult himself scouts
the popular apology offered for it in the mental
inferiority of the female sex, and a considerable
part of his volume is taken up with descriptions
of the numerous expedients, some of them dis-
playing extraordinary ingenuity, which the Roman
lawyers had devised for enabling Women to defeat
the ancient rules. Led by their theory of Natural
Law, the jurisconsults had evidently at this time
assumed the equality of the sexes as a principle
of their code of equity. The restrictions which
they attacked were, it is to be observed, restrictions
on the disposition of property, for which the
assent of the woman's guardians was still formally
required. Control of her person was apparently
quite obsolete.

Ancient law subordinates the woman to her
blood-relations, while a prime phenomenon of
modern jurisprudence has been her subordination
to her husband. The history of the change
is remarkable. It begins far back in the annals
of Rome. Anciently, there were three modes in
which marriage might be contracted according
to Roman usage, one involving a religious solemnity, the other two the observance of certain
secular formalities. By the religious marriage
or *Confarreation* ; by the higher form of civil
marriage, which was called *Coemption* ; and by
the lower form, which was termed *Usus*, the
Husband acquired a number of rights, over the

person and property of his wife, which were on the whole in excess of such as are conferred on him in any system of modern jurisprudence. But in what capacity did he acquire them ? Not as *Husband*, but as *Father*. By the Confarreation, Coemption, and Usus, the woman passed *in manum viri*, that is, in law she became the *Daughter* of her husband. She was included in his Patria Potestas. She incurred all the liabilities springing out of it while it subsisted, and surviving it when it had expired. All her property became absolutely his, and she was retained in tutelage after his death to the guardian whom he had appointed by will. These three ancient forms of marriage fell, however, gradually into disuse, so that at the most splendid period of Roman greatness, they had almost entirely given place to a fashion of wedlock—old apparently, but not hitherto considered reputable—which was founded on a modification of the lower form of civil marriage. Without explaining the technical mechanism of the institution now generally popular, I may describe it as amounting in law to a little more than a temporary deposit of the woman by her family. The rights of the family remained unimpaired, and the lady continued in the tutelage of guardians whom her parents had appointed and whose privileges of control overrode, in many material respects, the inferior authority of her husband. The consequence was that the situation of the Roman female, whether married or unmarried, became one of great personal and proprietary independence, for the tendency of the later law, as I have already hinted, was to reduce the power of the guardian to a nullity, while the form of marriage in fashion conferred on the husband no compensating superiority. But Christianity tended somewhat from the very first to narrow this remarkable liberty. Led at first by justifiable disrelish for the loose practices of the decaying heathen world, but afterwards hurried on by a passion of asceticism, the professors of the new faith looked with disfavour on a marital tie which was in fact the laxest the Western world has seen. The latest Roman law, so far as it is touched by the Constitutions of the Christian Emperors, bears some marks of a reaction against the liberal doctrines of the great Antonine jurisconsults. And the prevalent state of religious sentiment may explain why it is that modern jurisprudence, forged in the furnace of barbarian conquest, and formed by the fusion of Roman jurisprudence with patriarchal usage, has absorbed, among its rudiments, much more than usual of those rules concerning the position of women which belong peculiarly to an imperfect civilisation. During the troubled era which begins modern history, and while the laws of the German and Sclavonic immigrants remained superposed like a separate layer above the Roman jurisprudence of their provincial subjects, the women of the dominant races are seen everywhere under various forms of archaic guardianship, and the husband who takes a wife from any family except his own pays a money-price to her relations for the tutelage which they surrender to him. When we move onwards, and the code of the middle ages has been formed by the amalgamation of the two systems, the law relating to women carries the stamp of its double origin. The principle of the Roman jurisprudence is so far triumphant that unmarried females are generally (though there are local exceptions to the rule) relieved from the bondage of the family ; but the archaic principle of the barbarians has fixed the position of married women, and the husband has drawn to himself in his marital character the powers which had once belonged to his wife's male kindred, the only difference being that he no longer purchases his privileges. At this point therefore the modern law of Southern and Western Europe begins to be distinguished by one of its chief characteristics, the comparative freedom it allows to unmarried women and widows, the heavy disabilities it imposes on wives. It was very long before the subordination entailed on the other sex by marriage was sensibly diminished. The principal and most powerful solvent of the revived barbarism of Europe was always the codified jurisprudence of Justinian, wherever it was studied with that passionate enthusiasm which it seldom failed to awaken. It covertly but most efficaciously undermined the customs which it pretended merely to interpret. But the Chapter of law relating to married women was for the most part read by the light, not of Roman, but of Canon Law, which in no one particular departs so widely from the spirit of the secular jurisprudence as in the view it takes of the relations created by marriage. This was in part inevitable, since no society which preserves any tincture of Christian institution is likely to restore to married women the personal liberty conferred on them by the middle Roman law, but the proprietary disabilities of married females stand on quite a different basis from their personal incapacities, and it is by the tendency of their doctrines to keep alive and consolidate the former, that the expositors of the Canon Law have deeply injured civilisation. There are many vestiges of a struggle between the secular and ecclesiastical principles, but the Canon Law nearly everywhere prevailed. In some of the French provinces, married women, of a rank below nobility, obtained all the powers of dealing with property which Roman jurisprudence had allowed, and this local law has been largely followed by the Code Napoléon ; but the state of the Scottish law shows that scrupulous deference to the doctrines of the Roman jurisconsults did not always extend to mitigating the disabilities of wives. The systems however which are least indulgent to married women are invariably those which have followed the Canon Law exclusively, or those which, from the lateness of their contact with European civilisation, have never had their archaisms weeded out. The Danish and Swedish laws, harsh for many centuries to all females, are still much less favourable to wives than the generality of Continental codes. And yet more stringent in the proprietary incapacities it imposes is the English Common Law, which borrows far the greatest number of its fundamental principles from the jurisprudence of the Canonists. Indeed, the part of the Common Law which prescribes the legal situation of married women may serve to give an Englishman clear notions of the great institution which has been the principal subject of this chapter. I do not know how the operation and nature of the ancient Patria Potestas can be brought so vividly before the mind as by reflecting on the prerogatives attached to the husband by the pure English Common Law, and by recalling the rigorous consistency with which the view of a complete legal subjection on the part of the wife is carried by it, where it is untouched by equity or statutes, through every department of rights, duties, and remedies. The distance between the eldest and latest Roman law on the subject of Children under Power may be considered as equivalent to the difference between the Common Law and the jurisprudence of the Court of Chancery in the rules which they respectively apply to wives.

If we were to lose sight of the true origin of Guardianship in both its forms, and were to employ the common language on these topics, we should find ourselves remarking that, while the Tutelage of Women is an instance in which systems of archaic law push to an extravagant length the fiction of suspended rights, the rules which they lay down for the Guardianship of Male Orphans are an example of a fault in precisely the opposite direction. Such systems terminate the Tutelage of Males at an extraordinary early period. Under the ancient Roman law, which may be taken as their type, the son who was delivered from Patria Potestas by the death of his Father or Grandfather remained under guardianship till an epoch which for general purposes may be described as arriving with his fifteenth year; but the arrival of that epoch placed him at once in the full enjoyment

of personal and proprietary independence. The
period of minority appears therefore to have been
as unreasonably short as the duration of the
disabilities of women was preposterously long.
But, in point of fact, there was no element either
of excess or of shortcoming in the circumstances
which gave their original form to the two kinds
of guardianship. Neither the one nor the other of
them was based on the slightest consideration of
public or private convenience. The guardianship
of male orphans was no more designed originally
to shield them till the arrival of years of discretion
than the tutelage of women was intended to protect
the other sex against its own feebleness. The
reason why the death of the father delivered the
son from the bondage of the family was the son's
capacity for becoming himself the head of a new
family and the founder of a new Patria Potestas :
no such capacity was possessed by the woman,
and therefore she was *never* enfranchised. Accordingly the Guardianship of Male Orphans was a
contrivance for keeping alive the semblance of
subordination to the family of the Parent, up to
the time when the child was supposed capable of
becoming a parent himself. It was a prolongation of the Patria Potestas up to the period of
bare physical manhood. It ended with puberty,
for the rigour of the theory demanded that it
should do so. Inasmuch, however, as it did not
profess to conduct the orphan ward to the age of
intellectual maturity or fitness for affairs, it was
quite unequal to the purposes of general convenience ; and this the Romans seem to have
discovered at a very early stage of their social

progress. One of the very oldest monuments of Roman legislation is the *Lex Lætoria* or *Plætoria*, which placed all free males who were of full years and rights under the temporary control of a new class of guardians, called *Curatores*, whose sanction was required to validate their acts or contracts. The twenty-sixth year of the young men's age was the limit of this statutory supervision ; and it is exclusively with reference to the age of twenty-five that the terms " majority " and " minority " are employed in Roman law. *Pupil-age*, or *wardship*, in modern jurisprudence has adjusted itself with tolerable regularity to the simple principle of protection to the immaturity of youth both bodily and mental. It has its natural termination with years of discretion. But for protection against physical weakness, and for protection against intellectual incapacity, the Romans looked to two different institutions, distinct both in theory and design. The ideas attendant on both are combined in the modern idea of guardianship.

The Law of Persons contains but one other chapter which can be usefully cited for our present purpose. The legal rules by which systems of mature jurisprudence regulate the connection of *Master* and *Slave*, present no very distinct traces of the original condition common to ancient societies. But there are reasons for this exception. There seems to be something in the institution of Slavery which has at all times either shocked or perplexed mankind, however little habituated to reflection, and however slightly advanced in the cultivation of its moral instincts. The compunc-

tion which ancient communities almost unconsciously experienced appears to have always
resulted in the adoption of some imaginary
principle upon which a defence, or at least a
rationale, of slavery could be plausibly founded.
Very early in their history the Greeks explained
the institution as grounded on the intellectual
inferiority of certain races, and their consequent
natural aptitude for the servile condition. The
Romans, in a spirit equally characteristic, derived
it from a supposed agreement between the victor
and the vanquished, in which the first stipulated
for the perpetual services of his foe, and the other
gained in consideration the life which he had
legitimately forfeited. Such theories were not
only unsound but plainly unequal to the case for
which they affected to account. Still they exercised powerful influence in many ways. They
satisfied the conscience of the Master. They
perpetuated and probably increased the debasement of the Slave. And they naturally tended to
put out of sight the relation in which servitude
had originally stood to the rest of the domestic
system. This relation, though not clearly exhibited, is casually indicated in many parts of
primitive law, and more particularly in the
typical system—that of ancient Rome.

Much industry and some learning have been
bestowed in the United States of America on the
question whether the Slave was in the early stages
of society a recognised member of the Family.
There is a sense in which an affirmative answer
must certainly be given. It is clear, from the
testimony both of ancient law and of many

primeval histories, that the Slave might under certain conditions be made the Heir, or Universal Successor, of the Master, and this significant faculty, as I shall explain in the Chapter on Succession, implies that the Government and representation of the Family might, in a particular state of circumstances, devolve on the bondman. It seems, however, to be assumed in the American arguments on the subject that, if we allow Slavery to have been a primitive Family institution, the acknowledgment is pregnant with an admission of the moral defensibility of Negro-servitude at the present moment. What then is meant by saying that the Slave was originally included in the Family ? Not that his situation may not have been the fruit of the coarsest motives which can actuate man. The simple wish to use the bodily powers of another person as a means of ministering to one's own ease or pleasure is doubtless the foundation of Slavery, and as old as human nature. When we speak of the Slave as anciently included in the Family, we intend to assert nothing as to the motives of those who brought him into it or kept him there ; we merely imply that the tie which bound him to his master was regarded as one of the same general character with that which united every other member of the group to its chieftain. This consequence is, in fact, carried in the general assertion already made, that the primitive ideas of mankind were unequal to comprehending any basis of the connection *inter se* of individuals, apart from the relations of family. The Family consisted primarily of those who belonged to it by consanguinity, and next of those

who had been engrafted on it by adoption ; but
there was still a third class of persons who were
only joined to it by common subjection to its head,
and these were the Slaves. The born and the
adopted subjects of the chief were raised above
the Slave by the certainty that in the ordinary
course of events they would be relieved from
bondage and entitled to exercise powers of their
own ; but that the inferiority of the Slave was
not such as to place him outside the pale of the
Family, or such as to degrade him to the footing
of inanimate property, is clearly proved, I think,
by the many traces which remain of his ancient
capacity for inheritance in the last resort. It
would, of course, be unsafe in the highest degree to
hazard conjectures how far the lot of the Slave was
mitigated, in the beginnings of society, by having
a definite place reserved to him in the empire of
the Father. It is, perhaps, more probable that
the son was practically assimilated to the Slave,
than that the Slave shared any of the tenderness
which in later times was shown to the son. But
it may be asserted with some confidence of advanced and matured codes that, wherever servitude
is sanctioned, the Slave has uniformly greater
advantages under systems which preserve some
memento of his earlier condition than under those
which have adopted some other theory of his civil
degradation. The point of view from which jurisprudence regards the Slave is always of great
importance to him. The Roman law was arrested
in its growing tendency to look upon him more
and more as an article of property by the theory
of the Law of Nature ; and hence it is that,

wherever servitude is sanctioned by institutions which have been deeply affected by Roman jurisprudence, the servile condition is never intolerably wretched. There is a great deal of evidence that in those American States which have taken the highly Romanised code of Louisiana as the basis of their jurisprudence, the lot and prospects of the Negro-population were better in many material respects, until the letter of the fundamental law was overlaid by recent statutory enactments passed under the influence of panic, than under institutions founded on the English Common Law, which, as recently interpreted, has no true place for the Slave, and can only therefore regard him as a chattel.

We have now examined all parts of the ancient Law of Persons which fall within the scope of this treatise, and the result of the inquiry is, I trust, to give additional definiteness and precision to our view of the infancy of jurisprudence. The Civil laws of States first make their appearance as the Themistes of a patriarchal sovereign, and we can now see that these Themistes are probably only a developed form of the irresponsible commands which, in a still earlier condition of the race, the head of each isolated household may have addressed to his wives, his children, and his slaves. But, even after the State has been organised, the laws have still an extremely limited application. Whether they retain their primitive character as Themistes, or whether they advance to the condition of Customs or Codified Texts, they are binding not on individuals, but on Families. Ancient jurisprudence, if a perhaps deceptive

comparison may be employed, may be likened to
International Law, filling nothing, as it were,
excepting the interstices between the great groups
which are the atoms of society.   In a community
so situated, the legislation of assemblies and the
jurisdiction of Courts reach only to the heads of
families, and to every other individual the rule
of conduct is the law of his home, of which his
Parent is the legislator.   But the sphere of civil
law, small at first, tends steadily to enlarge itself.
The agents of legal change, Fictions, Equity, and
Legislation, are brought in turn to bear on the
primeval institutions, and at every point of the
progress, a greater number of personal rights and
a larger amount of property are removed from
the domestic forum to the cognisance of the public
tribunals.   The ordinances of the government
obtain gradually the same efficacy in private
concerns as in matters of state, and are no longer
liable to be overridden by the behests of a despot
enthroned by each hearthstone.   We have in the
annals of Roman law a nearly complete history
of the crumbling away of an archaic system, and
of the formation of new institutions from the recombined materials, institutions some of which
descended unimpaired to the modern world, while
others, destroyed or corrupted by contact with
barbarism in the dark ages, had again to be re-
covered by mankind.   When we leave this jurisprudence at the epoch of its final reconstruction
by Justinian, few traces of archaism can be discovered in any part of it except in the single
article of the extensive powers still reserved to
the living Parent. Everywhere else principles

of convenience, or of symmetry, or of simplification—new principles at any rate—have usurped the authority of the jejune considerations which satisfied the conscience of ancient times. Everywhere a new morality has displaced the canons of conduct and the reasons of acquiescence which were in unison with the ancient usages, because in fact they were born of them.

The movement of the progressive societies has been uniform in one respect. Through all its course it has been distinguished by the gradual dissolution of family dependency, and the growth of individual obligation in its place. The Individual is steadily substituted for the Family, as the unit of which civil laws take account. The advance has been accomplished at varying rates of celerity, and there are societies not absolutely stationary in which the collapse of the ancient organisation can only be perceived by careful study of the phenomena they present. But, whatever its pace, the change has not been subject to reaction or recoil, and apparent retardations will be found to have been occasioned through the absorption of archaic ideas and customs from some entirely foreign source. Nor is it difficult to see what is the tie between man and man which replaces by degrees those forms of reciprocity in rights and duties which have their origin in the Family. It is Contract. Starting, as from one terminus of history, from a condition of society in which all the relations of Persons are summed up in the relations of Family, we seem to have steadily moved towards a phase of social order in which all these relations arise from the free agreement of Individuals. In Western Europe the progress achieved in this direction has been considerable. Thus the status of the Slave has disappeared—it has been superseded by the contractual relation of the servant to his master. The status of the Female under Tutelage, if the tutelage be understood of persons other than her husband, has also ceased to exist ; from her coming of age to her marriage all the relations she may form are relations of contract. So too the status of the Son under Power has no true place in the law of modern European societies. If any civil obligation binds together the Parent and the child of full age, it is one to which only contract gives its legal validity. The apparent exceptions are exceptions of that stamp which illustrate the rule. The child before years of discretion, the orphan under guardianship, the adjudged lunatic, have all their capacities and incapacities regulated by the Law of Persons. But why ? The reason is differently expressed in the conventional language of different systems, but in substance it is stated to the same effect by all. The great majority of Jurists are constant to the principle that the classes of persons just mentioned are subject to extrinsic control on the single ground that they do not possess the faculty of forming a judgment on their own interests ; in other words, that they are wanting in the first essential of an engagement by Contract.

The word Status may be usefully employed to construct a formula expressing the law of progress thus indicated, which, whatever be its value, seems to me to be sufficiently ascertained. All the forms of Status taken notice of in the Law of Persons were derived from, and to some extent are still coloured by, the powers and privileges anciently residing in the Family. If then we employ Status, agreeably with the usage of the best writers, to signify these personal conditions only, and avoid applying the term to such conditions as are the immediate or remote result of agreement, we may say that the movement of the progressive societies has hitherto been a movement *from Status to Contract.*

NOTE I

MONTESQUIEU, BENTHAM, AND HISTORICAL METHOD

MAINE'S judgment of Montesquieu is, in effect, that, notwith standing inevitable defects of method and some individual faults, he came nearer than any other man to founding the historical and comparative study of institutions. It is true, as Sir Courtenay Ilbert has said in a fuller criticism ("The Romanes Lecture: 'Montesquieu,'" Oxford, 1904), that "his appreciation of the historical method was imperfect, and his application of it defective": at the same time his work "prepared for and gave an enormous stimulus to those methods of study which are now recognized as indispensable to any scientific treatment either of Law or of Politics" (*op. cit.* pp. 35-6).

In 1903, on quitting the chair which I had the honour of holding in succession to Maine at Oxford, I thus endeavoured to sum up Montesquieu's relation to these studies:—

"If we hesitate to call him the founder, it is only because neither his materials nor his methods of execution were adequate to do justice to his ideas. He aimed (if I may repeat my own words, first written many years ago) at constructing a comparative theory of legislation and institutions adapted to the political needs of different forms of government, and a comparative theory of politics and law based on wide observation of the actual systems of different lands and ages. Hobbes was before him in realising that history is not a series of accidents, but Montesquieu was the first of the moderns to proclaim that a nation's institutions are part of its history, and must be considered as such if we are to understand them rightly. Much of his history is sound, and many of his judgments are admirable. Yet he failed to construct a durable system, and ' L'Esprit des Lois ' cannot even be called a systematic book. The materials were still too scattered and uncertain to be safely handled on Montesquieu's grand scale. Perhaps he would have done better to confine himself to Western Europe. The main defects of his method may be reduced, I think, to two. First, he overrated the influence of climate and other external conditions, and underrated, if he did not wholly neglect, the effects of race and tradition. Next, he had not even an inkling of what is now a fundamental rule of this kind of enquiry: namely, that there is a normal course of development for communities as well as for individuals, and that institutions which belong to different stages are not commensurable terms in any scientific comparison. This is as much as to say that even Montesquieu could not wholly escape from the unhistorical dogmatism of his time. It is perhaps a minor drawback that he constantly seeks for reasons of deliberate policy to account for seemingly eccentric features of outlandish customs, rightly or wrongly reported by missionaries or others, instead of endeavouring to connect them with their historic and racial surroundings. But the result is that many chapters of his great work amount, taken by themselves, to little more than collections of anecdotes and conjectures in which the most incongruous elements, such as the customs of China and the laws of Spain, are brought together at random. Also Montesquieu is not free from the very common error, especially prevalent in the eighteenth century, of attributing a constant and infallible efficacy to forms of government. In short, Montesquieu saw the promised land afar off, but was not equipped for entering it. I do not wish to be understood as affecting to find any fault with him. The greatness of Montesquieu's conception was his own, and the shortcomings in execution were at the time necessary, or at least natural " (" The History of Comparative Jurisprudence, a farewell Public Lecture " : Journ. Soc. Comp. Legisl., 1903, at pp. 83-4).

The " historical theory " ascribed to Bentham (p. 127) seems to be not quite so unfruitful as Maine's criticism supposes. If it is said that societies modify their laws according to modifications of their views of general expediency, this must mean views formed by actual observation and experience, as opposed to the application of dogmatic or traditional rules ; and it must be implied that such views have a greater part in the changes of legal institutions than is avowed, or perhaps realised, by the actors and promoters. Doubtless Bentham underrated the power of tradition and custom. Probably he underrated it very much in the case of archaic societies. But his proposition, understood as above explained, is a substantial one and capable of discussion. It is not reducible to the truism that people make changes because they think change expedient, or in other words because they desire change ; it signifies that the reasons professed or admitted for making particular changes are often not the real or the most operative reasons. Apparently the passages to which Maine alludes are scattered about various works of Bentham's and not expressed in clear or positive terms ; it therefore does not seem practicable, in the absence of any specific reference, to identify them. But it was obviously natural for Bentham, with his thoroughgoing conviction that all ethical problems can be solved by the utilitarian calculus, to maintain that in fact the greater part of mankind are utilitarians without knowing it.

Maine's claim of scientific validity for the historical treatment of jurisprudence (p. 128) is now disputed by no one; indeed, if we now find any difficulty, it is in remembering that in 1861 it was still novel, and that its champion at that time had need of much insight and some boldness. His precepts as to the need of observing the caution approved by experience in other kinds of scientific enquiry, beginning with the best evidence and working gradually from what is known to what is obscure or unknown, are still in full force, and might easily be illustrated by the failure of ambitious reconstructions of later date whose authors have neglected them.

NOTE K

THE PATRIARCHAL THEORY

In the preface to the tenth edition, reprinted in all subsequent issues, Maine himself referred to the chapter on Theories of Primitive Society in "Early Law and Custom." The note on the Gens in the same volume (p. 286 sqq.) should also be consulted. In 1886 Maine replied in the Quarterly Review to the criticisms of the McLennan brothers (Q.R., vol. 162, p. 181); no secret was made of the authorship, though the practice of the Review, as it then stood, did not allow signature or public acknowledgment. It should be noted that the supposed ancient Slavonic poem cited at p. 196 of this article is a modern forgery: see Kovalevsky, "Modern Customs and Ancient Laws of Russia," p. 5. The last-named learned author made fuller contributions to the subject in his lectures delivered and published in French at Stockholm ("Tableau des origines et de l'évolution de la famille et de la propriété," 1890: some account of this book, which may not be easily accessible in England, was given in the Saturday Review of October 18 and 25, 1890). Still later Dr. Kohler of Berlin has dealt systematically with the whole topic of archaic marriage and kinship, following and applying Morgan's doctrine with less reserve than Lord Avebury and Dr. Tylor, who do not accept Morgan's inferences ("Zur Urgeschichte der Ehe: Totemismus, Gruppenehe, Mutterrecht," reprinted from "Ztschr. für vergleichende Rechtswissenschaft," Stuttgart, 1897: and see a more summary statement by the same learned author in the "Encyklopädie der Rechtswissenschaft," re-edited by him in 1904, vol. i. pp. 27 sqq.). Most English readers, however, will find in the latest edition (1902) of Lord Avebury's "Origin of Civilisation," and in Dr. E. B. Tylor's article on the Matriarchal Family System, Nineteenth Century i. 81

(1896), and in Mr. Andrew Lang's "The Secret of the Totem" (1905), the easiest and certainly not the least profitable guides, among writings published since Maine's death, to what is now known or conjectured in this extremely difficult inquiry.

Much trouble and confusion might have been saved if Maine had in the first place expressly confined his thesis, as for all practical purposes it was confined, to the Indo-European family of nations. Herbert Spencer, whose courteous treatment of "Ancient Law" set a good example not always followed, gave a hint of this long ago. When Maine wrote "Ancient Law" there were no trustworthy materials for dealing with the social history of other races on a large scale. It is certain that from the earliest times at which we have any distinct knowledge of Indo-European society we find families—or communities which may be considered as expanded families—tracing descent through males, and living under the authority, more or less tempered by custom, of the eldest male ascendant. The worship of ancestors in the male line is of extreme antiquity in every branch of the stock; it is in full force at this day among the Hindus, and there are quite recent traces of it elsewhere. This is enough for the historian of Indo-European institutions; for the remaining evidences of a different earlier system are mere survivals at best, and of no importance for any subsequent development, however interesting they may be for prehistoric anthropology. My own judgment, so far as I have been able to form one, is that many of them are no better than ambiguous. Further, it is to be observed that local survivals of "matriarchal" institutions, where their existence is made out, may quite possibly not be Indo-European at all, but belong to the customs of the non-Aryan tribes who were subdued by Aryan invaders in India, or in Eastern Europe, or in the Mediterranean countries. We have been asked to regard the Erinyes prosecuting Orestes for matricide as the champions of a more ancient "mother-right" against the paternal system : as if the natural tendency of that system were to treat matricide as venial. Surely the question whether the son is bound to take up the father's blood-feud even against his own mother is hard enough to make a dramatic problem under any system which admits private vengeance at all. But in any case the Erinyes were autochthonous deities, looking on the gods of Olympus as intruders (τοιαῦτα δρῶσιν οἱ νεώτεροι θεοί). If their failure in the suit against Orestes is a symbol of anything, it may well symbolise the triumph of Hellenic over aboriginal customs. The existence of non-Aryan elements in the Mycenaean and even the later historical civilisation of Greece is accepted for independent reasons by some of our best archaeologists (P. Gardner in Eng. Hist. Rev. xvi. 744). Again (to take a Semitic example) we are told that Gideon avenged the sons of his mother upon the kings of Midian (Judges viii. 19). But there was no one else to do it, and the men of Israel who, as we read only a few verses below, said unto Gideon: "Rule thou over us, both thou and thy son, and thy son's son also," were certainly familiar with succession through males. The German, Scandinavian, and Celtic tribal customs as disclosed in the earliest known history of those branches appear to be thoroughly paternal, though not without traces of preference for relatives on the mother's side.[1] Summing up the results, Dr. Tylor says (Nineteenth Century, xl. 94): "There is no proof that at any period the maternal system held exclusive possession of the human race, but the strength with which it kept its ground may be measured by its having encompassed the globe in space, and lasted on from remote antiquity in time." For different views as to the significance of some archaic Indo-European customs, see J. D. Mayne in L.Q.R. i. 485, 494, and Kovalevsky, "Droit coutumier Ossétien," Paris, 1893, p. 181. It is no doubt possible, as suggested by Mr. Kovalevsky, that survivals from an earlier system may be maintained under a later one for reasons different from the original ones. But if patriarchal reasons are enough to account for the custom as we find it, we can hardly assume that in a given case it was formerly matriarchal, merely because for all we know it might have been. This would be to assume the very thing to be proved, namely that the society in question was in fact maternal at some earlier time.

On the whole the safest opinion appears at present to be that the Indo-European race may have gone through a stage of "matriarchy" at some remote time, but at any rate before the great migration which dispersed the several branches. This was Ihering's conclusion in his brilliant posthumous work, "Vorgeschichte der Indo-Europäer" (p. 40 of Eng. tr., 62 of original). It would seem, again, that the transformation, if such a transformation there was, must not only have taken place very early, but must have been singularly rapid and complete. Thus we are brought face to face with Maine's original problem: How and why did the Indo-Europeans become progressive? In this connexion I cannot forbear from citing some profitable words of my lamented friend Professor F. W. Maitland, though their immediate subject-matter is the history not of the family but of property.

"Even had our anthropologists at their command material that would justify them in prescribing a normal programme for the human race and in decreeing that every independent portion of mankind must, if it is to move at all, move through one fated series of stages which may be designated as Stage *A*, Stage *B*, Stage *C*,

---

[1] It is now admitted that marriage by capture was part of the earliest Germanic law, but it is very doubtful whether it survived the introduction of Christianity in England. The Anglo-Saxon bride-price appears to have been paid not for the wife's person but for the rights of wardship (Hazeltine, "Zur Geschichte der Eheschliessung nach angelsächsischem Recht," Berlin, 1905).

and so forth, we still should have to face the fact that the rapidly progressive groups have been just those which have not been independent, which have not worked out their own salvation, but have appropriated alien ideas and have thus been enabled, for anything that we can tell, to leap from Stage A to Stage X without passing through any intermediate stages. Our Anglo-Saxon ancestors did not arrive at the alphabet, or at the Nicene Creed, by traversing a long series of 'stages'; they leapt to the one and to the other " (" Domesday Book and Beyond," p. 345).

The accident of borrowing one alphabet rather than another, or in one stage rather than another, may determine the affinities of a literature and a civilization for many generations. All the tendency of modern research is to show that deliberate imitation was earlier, easier, and commoner than scholars formerly supposed; and that people will imitate pretty odd things is amply shown by modern experience.

Maine was not the first to discover that the ancient Indo-European tribe or city, as the case may be, is an expanded family with the tie of actual kindred supplemented, so far as needful to keep the community together, by adoption or even by bolder fictions; indeed, the conception is in its essential points as old as Aristotle. But he was, I think, the first to call attention in an adequate manner to the general existence and importance of this feature in archaic society. His view has been strikingly confirmed by the researches in the history of Slavonic institutions which are mentioned in "Early Law and Custom" under the head of East European House Communities. The family element in the Indo-European community has now and then been unduly suffered to drop out of sight. Thus the exclusiveness of the archaic village or township is simply and adequately explained as the exclusiveness of a community which had been or pretended to be a clan, and no deeper mystery need be sought in the much discussed Salic rule *De Migrantibus*.

Maine's original thesis was further developed by himself in the lecture on Kinship as the Basis of Society in " The Early History of Institutions," pp. 64 sqq.

It is impossible here, and I hardly think it would be relevant if possible, to enter at large on discussion of the " matriarchal " or, as Dr. Tylor prefers to call it, maternal family system. But it may be pointed out that, whatever else it is or has been, primitive it is not. It goes along with an elaborate and complex nomenclature of kindred and affinity, of which the interpretation is much disputed,[1] and often though not always with other usages of the

---

[1] J. F. McLennan's opinion, which he intended to develop farther and prove in detail, was that this classification had nothing to do with consanguinity, but was a system of modes of salutation; and this is also maintained by Dr. Westermarck. Morgan, on the other hand, would allow no merit to McLennan's work and thought the term " exogamy," now generally adopted, useless. Professor Kohler,

most artificial kind, of which the explanation is no less conjectural, and as obscure to the modern historian as the facts to be
explained are repugnant to modern civilized manners.   Dr. Tylor
has observed that its real characteristic point is the continuance of
the wife in her own family, who do not lose her property or the
value of her work, and gain the husband's alliance.   If these or
such-like politic motives were the true determining causes of
" matriarchy "—and Dr. Tylor makes out a case which is none the
less strong for being simple and using the general known materials
of human nature instead of hypothetical superstitions—we are a
long way off from primitive man, and the problem of what came
before all this remains open.   Here Maine's appeal to the Homeric
description of the savage (not merely barbarous) Cyclopes is
probably nearer to the truth than the state of promiscuity—surely
the least likely state of nature ever heard of—which some anthropologists have postulated.   At any rate it has, in substance, Dr.
Tylor's support.   " The claim of the patriarchal system to have
belonged to primitive human life has not merely long acceptance
in its favour, but I venture to think that those who uphold it have
the weight of evidence on their side, provided that they do not
insist on its fully developed form having at first appeared, but are
content to argue that already in the earliest ages the man took his
wife to himself, and that the family was under his power and
protection, the law of male descent and all that belongs to it
gradually growing up afterwards on this basis. . . . Among the
great ancient and modern nations within the range of history, the
paternal system becomes so dominant as to be taken for granted,
and the existence of any other rule seems extraordinary "
(Nineteenth Century, xl. 84, 85).   So far as the evidence has gone,
the maternal system appears to be unstable when people who live
under it come into contact with paternal families: in such cases
the husband's predominance pretty soon begins to assert or re-
assert itself.   It is also remarkable that a received custom so lax
as not to seem to civilized administrators fit to rank as any kind
of marriage law has been found compatible with fairly strict
monogamy in practice (on both these points see H. H. Shephard,
" Marriage Law in Malabar," L.Q.R. viii. 314).   It seems fairly
certain that both the frequency and the importance of polyandry
have been exaggerated, and that, where it occurs, it can be
explained, by those who regard " group-marriage " as proved,
as a limiting case of group-marriage determined by special

and less decidedly Mr. Kovalevsky, are, I believe, the only recent authors prepared to accept as a whole the consequences drawn by Morgan himself from the
" classificatory " system.   Subject to what McLennan might have added if he had
lived, his particular line of objection just mentioned does not seem sufficient.   Mr.
Andrew Lang's conclusions are about equally remote from both schools .

conditions. Thus we are rather led to regard the maternal system as a product of social necessities, not yet very well understood, which, although they have prevailed at some time in many or most inhabited parts of the world, may be fairly called abnormal with respect to the most original and persistent instincts of mankind as a species. When the maternal is supplanted by the paternal society, those instincts come to their own again in surroundings that no longer demand the highly artificial discipline of matriarchy. Much more evidence is needed both as to the origins of the maternal family, and as to the causes and manner of its transformation into the paternal type, before anything like a comprehensive statement can be made. We should remember that, as Professor Maitland says, continuing the passage already quoted, "we are learning that the attempt to construct a normal programme for all portions of mankind is idle and unscientific." Probably no one would now maintain that either marriage by capture or matriarchy is primitive. Any such position is formally disclaimed, for example, by a recent learned and ingenious author, Dr. Richard Hildebrand, " Recht und Sitte auf den verschiedenen Kulturstufen," 1ter Teil, Jena, 1896. It is perhaps needless at this day to refute the formerly current opinion that the customs of savages are the result of degradation from a more ancient state of innocence or civilization. Partial backsliding into barbarism over a considerable range of both time and space is of course possible, as shown in the decline of the Roman and the Mogul empires. But trying to account for the systems of kinship (if it is kinship) investigated by Morgan as fallings off from monogamy or patriarchal polygamy is, if I may repeat an illustration I have already used in an earlier note, like expecting to find chalk under granite.

Finally Mr. Lang, in "The Secret of the Totem," agreeing in the main with Darwin on this point, wholly rejects the hypothesis of a promiscuous horde having been the earliest state of human life, and holds that "men, whatever their brutal ancestors may have done, when they became men indeed, lived originally in small anonymous local groups, and had, for a reason to be given "—the jealous despotism of the eldest male, as is explained in a later chapter—"the habit of selecting female mates from groups *not* their own." McLennan's explanation of exogamy is dismissed as wholly inadequate, and the facts supposed by Morgan and his school to establish a general epoch of " group-marriage " are treated as exceptional and belonging to a relatively advanced stage. I do not presume to appreciate Mr. Lang's theory, or make any critical comparison of it with those of other anthropologists who differ widely from Mr. Lang and from one another. But it is legitimate to observe that Mr. Lang, as well as Dr. Tylor, appears to justify Maine's opinion as to the primitive character of the Cyclopean family, and that it is less plausible now than it was twenty years ago to regard Maine as an old-fashioned literary scholar standing out against the lights of modern research. No doubt Maine, when he wrote "Ancient Law," conceived the transition from the savagery of the Cyclops to the archaic civilisation of a Roman paterfamilias under the Kings or the early Republic as having been a far more direct and simple process than we can at this day think probable. This is so common an incident of historical speculation, in the absence of full and trustworthy material, that there is nothing in it to derogate from Maine's credit.

With regard to the extreme form of paternal power which, as Maine says (p. 142), we may conveniently call by its later Roman name of Patria Potestas, it is not clear that it is a mere incident of family headship. Some competent persons, such as Mr. Kovalevsky, hold it to be derived from the notion that the wife is the husband's property, and therefore her offspring must be in his power too. If this be so, the right, being proprietary and not merely social, would belong exclusively to Private Law, and the "maxim of Roman jurisprudence that the Patria Potestas did not extend to the Jus Publicum" would be strictly logical as well as politic. But some, again, think that the paternal family itself was developed through marriage by capture or purchase, causing the wife so acquired to be regarded as the husband's chattel (Kohler, "Encykl. der Rechtswissenschaft," i. 30, 33; "Das Vaterrecht entwickelt sich . . . zunächst als Herrschaftsrecht: der Ehemann ist Herr der Frau und damit Herr ihrer Frucht"). Not that lordship in a rudimentary society can safely be identified with our modern legal ownership. *Dominus* is an ambiguous word except in strict Roman law. At all events we cannot disregard the testimony of Gaius that the Patria Potestas of the Roman family law was, in the time of Hadrian, singular among the Mediterranean nations; and, so far as we know anything of the provincial customs of the empire, they seem to have been not less but more archaic than the law of Rome. The responsibilities of the Roman paterfamilias, on the other hand, are not distinguishable in character or extent from those of the patriarch in other Indo-European family systems.

Another reason against regarding the Roman Patria Potestas as of the highest antiquity is that at an earlier time the paterfamilias was regarded not as owner, but as an administrator of the family property which in some sense already belonged to the heirs as well as himself. Indeed, this idea survived as late as the classical ages of Roman law in the untranslatable term of art *sui heredes*, of which "necessary heirs" is perhaps the most tolerable rendering, and the comments of the jurists upon it (Paulus in D. 28, 2, *de liberis et postumis*, 11, cited by Holmes, "The Common Law," p. 342). We are fully confirmed in this by the history of the Hindu Joint Family. In Bengal the change from the position of an administrator with large powers to that of an owner is known to have taken place in relatively modern times.

Finally, I venture to record, for what it may be worth, my impression that recent inquirers, with the notable exception of Mr. J. G. Frazer, have somewhat neglected the part of superstitions and magical or pseudo-scientific beliefs in the formation of social customs. There is no presumption whatever that the true explanation of any savage practice is that which to us appears most reasonable or natural. The fundamental difference between religion and magic has been explained by Lord Avebury and Sir Alfred Lyall. Religious offerings and ceremonies, apart from the higher ethical and philosophical developments of advanced theology, seek to propitiate supernatural powers, magical ritual to control both natural and supernatural agencies. The priest is, in the current phrase, a minister, that is to say a servant of whatever gods he worships; he begs their peace and alliance with tribute in his hand. The magician or wizard acts as a master; he aims at using the secrets of nature, or commanding for his own use or that of his clients, and at his own will, the " armies of angels that soar, legions of demons that lurk." Solomon's seal is magical, his dedication of the temple is religious. The facts that magic and religion are often intermixed, and that the priest is very apt to revert to the position of a mere thaumaturgist, do not appear to alter the importance of the distinction. But this has little, if anything, to do with the present subject.

NOTE L

STATUS AND CONTRACT

Maine's now celebrated dictum as to the movement from Status to Contract in progressive societies is perhaps to be understood as limited to the law of Property, taking that term in its widest sense as inclusive of whatever has a value measurable in exchange. With that limitation the statement is certainly just, and has not ceased to be significant. The movement is not yet complete, for example, in England, where the emancipation of married women's property has been proceeding in a piecemeal fashion for more than a generation, and is at present in a transitional state capable not only of raising hard questions but of producing, within a few years, decisions not easy to reconcile. As regards the actual definition of different personal conditions, and the more personal relations incidental to them, it does not seem that a movement from Status to Contract can be asserted with any generality. For example, the tendency of modern legislation has been to make the dissolution of marriage less difficult, and in some jurisdictions this has gone very far. But it has nowhere been enacted, and I do not think any legislator has yet seriously proposed, that the parties shall be free to settle for themselves, by the terms of the marriage contract, whether the marriage shall be dissoluble or not, and if so, on what grounds. Assimilation of marriage, as a personal relation, to partnership is not within the scope of practical jurisprudence. Again, a minor who has attained years of discretion cannot advance or postpone the date of his full age by contract with his parent or guardian, and we do not hear of any one proposing to confer such a power. The test which Maine suggests as alone justifying the preservation of disabilities—that the persons concerned do not possess the faculty of forming a judgment on their own interests—will hardly be received as adequate for either of the cases just put. In fact, the interests which these rules of law regard are not those of the parties alone. Paramount considerations of the stability of society, or the general convenience of third persons, override the freedom usually left to parties in their own affairs. The law of persons may be and has been cut short; but, so long as we recognise any differences at all among persons, we cannot allow their existence and nature to be treated merely as matter of bargain. Status may yield ground to Contract, but cannot itself be reduced to Contract. On the other hand Contract has made attacks on Property which have been repulsed. There was a time in the thirteenth century during which it seemed as if there was no rule of tenure that could not be modified by the agreement of parties. Our settled rules that only certain defined forms of interest in property can be created by private acts, our rule against perpetuities, are the answer of the Common Law to attempts to bring everything under private bargain and control. The importance of Contract in the feudal scheme of society is pointed out by Maine himself in this book, ch. ix *ad fin.* (cp. Pollock and Maitland, "H.E.L." ii. 230).

One department of the law of Persons is increasing, not diminishing, in importance, namely the law of corporations or "moral persons." We are beginning to find that the law cannot afford to ignore collective personality—that of a trade union, for example—where fact and usage have conferred a substantially corporate character on a more or less permanent social group. Modern company law is largely, no doubt, a law of contract; but of contract whose action is regulated and modified at every turn by the fact that one of the chief parts is born by a corporate and not an individual person.

Maine guarded his position, however, to a considerable extent in the final words of this chapter, for he seems not to include Marriage—at all events marriage among Western nations, which is preceded by and results from agreement of the parties—under the head of Status. And, if the term is thus restricted, the gravest apparent exception to Maine's dictum is removed. This, of course, involves a sensible narrowing of the term Status, a much discussed term which, according to the best modern expositions, includes the sum total of a man's personal rights and duties (Salmond, "Jurisprudence," 1902, pp. 253-7), or, to be verbally accurate, of his capacity for rights and duties (Holland, "Jurisprudence," 9th ed. p. 88). It is curious that the word "estate," which is nothing but the French form of "status," should have come to stand over against it in an almost opposite category. A man's *estate* is his measurable property; what we call his *status* is his position as a lawful man, a voter, and so forth. The liability of every citizen to pay rates and taxes is a matter of status; what a given citizen has to pay depends on his estate, or portions of it assigned as the measures of particular imposts. We have, too, an "estate" in land, which so far preserves the original associations of "status" that, as we have just noted, contract may not alter its incidents or nature. Again, as Professor Maitland has pointed out (Introduction to Gierke's "Political Theories of the Middle Age," Camb. 1900, p. xxv), the Roman Status has also become the State of modern public law, and in that form has refused to be reduced to a species of contract by the ingenious efforts of individualist philosophers, notwithstanding the widespread acceptance of the Social Contract for a century or more.

It is not clear how far Maine regarded the movement of which he spoke as a phase of the larger political individualism which prevailed in the eighteenth century and great part of the nineteenth, or what he would have thought of the reaction against this doctrine which we are now witnessing. At all events the questions at issue between publicists of various schools as to the proper limits of State interference with trade, or of State and municipal enterprise, do not seem to have much to do with simplifying the tenure and transfer of property, nor with removing obsolete personal disabilities.

Professor Dicey says indeed ("Law and Public Opinion in England," p. 283) that "the rights of workmen in regard to compensation for accidents have become a matter not of contract, but of status." But many other kinds of contracts have long had incidents attached to them by law, and those incidents are not always subject to be varied at the will of the parties. A mortgagor cannot enter into an agreement with the mortgagee which has the effect of making the mortgage irredeemable, or even tends that way by "clogging the equity of redemption." It would be a strong thing to say that this peculiar doctrine of English courts of equity has created a status of mortgagors.

The Trade Disputes Act, 1906, passed since this note was first published, may certainly be said to have conferred a new and unexampled status on combinations of both employers and workmen by exempting them in several respects from the operation of the general law; but the obligation of contracts is not directly affected, and it remains to be seen whether the Act represents any general movement of legislative ideas, or anything else than the pressure of very powerful interests astutely applied at a critical moment. On one or two points it only confirms what was already the better supported opinion.

CHAPTER VI

THE EARLY HISTORY OF TESTAMENTARY
SUCCESSION

IF an attempt were made to demonstrate in
England the superiority of the historical method
of investigation to the modes of inquiry concerning
Jurisprudence which are in fashion among us,
no department of Law would better serve as an
example than Testaments or Wills. Its capabili-
ties it owes to its great length and great continuity.
At the beginning of its history we find ourselves
in the very infancy of the social state, surrounded
by conceptions which it requires some effort of
mind to realise in their ancient form ; while here,
at the other extremity of its line of progress, we
are in the midst of legal notions which are nothing
more than those same conceptions disguised by
the phraseology and by the habits of thought
which belong to modern times, and exhibiting
therefore a difficulty of another kind, the difficulty
of believing that ideas which form part of our
everyday mental stock can really stand in need
of analysis and examination. The growth of the
Law of Wills between these extreme points can
be traced with remarkable distinctness. It was
much less interrupted at the epoch of the birth of
feudalism, than the history of most other branches
of law. It is, indeed, true that as regards all

provinces of jurisprudence, the break caused by
the division between ancient and modern history,
or in other words by the dissolution of the Roman
Empire, has been very greatly exaggerated. In-
dolence has disinclined many writers to be at the
pains of looking for threads of connection entangled
and obscured by the confusions of six troubled
centuries, while other inquirers, not naturally
deficient in patience and industry, have been misled
by idle pride in the legal system of their country,
and by consequent unwillingness to confess its
obligations to the jurisprudence of Rome.   But
these unfavourable influences have had comparatively little effect on the province of Testamentary
Law. The barbarians were confessedly strangers
to any such conception as that of a Will.   The
best authorities agree that there is no trace of it in
those parts of their written codes which comprise
the customs practised by them in their original
seats, and in their subsequent settlements on the
edge of the Roman Empire.   But soon after they
became mixed with the population of the Roman
provinces they appropriated from the Imperial
jurisprudence the conception of a Will, at first in
part, and afterwards in all its integrity.   The
influence of the Church had much to do with this
rapid assimilation. The ecclesiastical power had
very early succeeded to those privileges of custody
and registration of Testaments which several of
the heathen temples had enjoyed ; and even thus
early it was almost exclusively to private bequests
that the religious foundations owed their temporal
possessions.   Hence it is that the decrees of the
earliest Provincial Councils perpetually contain

anathemas against those who deny the sanctity of Wills. Here, in England, Church influence was certainly chief among the causes which by universal acknowledgment have prevented that discontinuity in the history of Testamentary Law which is sometimes believed to exist in the history of other provinces of Jurisprudence. The jurisdiction over one class of Will was delegated to the Ecclesiastical Courts, which applied to them, though not always intelligently, the principles of Roman jurisprudence ; and, though neither the Courts of Common Law nor the Court of Chancery owned any positive obligation to follow the Ecclesiastical tribunals, they could not escape the potent influence of a system of settled rules in course of application by their side. The English law of testamentary succession to personality has become a modified form of the dispensation under which the inheritances of Roman citizens were administered.

It is not difficult to point out the extreme difference of the conclusions forced on us by the historical treatment of the subject, from those to which we are conducted when, without the help of history, we merely strive to analyse our *primâ-facie* impressions. I suppose there is nobody who, starting from the popular or even the legal conception of a Will, would not imagine that certain qualities are necessarily attached to it. He would say, for example, that a Will necessarily takes effect *at death only*—that it is *secret*, not known as a matter of course to persons taking interests under its provisions—that it is *revocable, i e.* always capable of being superseded by a new act of testation. Yet I shall be able to show that there was a time when none of these characteristics belonged to a Will. The Testaments from which our Wills are directly descended at first took effect immediately on their execution ; they were not secret ; they were not revocable. Few legal agencies are, in fact, the fruit of more complex historical agencies than that by which a man's written intentions control the posthumous disposition of his goods. Testaments very slowly and gradually gathered round them the qualities I have mentioned ; and they did this from causes and under pressure of events which may be called casual, or which at any rate have no interest for us at present, except so far as they have effected the history of law.

At a time when legal theories were more abundant than at present—theories which, it is true, were for the most part gratuitous and premature enough, but which nevertheless rescued jurisprudence from that worse and more ignoble condition, not unknown to ourselves, in which nothing like a generalisation is aspired to, and law is regarded as a mere empirical pursuit—it was the fashion to explain the ready and apparently intuitive perception which we have of certain qualities in a Will, by saying that they were natural to it, or, as the phrase would run in full, attached to it by the Law of Nature. Nobody, I imagine, would affect to maintain such a doctrine when once it was ascertained that all these characteristics had their origin within historical memory ; at the same time vestiges of the theory of which the doctrine is an offshoot, linger in forms of expression

which we all of us use, and perhaps scarcely know
how to dispense with. I may illustrate this by
mentioning a position common in the legal literature of the seventeenth century. The jurists of
that period very commonly assert that the power
of Testation itself is of Natural Law, that it is a
right conferred by the Law of Nature. Their
teaching, though all persons may not at once see
the connection, is in substance followed by those
who affirm that the right of dictating or controlling
the posthumous disposal of property is a necessary
or natural consequence of the proprietary rights
themselves. And every student of technical jurisprudence must have come across the same view,
clothed in the language of a rather different
school, which, in its rationale of this department
of law, treats succession *ex testamento* as the mode
of devolution which the property of deceased
persons ought primarily to follow, and then proceeds to account for succession *ab intestato* as
the incidental provision of the lawgiver for the
discharge of a function which was only left un-
performed through the neglect or misfortune of
the deceased proprietor. These opinions are only
expanded forms of the more compendious doctrine
that Testamentary disposition is an institution
of the Law of Nature. It is certainly never quite
safe to pronounce dogmatically as to the range of
association embraced by modern minds when they
reflect on Nature and her Law ; but I believe that
most persons, who affirm that the Testamentary
Power is of Natural Law, may be taken to imply
either that, as a matter of fact, it is universal, or
that nations are prompted to sanction it by an

original instinct and impulse. With respect to the first of these positions, I think that, when explicitly set forth, it can never be seriously contended for in an age which has seen the severe restraints imposed on the Testamentary Power by the *Code Napoléon*, and has witnessed the steady multiplication of systems for which the French codes have served as a model. To the second assertion we must object that it is contrary to the best-ascertained facts in the early history of law, and I venture to affirm generally that, in all indigenous societies, a condition of jurisprudence in which Testamentary privileges are *not* allowed, or rather not contemplated, has preceded that later stage of legal development in which the mere will of the proprietor is permitted under more or less of restriction to override the claims of his kindred in blood.

The conception of a Will or Testament cannot be considered by itself. It is a member, and not the first, of a series of conceptions. In itself a Will is simply the instrument by which the intention of the testator is declared. It must be clear, I think, that before such an instrument takes its turn for discussion, there are several preliminary points to be examined—as for example, what is it, what sort of right or interest, which passes from a dead man on his decease ? to whom and in what form does it pass ? and how came it that the dead were allowed to control the posthumous disposition of their property ? Thrown into technical language, the dependence of the various conceptions which contribute to the notion of a Will is thus expressed. A Will or Testament is an instrument by which the devolution of an inheritance is prescribed. Inheritance is a form of universal succession. A universal succession is a succession to a *universitas juris*, or university of rights and duties. Inverting this order we have therefore to inquire what is a *universitas juris* ; what is a universal succession ; what is the form of universal succession which is called an inheritance ? And there are also two further questions, independent to some extent of the points I have mooted, but demanding solution before the subject of Wills can be exhausted. These are, how came an inheritance to be controlled in any case by the testator's volition, and what is the nature of the instrument by which it came to be controlled ?

The first question relates to the *universitas juris* ; that is a university (or bundle) of rights and duties. A *universitas juris* is a collection of rights and duties united by the single circumstance of their having belonged at one time to some one person. It is, as it were, the legal clothing of some given individual. It is not formed by grouping together *any* rights and *any* duties. It can only be constituted by taking all the rights and all the duties of a particular person. The tie which so connects a number of rights of property, rights of way, rights to legacies, duties of specific performance, debts, obligations, to compensate wrongs—which so connects all these legal privileges and duties together as to constitute them a *universitas juris*, is the *fact* of their having attached to some individual capable of exercising them. Without this *fact* there is no university of rights and duties. The expression *universitas juris* is

not classical, but for the notion jurisprudence
is exclusively indebted to Roman law; nor is it
at all difficult to seize. We must endeavour to
collect under one conception the whole set of
legal relations in which each one of us stands to
the rest of the world. These, whatever be their
character and composition, make up together a
universitas juris; and there is but little danger
of mistake in forming the notion, if we are only
careful to remember that duties enter into it quite
as much as rights. Our duties may overbalance
our rights. A man may owe more than he is
worth, and therefore if a money value is set on
his collective legal relations he may be what is
called insolvent. But for all that the entire group
of rights and duties which centres in him is not
the less a " juris universitas."

We come next to a " universal succession." A
universal succession is a succession to a *universitas
juris*. It occurs when one man is invested with
the legal clothing of another, becoming at the same
moment subject to all his liabilities and entitled to
all his rights. In order that the universal succession may be true and perfect, the devolution
must take place *uno ictu*, as the jurists phrase it.
It is of course possible to conceive one man
acquiring the whole of the rights and duties of
another at different periods, as for example by
successive purchases; or he might acquire them
in different capacities, part as heir, part as purchaser, part as legatee. But though the group
of rights and duties thus made up should in fact
amount to the whole legal personality of a particular individual, the acquisition would not be a

13

universal succession. In order that there may be a true universal succession, the transmission must be such as to pass the whole aggregate of rights and duties at the *same* moment and in virtue of the *same* legal capacity in the recipient. The notion of a universal succession, like that of a " juris universitas," is permanent in jurisprudence, though in the English legal system it is obscured by the great variety of capacities in which rights are acquired, and, above all, by the distinction between the two great provinces of English property, " realty " and " personalty." The succession of an assignee in bankruptcy to the entire property of the bankrupt is, however, a universal succession, though, as the assignee only pays debts to the extent of the assets, this is only a modified form of the primary notion. Were it common among us for persons to take assignments of *all* a man's property on condition of paying *all* his debts, such transfers would exactly resemble the universal successions known to the oldest Roman Law. When a Roman citizen *adrogated* a son, *i.e.*, took a man, not already under Patria Potestas, as his adoptive child, he succeeded *universally* to the adoptive child's estate, *i.e.*, he took all the property and became liable for all the obligations. Several other forms of universal succession appear in the primitive Roman Law, but infinitely the most important and the most durable of all was that one with which we are more immediately concerned, Hæreditas or Inheritance. Inheritance was a universal succession, occurring at a death. The universal successor was Hæres or Heir. He stepped at once into all the rights and all the duties of the dead man. He was instantly clothed with his entire legal person, and I need scarcely add that the special character of the Hæres remained the same, whether he was named by a Will or whether he took on an intestacy. The term Hæres is no more emphatically used of the Intestate than of the Testamentary Heir, for the manner in which a man became Hæres had nothing to do with the legal character he sustained. The dead man's universal successor, however he became so, whether by Will or by Intestacy, was his Heir. But the Heir was not necessarily a single person. A group of persons, considered in law as a single unit, might succeed as *co-heirs* to the Inheritance.

Let me now quote the usual Roman definition of an Inheritance. The reader will be in a position to appreciate the full force of the separate terms. *Hæreditas est successio in universum jus quod defunctus habuit* (" an inheritance is a succession to the entire legal position of a deceased man "). The notion was that, though the physical person of the deceased had perished, his legal personality survived and descended unimpaired on his Heir or Co-heirs, in whom his identity (so far as the law was concerned) was continued. Our own law, in constituting the Executor or Administrator the representative of the deceased to the extent of his personal assets, may serve as an illustration of the theory from which it emanated, but, although it illustrates, it does not explain it. The view of even the later Roman Law required a closeness of correspondence between the position of the deceased and of his Heir which is no feature of an English representation ; and, in the primitive jurisprudence everything turned on the continuity of succession. Unless provision was made in the will for the instant devolution of the testator's rights and duties on the Heir or Co-heirs, the testament lost all its effect.

In modern Testamentary jurisprudence, as in the later Roman Law, the object of first importance is the execution of the testator's intentions. In the ancient law of Rome the subject of corresponding carefulness was the bestowal of the Universal Succession. One of these rules seems to our eyes a principle dictated by common sense, while the other looks very much like an idle crotchet. Yet that without the second of them the first would never have come into being, is as certain as any proposition of the kind can be.

In order to solve this apparent paradox, and to bring into greater clearness the train of ideas which I have been endeavouring to indicate, I must borrow the results of the inquiry which was attempted in the earlier portion of the preceding chapter. We saw one peculiarity invariably distinguishing the infancy of society. Men are regarded and treated, not as individuals, but always as members of a particular group. Everybody is first a citizen, and then, as a citizen, he is a member of his order—of an aristocracy or a democracy, of an order of patricians or plebeians ; or, in those societies which an unhappy fate has afflicted with a special perversion in their course of development, of a caste. Next, he is a member of a gens, house, or clan ; and lastly, he is a member of his *family*. This last was the narrowest

and most personal relation in which he stood;
nor, paradoxical as it may seem, was he ever
regarded as *himself*, as a distinct individual. His
individuality was swallowed up in his family. I
repeat the definition of a primitive society given
before. It has for its units, not individuals, but
groups of men united by the reality or the fiction
of blood-relationship.

It is in the peculiarities of an undeveloped
society that we seize the first trace of a universal
succession. Contrasted with the organisation of
a modern state, the commonwealths of primitive
times may be fairly described as consisting of a
number of little despotic governments, each perfectly distinct from the rest, each absolutely controlled by the prerogative of a single monarch.
But though the Patriarch, for we must not yet
call him the Pater-familias, had rights thus extensive, it is impossible to doubt that he lay
under an equal amplitude of obligations. If he
governed the family, it was for its behoof. If he
was lord of its possessions, he held them as trustee
for his children and kindred. He had no privilege
or position distinct from that conferred on him by
his relation to the petty commonwealth which he
governed. The Family, in fact, was a Corporation;
and he was its representative or, we might almost
say, its Public officer. He enjoyed rights and
stood under duties, but the rights and duties
were, in the contemplation of his fellow-citizens
and in the eye of the law, quite as much those of
the collective body as his own. Let us consider
for a moment, the effect which would be produced
by the death of such a representative. In the eye

of the law, in the view of the civil magistrate, the demise of the domestic authority would be a perfectly immaterial event. The person representing the collective body of the family and primarily responsible to municipal jurisdiction would bear a different name; and that would be all. The rights and obligations which attached to the deceased head of the house would attach, without breach of continuity, to his successor; for, in point of fact, they would be the rights and obligations of the family, and the family had the distinctive characteristic of a corporation—that it never died. Creditors would have the same remedies against the new chieftain as against the old, for the liability being that of the still existing family would be absolutely unchanged. All rights available to the family would be as available after the demise of the headship as before it—except that the corporation would be obliged—if indeed language so precise and technical can be properly used of these early times—would be obliged to *sue* under a slightly modified name.

The history of jurisprudence must be followed in its whole course, if we are to understand how gradually and tardily society dissolved itself into the component atoms of which it is now constituted —by what insensible gradations the relation of man to man substituted itself for the relation of the individual to his family, and of families to each other. The point now to be attended to is that even when the revolution had apparently quite accomplished itself, even when the magistrate had in great measure assumed the place of the Pater-familias, and the civil tribunal substituted itself for the domestic forum, nevertheless the whole scheme of rights and duties administered by the judicial authorities remained shaped by the influence of the obsolete privileges and coloured in every part by their reflection.   There seems little question that the devolution of the Universitas Juris, so strenuously insisted upon by the Roman Law as the first condition of a testamentary or intestate succession, was a feature of the older form of society which men's minds have been unable to dissociate from the new, though with that newer phase it had no true or proper connection.   It seems, in truth, that the prolongation of a man's legal existence in his heir, or in a group of co-heirs, is neither more nor less than a characteristic of *the family* transferred by a fiction to *the individual*.   Succession in corporations is necessarily universal, and the family was a corporation. Corporations never die.   The decease of individual members makes no difference to the collective existence of the aggregate body, and does not in any way affect its legal incidents, its faculties or liabilities.   Now in the idea of a Roman universal succession all these qualities of a corporation seem to have been transferred to the individual citizen. His physical death is allowed to exercise no effect on the legal position which he filled, apparently on the principle that that position is to be adjusted as closely as possible to the analogies of a family, which, in its corporate character, was not of course liable to physical extinction.

I observe that not a few Continental jurists have much difficulty in comprehending the nature of the connection between the conceptions blended in a universal succession, and there is perhaps no topic in the philosophy of jurisprudence on which their speculations, as a general rule, possess so little value. But the student of English law ought to be in no danger of stumbling at the analysis of the idea which we are examining. Much light is cast upon it by a fiction in our own system with which all lawyers are familiar. English lawyers classify corporations as Corporations aggregate and Corporations sole. A Corporation aggregate is a true Corporation, but a Corporation sole is an individual, being a member of a series of individuals, who is invested by a fiction with the qualities of a Corporation. I need hardly cite the King or the Parson of a Parish as instances of Corporations sole. The capacity or office is here considered apart from the particular person who from time to time may occupy it, and, this capacity being perpetual, the series of individuals who fill it are clothed with the leading attribute of Corporations —Perpetuity. Now in the older theory of Roman Law the individual bore to the family precisely the same relation which in the rationale of English jurisprudence a Corporation sole bears to a Corporation aggregate. The derivation and association of ideas are exactly the same. In fact, if we say to ourselves that for purposes of Roman Testamentary Jurisprudence each individual citizen was a Corporation sole, we shall not only realise the full conception of an inheritance, but have constantly at command the clue to the assumption in which it originated. It is an axiom with us that the King never dies, being a Corporation sole. His capacities are instantly filled by his successor, and

the continuity of dominion is not deemed to have
been interrupted.   With the Romans it seemed an
equally simple and natural process, to eliminate
the fact of death from the devolution of rights
and obligations.   The testator lived on in his heir
or in the group of his co-heirs.   He was in law
the same person with them, and if any one in his
testamentary dispositions had even constructively
violated the principle which united his actual and
his posthumous existence, the law rejected the
defective instrument, and gave the inheritance to
the kindred in blood, whose capacity to fulfil the
conditions of heirship was conferred on them by
the law itself, and not by any document which by
possibility might be erroneously framed.

When a Roman citizen died intestate or leaving
no valid Will, his descendants or kindred became
his heirs according to a scale which will be presently described.   The person or class of persons
who succeeded did not simply *represent* the
deceased, but, in conformity with the theory just
delineated, they *continued* his civil life, his legal
existence.   The same results followed when the
order of succession was determined by a Will, but
the theory of the identity between the dead man
and his heirs was certainly much older than any
form of Testament or phase of Testamentary
jurisprudence.   This indeed is the proper moment
for suggesting a doubt which will press on us with
greater force the further we plumb the depths of
this subject—whether *wills* would ever have come
into being at all if it had not been for these remarkable ideas connected with universal succession.   Testamentary law is the application of a

principle which may be explained on a variety of philosophical hypotheses as plausible as they are gratuitous; it is interwoven with every part of modern society, and it is defensible on the broadest grounds of general expediency. But the warning can never be too often repeated, that the grand source of mistake in questions of jurisprudence is the impression that those reasons which actuate us at the present moment, in the maintenance of an existing institution, have necessarily anything in common with the sentiment in which the institution originated. It is certain that, in the old Roman Law of Inheritance, the notion of a will or testament is inextricably mixed up, I might almost say confounded, with the theory of a man's posthumous existence in the person of his heir.

The conception of a universal succession, firmly as it has taken root in jurisprudence, has not occurred spontaneously to the framers of every body of laws. Wherever it is now found, it may be shown to have descended from Roman law; and with it have come down a host of legal rules on the subject of Testaments and Testamentary gifts, which modern practitioners apply without discerning their relation to the parent theory. But, in the pure Roman jurisprudence, the principle that a man lives on in his Heir—the elimination, if we may so speak, of the fact of death—is too obviously for mistake the centre round which the whole Law of Testamentary and Intestate succession is circling. The unflinching sternness of the Roman law in enforcing compliance with the governing theory would in itself suggest that the theory grew out of something in the primitive

constitution of Roman society ; but we may push
the proof a good way beyond the presumption.
It happens that several technical expressions,
dating from the earliest institution of wills at
Rome, have been accidentally preserved to us.
We have in Gaius the formula of investiture by
which the universal successor was created. We
have the ancient name by which the person afterwards called Heir was at first designated. We
have further the text of the celebrated clause in
the Twelve Tables by which the Testamentary
power was expressly recognised, and the clauses
regulating Intestate Succession have also been
preserved. All these archaic phrases have one
salient peculiarity. They indicate that what
passed from the Testator to the Heir was the
Family, that is, the aggregate of rights and duties
contained in the Patria Potestas and growing out
of it. The material property is in three instances
not mentioned at all ; in two others, it is visibly
named as an adjunct or appendage of the Family.
The original Will or Testament was therefore an
instrument, or (for it was probably not at first
in writing) a proceeding, by which the devolution
of the *Family* was regulated. It was a mode of
declaring who was to have the chieftainship, in
succession to the Testator. When Wills are
understood to have this for their original object,
we see at once how it is that they came to be
connected with one of the most curious relics of
ancient religion and law, the *sacra*, or Family Rites.
These *sacra* were the Roman form of an institution
which shows itself wherever society has not
wholly shaken itself free from its primitive clothing.

They are the sacrifices and ceremonies by which
the brotherhood of the family is commemorated,
the pledge and the witness of its perpetuity.
Whatever be their nature—whether it be true or
not that in all cases they are the worship of some
mythical ancestor—they are everywhere employed
to attest the sacredness of the family relation ;
and therefore they acquire prominent significance
and importance, whenever the continuous existence
of the Family is endangered by a change in the
person of its chief. Accordingly, we hear most
about them in connection with demises of domestic
sovereignty. Among the Hindoos, the right to
inherit a dead man's property is exactly co-extensive with the duty of performing his obsequies.
If the rites are not properly performed or not
performed by the proper person, no relation is
considered as established between the deceased
and anybody surviving him ; the Law of Succession does not apply, and nobody can inherit the
property. Every great event in the life of a
Hindoo seems to be regarded as leading up to and
bearing upon these solemnities. If he marries, it
is to have children who may celebrate them after
his death ; if he has no children, he lies under the
strongest obligation to adopt them from another
family, " with a view," writes the Hindoo doctor,
" to the funeral cake, the water, and the solemn
sacrifice." The sphere preserved to the Roman
sacra in the time of Cicero, was not less in extent.
It embraced Inheritances and Adoptions. No
adoption was allowed to take place without due
provision for the *sacra* of the family from which
the adoptive son was transferred, and no Testa-

ment was allowed to distribute an Inheritance without a strict apportionment of the expenses of these ceremonies among the different co-heirs. The differences between the Roman law at this epoch, when we obtain our last glimpse of the *sacra*, and the existing Hindoo system, are most instructive. Among the Hindoos, the religious element in law has acquired a complete predominance. Family sacrifices have become the keystone of all the Law of Persons and much of the Law of Things. They have even received a monstrous extension, for it is a plausible opinion that the self-immolation of the widow at her husband's funeral, a practice continued to historical times by the Hindoos, and commemorated in the traditions of several Indo-European races, was an addition grafted on the primitive *sacra*, under the influence of the impression, which always accompanies the idea of sacrifice, that human blood is the most precious of all oblations. With the Romans, on the contrary, the legal obligation and the religious duty have ceased to be blended. The necessity of solemnising the *sacra* forms no part of the theory of civil law, but they are under the separate jurisdiction of the College of Pontiffs. The letters of Cicero to Atticus, which are full of allusions to them, leave no doubt that they constituted an intolerable burden on Inheritances ; but the point of development at which law breaks away from religion has been passed, and we are prepared for their entire disappearance from the later jurisprudence.

In Hindoo law there is no such thing as a true Will. The place filled by Wills is occupied by

Adoptions. We can now see the relation of the Testamentary Power to the Faculty of Adoption, and the reason why the exercise of either of them could call up a peculiar solicitude for the performance of the *sacra*. Both a Will and an Adoption threaten a distortion of the ordinary course of Family descent, but they are obviously contrivances for preventing the descent being wholly interrupted, when there is no succession of kindred to carry it on. Of the two expedients Adoption, the factitious creation of blood-relationship, is the only one which has suggested itself to the greater part of archaic societies. The Hindoos have indeed advanced one point on what was doubtless the antique practice, by allowing the widow to adopt when the father has neglected to do so, and there are in the local customs of Bengal some faint traces of the Testamentary powers. But to the Romans belongs pre-eminently the credit of inventing the Will, the institution which, next to the Contract, has exercised the greatest influence in transforming human society. We must be careful not to attribute to it in its earliest shape the functions which have attended it in more recent times. It was at first, not a mode of distributing a dead man's goods, but one among several ways of transferring the representation of the household to a new chief. The goods descend no doubt to the Heir, but that is only because the government of the family carries with it in its devolution the power of disposing of the common stock. We are very far as yet from that stage in the history of Wills in which they become powerful instruments in modifying society through the

stimulus they give to the circulation of property
and the plasticity they produce in proprietary
rights. No such consequences as these appear in
fact to have been associated with the Testamentary
power even by the latest Roman lawyers. It will
be found that Wills were never looked upon in
the Roman community as a contrivance for parting
Property and the Family, or for creating a variety
of miscellaneous interests, but rather as a means
of making a better provision for the members of
a household than could be secured through the
rules of Intestate succession. We may suspect
indeed that the associations of a Roman with the
practice of will-making were extremely different
from those familiar to us nowadays. The habit
of regarding Adoption and Testation as modes
of continuing the Family cannot but have had
something to do with the singular laxity of Roman
notions as to the inheritance of sovereignty. It
is impossible not to see that the succession of the
early Roman Emperors to each other was considered reasonably regular, and that, in spite of
all that had occurred, no absurdity attached to
the pretension of such Princes as Theodosius or
Justinian to style themselves Cæsar and Augustus.

When the phenomena of primitive societies
emerge into light, it seems impossible to dispute
a proposition which the jurists of the seventeenth
century considered doubtful, that Intestate Inheritance is a more ancient institution than
Testamentary Succession. As soon as this is
settled, a question of much interest suggests
itself, how and under what conditions were the
directions of a will first allowed to regulate the

devolution of authority over the household, and consequently the posthumous distribution of property. The difficulty of deciding the point arises from the rarity of Testamentary power in archaic communities. It is doubtful whether a true power of testation was known to any original society except the Roman. Rudimentary forms of it occur here and there, but most of them are not exempt from the suspicion of a Roman origin. The Athenian Will was, no doubt, indigenous, but then, as will appear presently, it was only an inchoate Testament. As to the Wills which are sanctioned by the bodies of law which have descended to us as the codes of the barbarian conquerors of imperial Rome, they are almost certainly Roman. The most penetrating German criticism has recently been directed to these *leges Barbarorum*, the great object of investigation being to detach those portions of each system which formed the customs of the tribe in its original home from the adventitious ingredients which were borrowed from the laws of the Romans. In the course of this process, one result has invariably disclosed itself, that the ancient nucleus of the code contains no trace of a Will. Whatever testamentary law exists, has been taken from Roman jurisprudence. Similarly, the rudimentary Testament which (as I am informed) the Rabbinical Jewish law provides for, has been attributed to contact with the Romans. The only form of Testament, not belonging to a Roman or Hellenic society, which can with any reason be supposed indigenous, is that recognised by the usages of the province of Bengal; and the

Testament of Bengal, which some have even supposed to be an invention of Anglo-Indian lawyers, is at most only a rudimentary Will.

The evidence, however, such as it is, seems to point to the conclusion that Testaments are at first only allowed to take effect on failure of the persons entitled to have the inheritance by right of blood genuine or fictitious. Thus, when Athenian citizens were empowered for the first time by the Laws of Solon to execute Testaments, they were forbidden to disinherit their direct male descendants. So, too, the Will of Bengal is only permitted to govern the succession so far as it is consistent with certain overriding claims of the family. Again, the original institutions of the Jews having provided nowhere for the privileges of Testatorship, the latter Rabbinical jurisprudence, which pretends to supply the *casus omissi* of the Mosaic law, allows the power of Testation to attach when all the kindred entitled under the Mosaic system to succeed have failed or are undiscoverable. The limitations by which the ancient German codes hedge in the testamentary jurisprudence which has been incorporated with them are also significant, and point in the same direction. It is the peculiarity of most of these German laws, in the only shape in which we know them, that, besides the *allod* or domain of each household, they recognise several subordinate kinds or orders of property, each of which probably represents a separate transfusion of Roman principles into the primitive body of Teutonic usage. The primitive German or allodial property is strictly reserved to the kindred. Not

14

only is it incapable of being disposed of by testament, but it is scarcely capable of being alienated by conveyance *inter vivos*. The ancient German law, like the Hindoo jurisprudence, makes the male children co-proprietors with their father, and the endowment of the family cannot be parted with except by the consent of all its members. But the other sorts of property, of more modern origin and lower dignity than the allodial possessions, are much more easily alienated than they, and follow much more lenient rules of devolution. Women and the descendants of women succeed to them, obviously on the principle that they lie outside the sacred precinct of the Agnatic brotherhood. Now, it is on these last descriptions of property, and on these only, that the Testaments borrowed from Rome were at first allowed to operate.

These few indications may serve to lend additional plausibility to that which in itself appears to be the most probable explanation of an ascertained fact in the early history of Roman Wills. We have it stated on abundant authority that Testaments, during the primitive period of the Roman State, were executed in the Comitia Calata, that is, in the Comitia Curiata, or Parliament of the Patrician Burghers of Rome, when assembled for Private Business. This mode of execution has been the source of the assertion, handed down by one generation of civilians to another, that every Will at one era of Roman history was a solemn legislative enactment. But there is no necessity whatever for resorting to an explanation which has the defect of attributing far too much precision to the proceedings of the ancient assembly. The proper key to the story concerning the execution of Wills in the Comitia Calata must no doubt be sought in the oldest Roman law of *intestate* succession. The canons of primitive Roman jurisprudence regulating the inheritance of relations from each other were, so long as they remained unmodified by the Edictal Law of the Prætor, to the following effect :—First, the *sui* or direct descendants who had never been emancipated succeeded. On the failure of the *sui*, the Nearest Agnate came into their place, that is, the nearest person or class of the kindred who was or might have been under the same Patria Potestas with the deceased. The third and last degree came next, in which the inheritance devolved on the *Gentiles*, that is, on the collective members of the dead man's *gens* or *House*. The House, I have explained already, was a fictitious extension of the family, consisting of all Roman Patrician citizens who bore the same name, and who on the ground of bearing the same name, were supposed to be descended from a common ancestor. Now the Patrician Assembly called the Comitia Curiata was a Legislature in which Gentes or Houses were exclusively represented. It was a representative assembly of the Roman people, constituted on the assumption that the constituent unit of the state was the Gens. This being so, the inference seems inevitable, that the cognisance of Wills by the Comitia was connected with the rights of the Gentiles, and was intended to secure them in their privilege of ultimate inheritance. The whole apparent anomaly is removed, if we suppose that a Testament could only be made when the Testator had no *gentiles* discoverable, or when they waived their claims, and that every Testament was submitted to the General Assembly of the Roman Gentes, in order that those aggrieved by its dispositions might put their veto upon it if they pleased, or by allowing it to pass might be presumed to have renounced their reversion. It is possible that on the eve of the publication of the Twelve Tables this vetoing power may have been greatly curtailed or only occasionally and capriciously exercised. It is much easier, however, to indicate the meaning and origin of the jurisdiction confided to the Comitia Calata, than to trace its gradual development or progressive decay.

The Testament to which the pedigree of all modern Wills may be traced is not, however, the Testament executed in the Calata Comitia, but another Testament designed to compete with it and destined to supersede it. The historical importance of this early Roman Will, and the light it casts on much of ancient thought, will excuse me for describing it at some length.

When the Testamentary power first discloses itself to us in legal history, there are signs that, like almost all the great Roman institutions, it was the subject of contention between the Patricians and the Plebeians. The effect of the political maxim, *Plebs Gentem non habet*, "a Plebeian cannot be a member of a house," was entirely to exclude the Plebeians from the Comitia Curiata. Some critics have accordingly supposed that a Plebeian could not have his Will read or recited to the Patrician Assembly, and was thus deprived of Testamentary privileges altogether. Others have been satisfied to point out the hardships of having to submit a proposed Will to the unfriendly jurisdiction of an assembly in which the Testator was not represented. Whatever be the true view, a form of Testament came into use, which has all the characteristics of a contrivance intended to evade some distasteful obligation. The Will in question was a conveyance *inter vivos*, a complete and irrevocable alienation of the Testator's family and substance to the person whom he meant to be his heir. The strict rules of Roman law must always have permitted such an alienation, but when the transaction was intended to have a posthumous effect, there may have been disputes whether it was valid for Testamentary purposes without the formal assent of the Patrician Parliament. If a difference of opinion existed on the point between the two classes of the Roman population, it was extinguished, with many other sources of heartburning, by the great Decemviral compromise. The text of the Twelve Tables is still extant which says, "*Pater familias uti de pecuniâ tutelâve rei suæ legâssit, ita jus esto*"—a law which can hardly have had any other object than the legitimation of the Plebeian Will.

It is well known to scholars that, centuries after the Patrician Assembly had ceased to be the legislature of the Roman State, it still continued to hold formal sittings for the convenience of private business. Consequently, at a period long subsequent to the publication of the Decemviral

Law, there is reason to believe that the Comitia Calata still assembled for the validation of Testaments. Its probable functions may be best indicated by saying that it was a Court of Registration, with the understanding, however, that the Wills exhibited were not *enrolled*, but simply recited to the members, who were supposed to take note of their tenor and to commit them to memory. It is very likely that this form of Testament was never reduced to writing at all, but at all events if the Will had been originally written, the office of the Comitia was certainly confined to hearing it read aloud, the document being retained afterwards in the custody of the Testator, or deposited under the safeguard of some religious corporation. This publicity may have been one of the incidents of the Testament executed in the Comitia Calata which brought it into popular disfavour. In the early years of the Empire the Comitia still held its meetings, but they seem to have lapsed into the merest form, and few Wills, or none, were probably presented at the periodical sitting.

It is the ancient Plebeian Will—the alternative of the Testament just described—which in its remote effects has deeply modified the civilisation of the modern world. It acquired at Rome all the popularity which the Testament submitted to the Calata Comitia appears to have lost. The key to all its characteristics lies in its descent from the *mancipium*, or ancient Roman conveyance, a proceeding to which we may unhesitatingly assign the parentage of two great institutions without which modern society can scarcely be supposed capable of holding together, the Contract and the Will. The Mancipium, or, as the word would exhibit itself in later Latinity, the Mancipation, carries us back by its incidents to the infancy of civil society. As it sprang from times long anterior, if not to the invention, at all events to the popularisation, of the art of writing, gestures, symbolical acts, and solemn phrases take the place of documentary forms, and a lengthy and intricate ceremonial is intended to call the attention of the parties to the importance of the transaction, and to impress it on the memory of the witnesses. The imperfection, too, of oral, as compared with written testimony necessitates the multiplication of the witnesses and assistants beyond what in later times would be reasonable or intelligible limits.

The Roman Mancipation required the presence first of all of the parties, the vendor and vendee, or we should perhaps rather say, if we are to use modern legal language, the grantor and grantee. There were also no less than *five* witnesses ; and an anomalous personage, the Libripens, who brought with him a pair of scales to weigh the uncoined copper money of ancient Rome. The Testament we are considering—the Testament *per æs et libram*, " with the copper and the scales," as it long continued to be technically called—was an ordinary Mancipation with no change in the form and hardly any in words. The Testator was the grantor ; the five witnesses and the libripens were present ; and the place of grantee was taken by a person known technically as the *familiæ emptor*, the Purchaser of the Family.

The ordinary ceremony of a Mancipation was then proceeded with. Certain formal gestures were made and sentences pronounced. The *Emptor familiæ* simulated the payment of a price by striking the scales with a piece of money, and finally the Testator ratified what had been done in a set form of words called the " Nuncupatio " or publication of the transaction, a phrase which, I need scarcely remind the lawyer, has had a long history in Testamentary jurisprudence. It is necessary to attend particularly to the character of the person called *familiæ emptor*. There is no doubt that at first he was the Heir himself. The Testator conveyed to him outright his whole " familia," that is, all the rights he enjoyed over and through the family ; his property, his slaves, and all his ancestral privileges, together, on the other hand, with all his duties and obligations.

With these data before us, we are able to note several remarkable points in which the Mancipatory Testament, as it may be called, differed in its primitive form from a modern Will. As it amounted to a conveyance *out-and-out* of the Testator's estate, it was not *revocable*. There could be no new exercise of a power which had been exhausted.

Again, it was not secret. The Familiæ Emptor, being himself the Heir, knew exactly what his rights were, and was aware that he was irreversibly entitled to the inheritance ; a knowledge which the violences inseparable from the best-ordered ancient society rendered extremely dangerous. But perhaps the most surprising consequences of this relation of Testaments to Conveyances

was the immediate vesting of the Inheritance
in the Heir. This has seemed so incredible to
not a few civilians, that they have spoken of the
Testator's estate as vesting conditionally on the
Testator's death, or as granted to him from a
time uncertain, *i.e.*, the death of the grantor.
But down to the latest period of Roman jurisprudence there was a certain class of transactions
which never admitted of being directly modified
by a condition, or of being limited to or from a
point of time. In technical language they did
not admit *conditio* or *dies*. Mancipation was one
of them, and therefore, strange as it may seem,
we are forced to conclude that the primitive
Roman Will took effect at once, even though
the Testator survived his act of Testation. It
is indeed likely that Roman citizens originally
made their Wills only in the article of death,
and that a provision for the continuance of the
Family effected by a man in the flower of life
would take the form rather of an Adoption than
of a Will. Still we must believe that, if the
Testator did recover, he could only continue to
govern his household by the sufferance of his
Heir.

Two or three remarks should be made before
I explain how these inconveniences were remedied,
and how Testaments came to be invested with
the characteristics now universally associated
with them. The Testament was not necessarily
written : at first, it seems to have been invariably
oral, and, even in later times, the instrument
declaratory of the bequests was only incidentally
connected with the Will and formed no essential

part of it. It bore in fact exactly the same relation to the Testament which the deed leading the uses bore to the Fines and Recoveries of old English law, or which the charter of feoffment bore to the feoffment itself. Previously, indeed, to the Twelve Tables, no writing would have been of the slightest use, for the Testator had no power of giving legacies, and the only persons who could be advantaged by a will were the Heir or Co-heirs. But the extreme generality of the clause in the Twelve Tables soon produced the doctrine that the heir must take the inheritance burdened by any directions which the Testator might give him, or, in other words, take it subject to legacies. Written testamentary instruments assumed thereupon a new value, as a security against the fraudulent refusal of the heir to satisfy the legatees ; but to the last it was at the Testator's pleasure to rely exclusively on the testimony of the witnesses, and to declare by word of mouth the legacies which the *familiæ emptor* was commissioned to pay.

The terms of the expression *Emptor familiæ* demand notice. "Emptor" indicates that the Will was literally a sale, and the word "familiæ," when compared with the phraseology in the Testamentary clause in the Twelve Tables, leads us to some instructive conclusions. "Familia," in classical Latinity, means always a man's slaves. Here, however, and generally in the language of ancient Roman law, it includes all persons under his Potestas, and the Testator's material property or substance is understood to pass as an adjunct or appendage of his household. Turning to the law of the Twelve Tables, it will be seen that it speaks of *tutela rei suæ*, " the guardianship of his substance," a form of expression which is the exact reverse of the phrase just examined.   There does not therefore appear to be any mode of escaping from the conclusion, that even at an era so comparatively recent as that of the Decemviral compromise, terms denoting " household " and " property " were blended in the current phrase-ology. If a man's household had been spoken of as his property we might have explained the expression as pointing to the extent of the Patria Potestas, but, as the interchange is reciprocal, we must allow that the form of speech carries us back to the primeval period in which property is owned by the family, and the family is governed by the citizen, so that the members of the community do not own their property *and* their family, but rather own their property *through* their family.

At an epoch not easy to settle with precision, the Roman Prætors fell into the habit of acting upon Testaments solemnised in closer conformity with the spirit than the letter of the law. Casual dispensations became insensibly the established practice, till at length a wholly new form of Will was matured and regularly engrafted on the Edictal Jurisprudence. The new or *Prætorian* Testament derived the whole of its impregnability from the *Jus Honorarium* or Equity of Rome. The Prætor of some particular year must have inserted a clause in his Inaugural Proclamation declaratory of his intention to sustain all Testaments which should have been executed with such and such solemnities ; and, the reform having been found advantageous, the article relating to it must have been again introduced by the Prætor's successor, and repeated by the next in office, till at length it formed a recognised portion of that body of jurisprudence which from these successive incorporations was styled the Perpetual or Continuous Edict. On examining the conditions of a valid Prætorian Will they will be plainly seen to have been determined by the requirements of the Mancipatory Testament, the innovating Prætor having obviously prescribed to himself the retention of the old formalities just so far as they were warrants of genuineness or securities against fraud. At the execution of the Mancipatory Testament seven persons had been present besides the Testator. Seven witnesses were accordingly essential to the Prætorian Will; two of them corresponding to the *libripens* and *familiæ emptor*, who were now stripped of their symbolical character, and were merely present for the purpose of supplying their testimony. No emblematic ceremony was gone through; the Will was merely recited; but then it is probable (though not absolutely certain) that a written instrument was necessary to perpetuate the evidence of the Testator's dispositions. At all events, whenever a writing was read or exhibited as a person's last Will, we know certainly that the Prætorian Court would not sustain it by special intervention, unless each of the seven witnesses had severally affixed his seal to the outside. This is the first appearance of *sealing* in the history of jurisprudence, considered as a mode of authentication. The use of seals, however, as mere fastenings, is doubtless of much higher antiquity ; and it appears to have been known to the Hebrews. We may observe, that the seals of the Roman Wills, and other documents of importance, did not only serve as the index of the present or assent of the signatary, but were also literally fastenings which had to be broken before the writing could be inspected.

The Edictal Law would therefore enforce the dispositions of a Testator, when, instead of being symbolised through the forms of mancipation, they were simply evidenced by the seals of seven witnesses. But it may be laid down as a general proposition, that the principal qualities of Roman property were incommunicable except through processes which were supposed to be coeval with the origin of the Civil Law. The Prætor therefore could not confer an *Inheritance* on anybody. He could not place the Heir or Co-heirs in that very relation in which the Testator had himself stood to his own rights and obligations. All he could do was to confer on the person designated as Heir the practical enjoyment of the property bequeathed, and to give the force of legal acquittances to his payments of the Testator's debts. When he exerted his powers to these ends, the Prætor was technically said to communicate the *Bonorum Possessio*. The Heir specially inducted under these circumstances, or *Bonorum Possessor*, had every proprietary privilege of the Heir by the Civil Law. He took the profits and he could alienate, but then, for all his remedies for redress against wrong, he must go, as we should phrase it, not to the Common Law, but to the Equity side of the Prætorian Court. No great chance of error would be incurred by describing him as having an *equitable* estate in the inheritance ; but then, to secure ourselves against being deluded by the analogy, we must always recollect that in one year the *Bonorum Possessio* was operated upon by a principle of Roman Law known as Usucapion, and the Possessor became Quiritarian owner of all the property comprised in the inheritance.

We know too little of the older law of Civil Process to be able to strike the balance of advantage and disadvantage between the different classes of remedies supplied by the Prætorian Tribunal. It is certain, however, that, in spite of its many defects, the Mancipatory Testament by which the *universitas juris* devolved at once and unimpaired was never entirely superseded by the new Will ; and at a period less bigoted to antiquarian forms, and perhaps not quite alive to their significance, all the ingenuity of the Jurisconsults seems to have been expended on the improvement of the more venerable instrument. At the era of Gaius, which is that of the Antonine Cæsars, the great blemishes of the Mancipatory Will had been removed. Originally, as we have seen, the essential character of the formalities had required that the Heir himself should be the Purchaser of the Family, and the consequence was that he not only instantly acquired a vested interest in the Testator's Property but was formally made aware of his rights. But the age of Gaius permitted some unconcerned person to officiate as Purchaser of the Family. The Heir, therefore, was not necessarily informed of the succession to which he was destined ; and Wills thenceforward acquired the property of *secrecy*. The substitution of a stranger for the actual Heir in the functions of " Familiæ Emptor " had other ulterior consequences. As soon as it was legalised, a Roman Testament came to consist of two parts or stages,—a Conveyance, which was a pure form, and a Nuncupatio, or Publication. In this latter passage of the proceeding, the Testator either orally declared to the assistants the wishes which were to be executed after his death, or produced a written document in which his wishes were embodied. It was not probably till attention had been quite drawn off from the imaginary Conveyance, and concentrated on the Nuncupatio as the essential part of the transaction, that Wills were allowed to become *revocable*.

I have thus carried the pedigree of Wills some way down in legal history. The root of it is the old Testament " with the copper and the scales," founded on a Mancipation or Conveyance. This ancient Will has, however, manifold defects, which are remedied, though only indirectly, by the Prætorian law. Meantime the ingenuity of the Jurisconsults effects, in the Common-Law Will or Mancipatory Testament, the very improvements which the Prætor may have concurrently carried out in Equity. These last ameliorations depend, however, on mere legal dexterity, and we see accordingly that the Testamentary Law of the day of Gaius or Ulpian is only transitional. What changes next ensued we know not ; but at length just before the reconstruction of the jurisprudence by Justinian, we find the subjects of the Eastern

Roman Empire employing a form of Will of which the pedigree is traceable to the Prætorian Testament on one side, and to the Testament " with the copper and the scales," on the other. Like the Testament of the Prætor, it required no Mancipation, and was invalid unless sealed by seven witnesses. Like the Mancipatory Will, it passed the Inheritance and not merely a *Bonorum Possessio*. Several, however, of its most important features were annexed by positive enactments, and it is out of regard to this threefold derivation from the Prætorian Edict, from the Civil Law, and from the Imperial Constitutions, that Justinian speaks of the Law of Wills in his own day as *Jus Tripertitum*. The new Testament thus described is the one generally known as the Roman Will. But it was the Will of the Eastern Empire only ; and the researches of Savigny have shown that in Western Europe the old Mancipatory Testament, with all its apparatus of conveyance, copper, and scales, continued to be the form in use far down in the Middle Ages.

NOTE M

TESTAMENTARY SUCCESSION

THE burden of this chapter is that the Will or Testament of modern law, with its specific characters of being secret, revocable, and posthumous in operation, is unknown to archaic law, and is of comparatively recent introduction wherever we find it. Maine's position is amply confirmed by later historical research, and one or two seeming exceptions which he felt bound to notice have been removed.

Jurists of the seventeenth century, we read in Maine's text, resorted to the law of nature to explain and justify testamentary power. This is almost enough of itself to show that no such power was commonly found in customary law. For the doctrine of natural law was, as we have already seen, a progressive and rationalist doctrine. Its use was to override the commonplace objections founded on lack of authority or even on the existence of contrary custom; and at the time of the Renaissance and even earlier it served speculative publicists in much the same way as the principle of utility (with which it has considerable affinities) has served modern reformers. In fact, the whole conception of individual succession to property, even without a will, is relatively modern. The archaic Indo-European family was, Maine tells us, a corporation, of which the patriarch for the time being was the representative or public officer—or at most, we may add, managing director. Evidently we are not meant to take this statement as if a definite legal doctrine of persons, much less artificial persons, was to be ascribed to the patriarchal stage of society. For in that stage, as Maine also says, a man was not yet regarded as an individual, but only as a member of his family and class; and this is still true to a great extent in Hindu law. Now the modern doctrine of corporations assumes that the "natural person" or individual, considered as a subject of rights and duties, or "lawful man," as our English books say, is the normal unit of legal institutions, and that the collective personality of a group of men acting in a common interest or duty and behaving like an individual is something which needs to be explained. But for archaic society the collective body and not the individual is the natural person.

We find the same conditions existing in full force among the German tribes in a much later period of time than that which Maine is directly considering in this chapter. A recent learned writer in France, dealing with precisely the same subject as it occurs in the medieval history of French law, has forcibly contrasted the Roman conception, as it was established in the classical law of the empire, with the German.

"Le droit romain consacre le triomphe de l'individualisme ; la volonté personnelle du chef de famille, voilà le facteur juridique essentiel, l'agent de toutes les transactions, la force créatrice de tous les droits. Cette volonté est si respectée et si puissante, qu'elle continue d'agir après la disparition de celui qui l'a exprimée. Le père règle le sort de sa fortune et de sa famille pour le temps où il ne sera plus, et cela par un acte souverainement libre, qu'il est toujours à même de modifier. . . . L'individu *sui juris* est, dans le monde romain, l'unité juridique et social.

"Chez les Germains, c'est bien plutôt la famille. Il serait sans doute excessif, surtout pour le temps des Leges [the custumals collectively known as 'Leges Barbarorum '], de déclarer en termes absolus que la famille est tout et que l'individu n'est rien; la vérité sous cette forme serait exagérée et dénaturée. Mais il est certain cependant que l'exaltation de l'individu est beaucoup moins

15

complète qu'à Rome, et que d'autre part la famille forme une association, une sorte d'être collectif armé de droits inconnus des jurisconsultes de l'Empire. L'énergie individuelle est limitée dans le temps, et les Germains ne peuvent pas concevoir qu'elle s'exerce au. delà de la tombe; sitôt l'homme mort, toutes ses volontés s'évanouissent. Au même moment ses prérogatives juridiques sont recouvertes et absorbées par celles de ses parents, car de son vivant même sa famille jouissait de droits autonomes qu'il ne dépendait pas de lui de supprimer: sa mort les développe, mais elle ne les crée pas" (Auffroy, "Evolution du testament en France," Paris, 1899, pp.173-4. Cf. Brunner, "Grundzüge der deutschen Rechtsgeschichte," § 56; "Das germanische Erbrecht war ein Familienrecht." For examples of analogous customs among various uncivilized tribes, see Lord Avebury, "Origin of Civilisation," 6th ed. pp. 489-91.

The suggestion in Maine's text of regarding the Roman ancestor in his representative character as a kind of corporation sole may be helpful to English students, but we can hardly trust it to throw light on the actual formation of Roman legal ideas. For our English category of corporations sole is not only, as Maine calls it, a fiction, but modern, anomalous, and of no practical use. When a parson or other solely corporate office-holder dies, there is no one to act for the corporation until a successor is appointed, and, when appointed, that successor can do nothing which he could not do without being called a corporation sole. In the case of the parson even the continuity of the freehold is not saved, and it is said to be in abeyance in the interval. As for the king, or "the Crown," being a corporation sole, the language of our books appears to be nothing but a clumsy and, after all, ineffective device to avoid openly personifying the State. The problems of federal politics in Canada and Australia threaten to make the fiction complex. Is "the Crown" a trustee for Dominion and Province, for Commonwealth and State, with possibly conflicting interests? or is there one indivisible Crown being or having several persons for different purposes? (F. W. Maitland, L.Q.R. xvi. 335, xvii. 131; W. Harrison Moore, L.Q.R. xx. 351; Markby, "Elements of Law," §145). The whole thing seems to have arisen from the technical difficulty of making grants to a parson and his successors after the practice of making them to God and the patron saint had been discontinued, as tending to bring the saints into the unseemly position of litigants before secular courts. All this we may now think makes for historical curiosity rather than philosophical edification.

But in any case the chief part of Maine's argument, his insistence on "the theory of a man's posthumous existence in the person of his heir," and the intimate connection of that theory with the ancestor's representative character as head of the family, goes to the root of the matter. Mr. Justice Holmes, now of the Supreme

Court of the United States, writing twenty years after Maine, summed this up with concise elegance ("The Common Law," p. 343):

"If the family was the owner of the property administered by a *paterfamilias*, its rights remained unaffected by the death of its temporary head. The family continued, although the head died. And when, probably by a gradual change, the *paterfamilias* came to be regarded as owner, instead of a simple manager of the family rights, the nature and continuity of those rights did not change with the title to them. The *familia* continued to the heirs as it was left by the ancestor. . . .

"The aggregate of the ancestor's rights and duties, or, to use the technical phrase, the total *persona* sustained by him, was early separated from his natural personality. For this *persona* was but the aggregate of what had formerly been family rights and duties, and was originally sustained by any individual only as the family head. Hence it was said to be continued by the inheritance ; and when the heir assumed it, he had his action in respect of injuries previously committed."

Maine proceeds to trace the development of the Roman testament from a distribution of property, taking effect at once, made in contemplation of impending death or great peril, and requiring, in its earliest form, something like legislative sanction (cp. Girard, "Manuel," pp. 792-5), through the intermediate stage of a conveyance reserving a life interest, which may be seen in the provincial customs of the Roman Empire, and much later in medieval and even modern systems. Muirhead ("Historical Introduction to the Pirvate Law of Rome," pp. 66, 168) pointed out a remedy for the difficulty suggested at p. 217, that a will by mancipation must have left the testator penniless. Usufruct might very well be reserved on a mancipation, Gai. ii. 33, "and a reservation of a life interest in one's own *familia* would possibly be construed even more liberally than an ordinary usufruct." Still, usufruct is not among the earliest institutions, and it would be rash to say that the difficulty may not have been real at one time. But men have been driven all over the world, by an imperfect state of property law or by special reasons for avoiding publicity, to put very large trust in the honour of chosen friends and assistants; and there is nothing about the Roman *familiae emtor* in his most archaic stage to surprise an English student who has made acquaintance with our medieval feoffee to uses. Indian practice will furnish a parallel in the *benámi* (literally, "anonymous") conveyances to a nominal purchaser, to hold on a secret trust for the real one, which appear to have survived the original reasons for them. Sohm, however, holds ("Institutes," § 112, pp. 543, 544, in Ledlie's translation, 3rd ed.) that the testament *per aes et libram* was coupled with a mandate to the *familiae emtor*, which was binding under the well-known provision of the Twelve Tables, "uti lingua nuncupassit ita ius esto." This would of course simplify the matter. The same learned author's suggestion that the institution of an heir was a modified form of adoption—that is, an adoption deferred to the testator's death—does not seem to be generally accepted (Girard, "Manuel," p. 793).

What is said in this chapter about Hindu law would no doubt have been fuller if a convenient and trustworthy text-book like Mr. Mayne's had existed at the time when it was written. I am not aware, however, that any modification is needed except on one point, namely that the strict determination of the order of succession among an ancestor's next of kin according to the spiritual efficacy of their sacrifices is found only in the school of Bengal. This has been thought to be a deliberate Brahmanical innovation; but lately two learned Indian scholars, Mr. Justice Mitra of the High Court of Calcutta and Mr. S. S. Setlur, have rejected that view; the former of them asserts, but the latter denies, that the peculiar doctrines in question are of Buddhistic origin (see L.Q.R. xxi. 380, xxii. 50, xxiii. 202). As Maine himself said in 1883, "we now can discern something of the real relation which the sacerdotal Hindu law bears to the true ancient law of the race" ("Early Law and Custom," p. 194; see also the chapter on Ancestor Worship and Inheritance). The general importance of keeping up the family ritual both in Hindu and in other archaic law remains undoubted. Some addition has to be made as regards the Hindu will. Quite unknown to early Hindu law, will-making came into use in modern times, though not in imitation of European practice according to the best authorities, and was not recognised in any of the Presidency Courts before 1832, when it was allowed in Bengal. When "Ancient Law" was published the law was not yet quite settled in Madras and Bombay; but the courts of those Presidencies followed the same course within a few years. Apparently the first form of the Bengal will was a gift *mortis causa* to religious uses. The reader will perceive the resemblance to the development of the testament of chattels, under ecclesiastical influence, in medieval English law. The English history, however, is for the most part too complex and peculiar to throw much light on the normal type of evolution. As for the Anglo-Saxon will, even if it can be assimilated to modern wills, which is doubtful, it was a special and anomalous kind of document, and disappeared after the Norman Conquest. Probably language is still to be found in popular books asserting or implying that before the Conquest there was general freedom of alienation; but this is due to pure misunderstanding, the privileged class of transactions which are recorded in the Anglo-Saxon charters having been taken as typical and indigenous. Early English "post obit gifts" (Pollock and Maitland, "H.E.L." ii. 317. sqq., and see Note Q below) do present some analogy to the Roman will by mancipation; and this appears in a strengthened form in the conveyance to feoffees to uses to be declared by the feoffee's will which was common in the later Middle Ages. In the thirteenth century divers learned clerks made an ingenious and, it seems, almost a successful attempt to create posthumous disposing power by grants *inter vivos*, containing in what we now call the "habendum" such words as "cuicunque dare vel etiam legare voluerit." A clause so framed is quite common in deeds of the third and even fourth quarters of that century, and inconsistent utterances in Bracton show that learned opinion fluctuated (18*b*, 412*b*, *pro*, 49*a*, fuller and seemingly more deliberate, *contra*, cp. Pollock and Maitland, ii. 27). We may believe [1] that for some time and to some extent the power such clauses purported to confer was exercised without objection. But this was a transitory experiment, and has nothing to do with any real testamentary distribution or succession. Local customs to devise land or, at any rate, purchased land existed, but their origin and early history are still obscure.

In Scotland we find the most remarkable illustration of the præ-testamentary stage, as we may call it, of property law Properly there is no such term as Will in Scots law, and there was no true will of lands before 1868. "Heritage could only be transmitted by a deed containing words of *de praesenti* disposition, and the use of the word 'dispone' was essential" (Green's "Encycl. of the Law of Scotland," s.v. *Will.*). The accustomed form was (and apparently still is, notwithstanding that it is no longer necessary) a "trust disposition and settlement," a present conveyance reserving a life interest to the grantor. Scotland, in fact, is the last home of the old Germanic *Vergabung von Todes wegen* (Goffin, "The Testamentary Executor," 1901, pp. 19, 99). It may survive many generations yet, for aught we know, as in the customs of Egypt and other parts of the Roman Empire essentially similar forms continued in use long after true wills had become familiar in the law of Rome. Original examples of the second century A.D. found at Naucratis might be seen in London some years ago. Notwithstanding the marks of Roman influence which the modern English will bears, its practical scope and effect remain as different as possible from those of the Roman testament. As a rule the wills of Englishmen having any considerable property to dispose of aim not at investing any one person with the whole of the testator's control over his estate, subject to payment of debts and legacies, but rather at postponing absolute control and preserving the estate under the sanction of a trust which will

---

[1] Extant wills of the period which purport to devise parcels of land (Madox, Form. Anglic. DCCLXVIII., DCCLXIX., DCCLXXI.) are not conclusive as to the practice in the absence of a known previous grant with which they can be connected, as other explanations are possible.

not be finally determined while any child of the testator is a minor or his widow living. The capital is to be intact as long as possible, while the income is enjoyed or applied according to the testator's directions. If any one is at all like a Roman heir, it is the executor, who does not necessarily take any beneficial interest, and whose origin is quite different (Goffin, *op. cit.* p. 33; O. W. Holmes, L.Q.R. i. 165-6; Gierke, "Grundzüge des deutschen Privatrechts," § 126, in "Encykl. d. Rechtswiss." i. 555). The Roman horror of intestacy mentioned in the early part of the following chapter was equalled or surpassed among medieval Englishmen (Pollock and Maitland, ii. 356); but the reason was not one that would have occurred to any Roman from the time of Labeo to that of Justinian, being the danger to the intestate's soul if he died without having assigned a fitting part of his estate to pious uses (Du Cange *s.v. intestatio*).

CHAPTER VII

ANCIENT AND MODERN IDEAS RESPECTING WILLS AND SUCCESSIONS

ALTHOUGH there is much in the modern European Law of Wills which is intimately connected with the oldest rules of Testamentary disposition practised among men, there are nevertheless some important differences between ancient and modern ideas on the subject of Wills and Successions. Some of the points of difference I shall endeavour to illustrate in this chapter.

At a period, removed several centuries from the era of the Twelve Tables, we find a variety of rules engrafted on the Roman Civil Law with the view of limiting the disinherison of children; we have the jurisdiction of the Prætor very actively exerted in the same interest; and we are also presented with a new remedy, very anomalous in character and of uncertain origin, called the Querela Inofficiosi Testamenti, "the Plaint of an Unduteous Will," directed to the reinstatement of the issue in inheritances from which they had been unjustifiably excluded by a father's Testament. Comparing this condition of the law with the text of the Twelve Tables which concedes in terms the utmost liberty of Testation, several writers have been tempted to interweave a good deal of dramatic incident into their history of the Law Testamentary. They tell us of the boundless license of disinherison in which the heads of families instantly began to indulge, of the scandal and injury to public morals which the new practices engendered, and of the applause of all good men which hailed the courage of the Prætor in arresting the progress of paternal depravity. This story, which is not without some foundation for the principal fact it relates, is often so told as to disclose very serious misconceptions of the principles of legal history. The Law of the Twelve Tables is to be explained by the character of the age in which it was enacted. It does not license a tendency which a later era thought itself bound to counteract, but it proceeds on the assumption that no such tendency exists, or perhaps we should say, in ignorance of the possibility of its existence. There is no likelihood that Roman citizens began immediately to avail themselves freely of the power to disinherit. It is against all reason and sound appreciation of history to suppose that the yoke of family bondage, still patiently submitted to, as we know, where its pressure galled most cruelly, would be cast off in the very particular in which its incidence in our own day is not otherwise than welcome. The Law of the Twelve Tables permitted the execution of Testaments in the only case in which it was thought possible that they could be executed, viz., on failure of children and proximate kindred. It did not forbid the disinherison of direct descendants, inasmuch as it did not legislate against a contingency which no Roman lawgiver of that era could have contemplated. No doubt, as the offices of family affection progressively lost the aspect of primary personal duties, the disinherison of children was occasionally attempted. But the interference of the Prætor, so far from being called for by the universality of the abuse, was doubtless first prompted by the fact that such instances of unnatural caprice were few and exceptional, and at conflict with the current morality.

The indications furnished by this part of Roman Testamentary Law are of a very different kind. It is remarkable that a Will never seems to have been regarded by the Romans as a means of *disinheriting* a Family, or of affecting the unequal distribution of a patrimony. The rules of law preventing its being turned to such a purpose, increase in number and stringency as the jurisprudence unfolds itself ; and these rules correspond doubtless with the abiding sentiment of Roman society, as distinguished from occasional variations of feeling in individuals. It would rather seem as if the Testamentary Power were chiefly valued for the assistance it gave in *making provision* for a Family, and in dividing the inheritance more evenly and fairly than the Law of Intestate Succession would have divided it. If this be the true reading of the general sentiment on the point, it explains to some extent the singular horror of Intestacy which always characterised the Roman. No evil seems to have been considered a heavier visitation than the forfeiture of Testamentary privileges ; no curse appears to have been bitterer than that which imprecated on an enemy that he might die without a Will.

The feeling has no counterpart, or none that is easily recognisable, in the forms of opinion which exist at the present day. All men at all times will doubtless prefer chalking out the destination of their substance to having their office performed for them by the law; but the Roman passion for Testacy is distinguished from the mere desire to indulge caprice by its intensity; and it has, of course, nothing whatever in common with that pride of family, exclusively the creation of feudalism, which accumulates one description of property in the hands of a single representative. It is probable, à priori, that it was something in the rules of Intestate Succession which caused this vehement preference for the distribution of property under a Testament over its distribution by law. The difficulty, however, is, that on glancing at the Roman Law of Intestate Succession in the form which it wore for many centuries before Justinian shaped it into that scheme of inheritance which has been almost universally adopted by modern lawgivers, it by no means strikes one as remarkably unreasonable or inequitable. On the contrary, the distribution it prescribes is so fair and rational, and differs so little from that with which modern society has been generally contented, that no reason suggests itself why it should have been regarded with extraordinary distaste, especially under a jurisprudence which pared down to a narrow compass the testamentary privileges of persons who had children to provide for. We should rather have expected that, as in France at this moment, the heads of families would generally save themselves the trouble of executing a Will, and allow the Law to do as it pleased with their assets. I think, however, if we look a little closely at the pre-Justinianean scale of Intestate Succession, we shall discover the key to the mystery. The texture of the law consists of two distinct parts. One department of rules comes from the Jus Civile, the Common-Law of Rome; the other from the Edict of the Prætor. The Civil Law, as I have already stated for another purpose, calls to the inheritance only three orders of successors in their turn; the Unemancipated children, the nearest class of Agnatic kindred, and the Gentiles. Between these three orders, the Prætor interpolates various classes of relatives, of whom the Civil Law took no notice whatever. Ultimately, the combination of the Edict and of the Civil Law forms a table of succession not materially different from that which has descended to the generality of modern codes.

The point for recollection is, that there must anciently have been a time at which the rules of the Civil Law determined the scheme of Intestate Succession exclusively, and at which the arrangements of the Edict were non-existent, or not consistently carried out. We cannot doubt that, in its infancy, the Prætorian jurisprudence had to contend with formidable obstructions, and it is more than probable that, long after popular sentiment and legal opinion had acquiesced in it, the modifications which it periodically introduced were governed by no certain principles, and fluctuated with the varying

bias of successive magistrates. The rules of
Intestate Succession, which the Romans must
at this period have practised, account, I think—
and more than account—for that vehement distaste
for an Intestacy to which Roman society during
so many ages remained constant. The order of
succession was this: on the death of a citizen,
having no will or no valid will, his Unemancipated
children became his Heirs. His *emancipated* sons
had no share in the inheritance. If he left no
direct descendants living at his death, the nearest
grade of the Agnatic kindred succeeded, but no
part of the inheritance was given to any relative
united (however closely) with the dead man
through female descents. All the other branches
of the family were excluded, and the inheritance
escheated to the *Gentiles*, or entire body of Roman
citizens bearing the same name with the deceased.
So that on failing to execute an operative Testament, a Roman of the era under examination
left his emancipated children absolutely without
provision, while, on the assumption that he died
childless, there was imminent risk that his possessions would escape from the family altogether,
and devolve on a number of persons with whom
he was merely connected by the sacerdotal fiction
that assumed all members of the same *gens* to be
descended from a common ancestor. The prospect
of such an issue is in itself a nearly sufficient
explanation of the popular sentiment; but, in
point of fact, we shall only half understand it,
if we forget that the state of things I have been
describing is likely to have existed at the very
moment when Roman society was in the first

stage of its transition from its primitive organisation in detached families. The empire of the father had indeed received one of the earliest blows directed at it through the recognition of Emancipation as a legitimate usage, but the law, still considering the Patria Potestas to be the root of family connection, persevered in looking on the emancipated children as strangers to the rights of kinship and aliens from the blood. We cannot, however, for a moment suppose that the limitations of the family imposed by legal pedantry had their counterpart in the natural affection of parents. Family attachments must still have retained that nearly inconceivable sanctity and intensity which belonged to them under the Patriarchal system ; and so little are they likely to have been extinguished by the act of emancipation, that the probabilities are altogether the other way. It may be unhesitatingly taken for granted that enfranchisement from the father's power was a demonstration, rather than a severance, of affection—a mark of grace and favour accorded to the best-beloved and most esteemed of the children. If sons thus honoured above the rest were absolutely deprived of their heritage by an Intestacy, the reluctance to incur it requires no farther explanation. We might have assumed *à priori* that the passion for Testacy was generated by some moral injustice entailed by the rules of Intestate succession ; and here we find them at variance with the very instinct by which early society was cemented together. It is possible to put all that has been urged in a very succinct form. Every dominant sentiment of the primitive

Romans was entwined with the relations of the family. But what was the Family? The Law defined it one way—natural affection another. In the conflict between the two, the feeling we would analyse grew up, taking the form of an enthusiasm for the institution by which the dictates of affection were permitted to determine the fortunes of its object.

I regard, therefore, the Roman horror of Intestacy as a monument of a very early conflict between ancient law and slowly changing ancient sentiment on the subject of the Family. Some passages in the Roman Statute-Law, and one statute in particular which limited the capacity for inheritance possessed by women, must have contributed to keep alive the feeling; and it is the general belief that the system of creating Fidei-Commissa, or bequests in trust, was devised to evade the disabilities imposed by those statutes. But the feeling itself, in its remarkable intensity, seems to point back to some deeper antagonism between law and opinion; nor is it at all wonderful that the improvements of jurisprudence by the Prætor should not have extinguished it. Everybody conversant with the philosophy of opinion is aware that a sentiment by no means dies out, of necessity, with the passing away of the circumstances which produced it. It may long survive them; nay, it may afterwards attain to a pitch and climax of intensity which it never attained during their actual continuance.

The view of a Will which regards it as conferring the power of diverting property from the Family, or of distributing it in such uneven

proportions as the fancy or good sense of the
Testator may dictate, is not older than that later
portion of the Middle Ages in which Feudalism
had completely consolidated itself.   When modern
jurisprudence first shows itself in the rough,
Wills are rarely allowed to dispose with absolute
freedom of a dead man's assets.   Wherever at
this period the descent of property was regulated
by Will—and over the greater part of Europe
movable or personal property was the subject
of Testamentary disposition—the exercise of the
Testamentary power was seldom allowed to
interfere with the right of the widow to a definite
share, and of the children to certain fixed proportions, of the devolving inheritance.   The shares
of the children, as their amount shows, were
determined by the authority of Roman law.   The
provision for the widow was attributable to the
exertions of the Church, which never relaxed its
solicitude for the interest of wives surviving their
husbands—winning, perhaps, one of the most
arduous of its triumphs when, after exacting
for two or three centuries an express promise
from the husband at marriage to endow his wife,
it at length succeeded in engrafting the principle
of Dower on the Customary Law of all Western
Europe.   Curiously enough, the dower of lands
proved a more stable institution than the analogous and more ancient reservation of certain
shares of the personal property to the widow and
children.   A few local customs in France maintained the right down to the Revolution, and
there are traces of similar usages in England;
but on the whole the doctrine prevailed that

movables might be freely disposed of by Will, and, even when the claims of the widow continued to be respected, the privileges of the children were obliterated from jurisprudence. We need not hesitate to attribute the change to the influence of Primogeniture. As the Feudal law of land practically disinherited all the children in favour of one, the equal distribution even of those sorts of property which might have been equally divided ceased to be viewed as a duty. Testaments were the principal instruments employed in producing inequality, and in this condition of things originated the shade of difference which shows itself between the ancient and the modern conception of a Will. But, though the liberty of bequest, enjoyed through Testaments, was thus an accidental fruit of Feudalism, there is no broader distinction than that which exists between a system of free Testamentary disposition and a system, like that of the Feudal land-law, under which property descends compulsorily in prescribed lines of devolution. This truth appears to have been lost sight of by the authors of the French Codes. In the social fabric which they determined to destroy, they saw Primogeniture resting chiefly on Family settlements, but they also perceived that Testaments were frequently employed to give the eldest son precisely the same preference which was reserved to him under the strictest of entails. In order, therefore, to make sure of their work, they not only rendered it impossible to prefer the eldest son to the rest in marriage-arrangements, but they almost expelled Testamentary succession from the law, lest it should

be used to defeat their fundamental principle
of an equal distribution of property among
children at the parent's death. The result is
that they have established a system of small
perpetual entails which is infinitely nearer akin
to the system of feudal Europe than would be
a perfect liberty of bequest. The land-law of
England, "the Herculaneum of Feudalism," is
certainly much more closely allied to the land-law
of the Middle Ages than that of any Continental
country, and Wills with us are frequently used
to aid or imitate that preference of the eldest
son and his line which is a nearly universal feature
in marriage settlements of real property. But
nevertheless feeling and opinion in this country
have been profoundly affected by the practice
of Free Testamentary disposition ; and it appears
to me that the state of sentiment in a great part
of French society, on the subject of the conserva-
tion of property in families, is much liker that
which prevailed throughout Europe two or three
centuries ago than are the current opinions of
Englishmen.

The mention of Primogeniture introduces one
of the most difficult problems of historical jurisprudence. Though I have not paused to explain
my expressions, it may have been noticed that I
have frequently spoken of a number of " co-heirs "
as placed by the Roman Law of Succession on the
same footing with a single Heir. In point of fact,
we know of no period of Roman jurisprudence at
which the place of the Heir, or Universal Successor,
might not have been taken by a group of co-heirs.
This group succeeded as a single unit, and the

assets were afterwards divided among them in a separate legal proceeding. When the Succession was *ab intestato*, and the group consisted of the children of the deceased, they each took an equal share of the property ; nor, though males had at one time some advantages over females, is there the faintest trace of Primogeniture. The mode of distribution is the same throughout archaic jurisprudence. It certainly seems that, when civil society begins and families cease to hold together through a series of generations, the idea which spontaneously suggests itself is to divide the domain equally among the members of each successive generation, and to reserve no privilege to the eldest son or stock. Some peculiarly significant hints as to the close relation of this phenomenon to primitive thought are furnished by systems yet more archaic than the Roman. Among the Hindoos, the instant a son is born, he acquires a vested right in his father's property, which cannot be sold without recognition of his joint-ownership. On the son's attaining full age, he can sometimes compel a partition of the estate, even against the consent of the parent ; and, should the parent acquiesce, one son can always have a partition even against the will of the others. On such partition taking place, the father has no advantage over his children, except that he has two of the shares instead of one. The ancient law of the German tribes was exceedingly similar. The *allod* or domain of the family was the joint property of the father and his sons. It does not, however, appear to have been habitually divided even at the death of the parent, and in the same

way the possessions of a Hindoo, however divisible
theoretically, are so rarely distributed in fact, that
many generations constantly succeed each other
without a partition taking place, and thus the
Family in India has a perpetual tendency to expand
into the Village Community, under conditions
which I shall hereafter attempt to elucidate. All
this points very clearly to the absolutely equal division of assets among the male children at death as
the practice most usual with society at the period
when family dependency is in the first stages of
disintegration. Here then emerges the historical
difficulty of Primogeniture. The more clearly we
perceive that, when the Feudal institutions were
in process of formation, there was no source in
the world whence they could derive their elements
but the Roman Law of the provincials on the one
hand and the archaic customs of the barbarians
on the other, the more are we perplexed at first
sight by our knowledge that neither Roman nor
barbarian was accustomed to give any preference
to the eldest son or his line in the succession to
property.

Primogeniture did not belong to the Customs
which the barbarians practised on their first
establishment within the Roman Empire. It is
known to have had its origin in the *benefices* or
beneficiary gifts of the invading chieftains. These
benefices, which were occasionally conferred by
the earlier immigrant kings, but were distributed
on a great scale by Charlemagne, were grants of
Roman provincial land to be holden by the
beneficiary on condition of military service. The
allodial proprietors do not seem to have followed

their sovereign on distant or difficult enterprises, and all the grander expeditions of the Frankish chiefs and of Charlemagne were accomplished with forces composed of soldiers either personally dependent on the royal house or compelled to serve it by the tenure of their land. The benefices, however, were not at first in any sense hereditary. They were held at the pleasure of the grantor, or at most for the life of the grantee ; but still, from the very outset, no effort seems to have been spared by the beneficiaries to enlarge the tenure, and to continue their lands in their family after death.   Through the feebleness of Charlemagne's successors, these attempts were universally successful, and the Benefice gradually transformed itself into the hereditary Fief. But, though the fiefs were hereditary, they did not necessarily descend to the eldest son.   The rules of succession which they followed were entirely determined by the terms agreed upon between the grantor and the beneficiary, or imposed by one of them on the weakness of the other. The original tenures were therefore extremely various ; not indeed so capriciously various as is sometimes asserted, for all which have hitherto been described present some combination of the modes of succession familiar to Romans and to barbarians, but still exceedingly miscellaneous. In some of them the eldest son and his stock undoubtedly succeeded to the fief before the others, but such successions, so far from being universal, do not even appear to have been general. Precisely the same phenomena recur during that more recent transmutation of European society which entirely substituted the feudal form of property for the domainia (or Roman) and the allodial (or German). The allods were wholly absorbed by the fiefs. The greater allodial proprietors transformed themselves into feudal lords by conditional alienations of portions of their land to dependants ; the smaller sought an escape from the oppressions of that terrible time by surrendering their property to some powerful chieftain, and receiving it back at his hands on condition of service in his wars. Meantime, that vast mass of the population of Western Europe whose condition was servile or semi-servile—the Roman and German personal slaves, the Roman *coloni* and the German *lidi*—were concurrently absorbed by the feudal organisation, a few of them assuming a menial relation to the lords, but the greater part receiving lands on terms which in those centuries were considered degrading. The tenures created during this era of universal infeudation were as various as the conditions which the tenants made with their new chiefs or were forced to accept from them. As in the case of the benefices, the succession to some, but by no means all, of the estates followed the rule of Primogeniture. No sooner, however, has the feudal system prevailed throughout the West, than it becomes evident that Primogeniture has some great advantage over every other mode of succession. It spread over Europe with remark-able rapidity, the principal instrument of diffusion being Family Settlements, the Pactes de Famille of France and Haus-Gesetze of Germany, which universally stipulated that lands held by knightly service should descend to the eldest son. Ultimately the law resigned itself to follow inveterate practice, and we find that in all the bodies of Customary Law, which were gradually built up, the eldest son and stock are preferred in the succession to estates of which the tenure is free and military. As to lands held by servile tenures (and originally all tenures were servile which bound the tenant to pay money or bestow manual labour), the system of succession prescribed by custom differed greatly in different countries and different provinces. The more general rule was that such lands were divided equally at death among all the children, but still in some instances the eldest son was preferred, in some the youngest. But Primogeniture usually governed the inheritance of that class of estates, in some respects the most important of all, which were held by tenures that, like the English Socage, were of later origin than the rest, and were neither altogether free nor altogether servile.

The diffusion of Primogeniture is usually accounted for by assigning what are called Feudal reasons for it. It is asserted that the feudal superior had a better security for the military service he required when the fief descended to a single person, instead of being distributed among a number on the decease of the last holder. Without denying that this consideration may partially explain the favour gradually acquired by Primogeniture, I must point out that Primogeniture became a custom of Europe much more through its popularity with the tenants than through any advantage it conferred on the lords. For its origin, moreover, the reason given does not account

at all. Nothing in law springs entirely from a
sense of convenience. There are always certain
ideas existing antecedently on which the sense of
convenience works, and of which it can do no more
than form some new combination ; and to find
these ideas in the present case is exactly the
problem.

A valuable hint is furnished to us from a
quarter fruitful of such indications. Although in
India the possessions of a parent are divisible at
his death, and may be divisible during his life,
among all his male children in equal shares, and
though this principle of the equal distribution of
property extends to every part of the Hindoo institutions, yet wherever *public office* or *political
power* devolves at the decease of the last Incum-
bent, the succession is nearly universally according
to the rules of Primogeniture. Sovereignties
descend therefore to the eldest son, and where
the affairs of the Village Community, the corporate
unit of Hindoo society, are confided to a single
manager, it is generally the eldest son who takes
up the administration at his parent's death. All
offices, indeed, in India, tend to become hereditary,
and, when their nature permits it, to vest in the
eldest member of the oldest stock. Comparing
these Indian successions with some of the ruder
social organisations which have survived in Europe
almost to our own day, the conclusion suggests
itself that, when Patriarchal power is not only
domestic but *political*, it is not distributed among
all the issue at the parent's death, but is the
birthright of the eldest son. The chieftainship of
a Highland clan, for example, followed the order

of Primogeniture. There seems, in truth, to be a form of family dependency still more archaic than any of those which we know from the primitive records of organised civil societies. The Agnatic Union of the kindred in ancient Roman law, and a multitude of similar indications, point to a period at which all the ramifying branches of the family tree held together in one organic whole ; and it is no presumptuous conjecture, that, when the corporation thus formed by the kindred was in itself an independent society, it was governed by the eldest male of the oldest line. It is true that we have no actual knowledge of any such society. Even in the most elementary communities, family-organisations, as we know them, are at most *imperia in imperio*. But the position of some of them, of the Celtic clans in particular, was sufficiently near independence within historical times to force on us the conviction that they were once separate *imperia*, and that Primogeniture regulated the succession to the chieftainship. It is, however, necessary to be on our guard against modern associations with the term of law. We are speaking of a family-connection still closer and more stringent than any with which we are made acquainted by Hindoo society or ancient Roman law. If the Roman Paterfamilias was visible steward of the family possessions, if the Hindoo father is only joint sharer with his sons, still more emphatically must the true patriarchal chieftain be merely the administrator of a common fund.

The examples of succession by Primogeniture which were found among the Benefices may, therefore, have been imitated from a system of family-

government known to the invading races, though
not in general use. Some ruder tribes may have
still practised it, or, what is still more probable,
society may have been so slightly removed from
its more archaic condition that the minds of some
men spontaneously recurred to it, when they were
called upon to settle the rules of inheritance for
a new form of property. But there is still the
question, Why did Primogeniture gradually supersede every other principle of succession ? The
answer, I think, is, that European society decidedly retrogaded during the dissolution of the
Carlovingian empire. It sank a point or two back
even from the miserably low degree which it had
marked during the earlier barbarian monarchies.
The great characteristic of the period was the
feebleness, or rather the abeyance, of kingly and
therefore of civil authority ; and hence it seems
as if, civil society no longer cohering, men universally flung themselves back on a social organisation older than the beginnings of civil communities.
The lord with his vassals, during the ninth and
tenth centuries, may be considered as a patriarchal
household, recruited, not as in the primitive times
by Adoption, but by Infeudation ; and to such a
confederacy, succession by Primogeniture was a
source of strength and durability. So long as
the land was kept together on which the entire
organisation rested, it was powerful for defence
and attack ; to divide the land was to divide the
little society, and voluntarily to invite aggression
in an era of universal violence. We may be
perfectly certain that into this preference for
Primogeniture there entered no idea of disin-

heriting the bulk of the children in favour of one.
Everybody would have suffered by the division
of the fief. Everybody was a gainer by its
consolidation. The Family grew stronger by the
concentration of power in the same hands ; nor is
it likely that the lord who was invested with the
inheritance had any advantage over his brethren
and kinsfolk in occupations, interests, or indulgences. It would be a singular anachronism to
estimate the privileges succeeded to by the heir
of a fief, by the situation in which the eldest son
is placed under an English strict settlement.

I have said that I regard the early feudal con-
federacies as descended from an archaic form of
the Family, and as wearing a strong resemblance
to it. But then in the ancient world, and in the
societies which have not passed through the cru-
cible of feudalism, the Primogeniture which seems
to have prevailed never transformed itself into
the Primogeniture of the later feudal Europe.
When the group of kinsmen ceased to be governed
through a series of generations by a hereditary
chief, the domain which had been managed for all
appears to have been equally divided among all.
Why did this not occur in the feudal world ? If
during the confusions of the first feudal period
the eldest son held the land for the behoof of the
whole family, why was it that when feudal Europe
had consolidated itself, and regular communities
were again established, the whole family did not
resume that capacity for equal inheritance which
had belonged to Roman and German alike ? The
key which unlocks this difficulty has rarely been
seized by the writers who occupy themselves in

tracing the genealogy of Feudalism. They perceive the materials of the feudal institutions, but
they miss the cement. The ideas and social forms
which contributed to the formation of the system
were unquestionably barbarian and archaic, but
as soon as Courts and lawyers were called in to
interpret and define it, the principles of interpretation which they applied to it were those of the
latest Roman jurisprudence, and were therefore
excessively refined and matured. In a patriarch-
ally governed society, the eldest son may succeed
to the government of the Agnatic group, and to
the absolute disposal of its property. But he is
not therefore a true proprietor. He has correlative duties not involved in the conception of
proprietorship, but quite undefined and quite
incapable of definition. The later Roman jurisprudence, however, like our own law, looked upon
uncontrolled power over property as equivalent
to ownership, and did not, and, in fact, could not,
take notice of liabilities of such a kind, that the
very conception of them belonged to a period
anterior to regular law. The contact of the refined and the barbarous notion had inevitably
for its effect the conversion of the eldest son into
legal proprietor of the inheritance. The clerical
and secular lawyers so defined his position from
the first ; but it was only by insensible degrees
that the younger brother, from participating on
equal terms in all the dangers and enjoyments of
his kinsman, sank into the priest, the soldier of
fortune, or the hanger-on of the mansion. The
legal revolution was identical with that which
occurred on a smaller scale, and in quite recent

times, through the greater part of the Highlands of Scotland. When called in to determine the legal powers of the chieftain over the domains which gave sustenance to the clan, Scottish jurisprudence had long since passed the point at which it could take notice of the vague limitations on completeness of dominion imposed by the claims of the clansmen, and it was inevitable therefore that it should convert the patrimony of many into the estate of one.

For the sake of simplicity, I have called the mode of succession Primogeniture whenever a single son or descendant succeeds to the authority over a household or society. It is remarkable, however, that in the few very ancient examples which remain to us of this sort of succession, it is not always the eldest son, in the sense familiar to us, who takes up the representation. The form of Primogeniture which has spread over Western Europe has also been perpetuated among the Hindoos, and there is every reason to believe that it is the normal form. Under it, not only the eldest son, but the eldest line is always preferred. If the eldest son fails, his eldest son has precedence not only over brothers but over uncles ; and, if he too fails, the same rule is followed in the next generation. But when the succession is not merely to *civil* but to *political* power, a difficulty may present itself which will appear of greater magnitude according as the cohesion of society is less perfect. The chieftain who last exercised authority may have outlived his eldest son, and the grandson who is primarily entitled to succeed may be too young and immature to undertake the actual guidance of the community, and the administration of its affairs. In such an event, the expedient which suggests itself to the more settled societies is to place the infant heir under guardianship till he reaches the age of fitness for government. The guardianship is generally that of the male Agnates ; but it is remarkable that the contingency supposed is one of the rare cases in which ancient societies have consented to the exercise of power by women, doubtless out of respect to the overshadowing claims of the mother. In India, the widow of a Hindoo sovereign governs in the name of her infant son, and we cannot but remember that the custom regulating succession to the throne of France—which, whatever be its origin, is doubtless of the highest antiquity—preferred the queen-mother to all other claimants for the Regency, at the same time that it rigorously excluded all females from the throne. There is, however, another mode of obviating the inconvenience attending the devolution of sovereignty on an infant heir, and it is one which would doubtless occur spontaneously to rudely organised communities. This is to set aside the infant heir altogether, and confer the chieftainship on the eldest surviving male of the first generation. The Celtic clan-associations, among the many phenomena which they preserved of an age in which civil and political society were not yet even rudimentarily separated, have brought down this rule of succession to historical times. With them, it seems to have existed in the form of a positive canon, that, failing the eldest son, his next brother

succeeds in priority to all grandsons, whatever
be their age at the moment when the sovereignty
devolves. Some writers have explained the principle by assuming that the Celtic customs took
the last chieftain as a sort of root or stock, and
then gave the succession to the descendant who
should be least remote from him ; the uncle thus
being preferred to the grandson as being nearer
to the common root. No objection can be taken
to this statement if it be merely intended as a
description of the system of succession ; but it
would be a serious error to conceive the men
who first adopted the rule as applying a course
of reasoning which evidently dates from the time
when feudal schemes of succession began to be
debated among lawyers. The true origin of the
preference of the uncle to the grandson is doubtless
a simple calculation on the part of rude men
in a rude society that it is better to be governed
by a grown chieftain than by a child, and that
the younger son is more likely to have come
to maturity than any of the eldest son's descendants. At the same time, we have some evidence
that the form of Primogeniture with which we
are best acquainted is the primary form, in the
tradition that the assent of the clan was asked
when an infant heir was passed over in favour
of his uncle. There is a tolerably well authenti-
cated instance of this ceremony in the annals
of the Scottish Macdonalds ; and Irish Celtic
antiquities, as interpreted by recent inquirers,
are said to disclose many traces of similar practices. The substitution by means of election,
of a " worthier " Agnatic relative for an elder

is not unknown, too, in the system of the Indian Village Communities.

Under Mahometan law, which has probably preserved an ancient Arabian custom, inheritances of property are divided equally among sons, the daughters taking a half share ; but if any of the children die before the division of the inheritance, leaving issue behind, these grandchildren are entirely excluded by their uncles and aunts. Consistently with this principle, the succession, when political authority devolves, is according to the form of Primogeniture which appears to have obtained among the Celtic societies. In the two great Mahometan families of the West, the rule is believed to be, that the uncle succeeds to the throne in preference to the nephew, though the latter be the son of an elder brother ; but though this rule has been followed quite recently both in Egypt and in Turkey, I am informed that there has always been some doubt as to its governing the devolution of the Turkish sovereignty. The policy of the Sultans has in fact generally prevented cases for its application from occurring, and it is possible that their wholesale massacres of their younger brothers may have been perpetrated quite as much in the interest of their children as for the sake of making away with dangerous competitors for the throne. It is evident, however, that in polygamous societies the form of Primogeniture will always tend to vary. Many considerations may constitute a claim on the succession, the rank of the mother, for example, or her degree in the affections of the father. Accordingly, some of the Indian

Mahometan sovereigns, without pretending to any distinct testamentary power, claim the right of nominating the son who is to succeed. The *blessing* mentioned in the Scriptural history of Isaac and his sons has sometimes been spoken of as a will, but it seems rather to have been a mode of naming an eldest son.

NOTE N

PRIMOGENITURE

MUCH has been written in recent years about the origins of medieval jurisdiction and land tenure, and the peculiar complication of tenure with personal lordship and jurisdiction which we call feudalism; we mention, almost at random, the names of Brunner, Waitz, Fustel de Coulanges, Flach, Luchaire; but there is nothing to throw doubt on the general soundness of the luminous sketch given in this chapter. Maine returns to the subject in the latter part of ch. viii. At the end of that chapter an opinion is adopted, it seems from Kemble, that "some shade of servile debasement" attached to a Germanic king's or chieftain's personal companions. I have never been able to discover Kemble's authority for this supposition, or to meet with any other acceptance of it. See, *contra*, Konrad Maurer in "Kritische Überschau," ii. 391.

Further observations on Primogeniture by Maine himself will be found in "The Early History of Institutions," pp. 124, 198-205. We may add to the brief mention of "parage" at p. 205 that the "paragium" of the Norman custumals has an important part in the Anglo-Norman nomenclature of Domesday Book. Groups of co-heirs holding "in paragio," and represented, for the purposes of the service due to their lord, by one of them who is sometimes called the senior, are common in several counties (Maitland, "Domesday Book and Beyond," p. 145; Pollock and Maitland, "H.E.L." ii. 263-4, 276; Pollock in Eng. Hist. Rev. 1896, xi. 228, note 65). This arrangement is a strong illustration of the practical convenience of primogeniture for the lord when feudal service was really military service. Maine's view that primogeniture originally had an official character seems to be thoroughly accepted; it would probably be found, if we had all the facts, that the occasional examples of primogeniture in servile or inferior tenures are to be explained by the tenement having been attached to some manorial or communal office. It would seem that, whether for reasons of convenience or because men liked to imitate the fashion of their lords, the general introduction of primogeniture in England was to some extent a popular movement. In 1255 the burgesses of Leicester alleged that they were being ruined by partible tenures, and procured a charter from their lord, Simon de Montfort, which Henry III. shortly afterwards confirmed, to change the course of descent to primogeniture (" Records of the Borough of Leicester," ed. Bateson, Nos. xxiii. xxiv., the latter indorsed " carta quod hereditas sit ad communem legem "). On the whole subject Mr. Evelyn Cecil's book " Primogeniture : A Short History of its Development in Various Countries, and its Practical Effects," Lond. 1895, may be studied with advantage.

CHAPTER VIII

THE EARLY HISTORY OF PROPERTY

THE Roman Institutional Treatises, after giving their definition of the various forms and modifications of ownership, proceed to discuss the Natural Modes of Acquiring Property. Those who are unfamiliar with the history of jurisprudence are not likely to look upon these " natural modes " of acquisition as possessing, at first sight, either much speculative or much practical interest. The wild animal which is snared or killed by the hunter, the soil which is added to our field by the imperceptible deposits of a river, the tree which strikes its roots into our ground, are each said by the Roman lawyers to be acquired by us *naturally*. The older jurisconsults had doubtless observed that such acquisitions were universally sanctioned by the usages of the little societies around them, and thus the lawyers of a later age, finding them classed in the ancient Jus Gentium, and perceiving them to be of the simplest description, allotted them a place among the ordinances of Nature. The dignity with which they were invested has gone on increasing in modern times till it is quite out of proportion to their original importance. Theory has made them its favourite food, and has enabled them to exercise the most serious influence on practice.

It will be necessary for us to attend to one
only among these " natural modes of acquisition,"
Occupatio or Occupancy.   Occupancy is the ad-
visedly taking possession of that which at the
moment is the property of no man, with the view
(adds the technical definition) of acquiring property in it for yourself.   The objects which the
Roman lawyers called *res nullius*—things which
have not or have never had an owner—can only
be ascertained by enumerating them.   Among
things which *never had* an owner are wild animals,
fishes, wild fowl, jewels disinterred for the first
time, and lands newly discovered or never before
cultivated.   Among things which *have not* an
owner are movables which have been abandoned,
lands which have been deserted, and (an anomalous but most formidable item) the property of
an enemy.   In all these objects the full rights
of dominion were acquired by the *Occupant*, who
first took possession of them with the intention
of keeping them as his own—an intention which,
in certain cases, had to be manifested by specific
acts.   It is not difficult, I think, to understand
the universality which caused the practice of
Occupancy to be placed by one generation of
Roman lawyers in the Law common to all Nations,
and the simplicity which occasioned its being
attributed by another to the Law of Nature.
But for its fortunes in modern legal history we
are less prepared by *à priori* considerations.   The
Roman principle of Occupancy, and the rules
into which the jurisconsults expanded it, are the
source of all modern International Law on the
subject of Capture in War and of the acquisition

of sovereign rights in newly discovered countries. They have also supplied a theory of the Origin of Property, which is at once the popular theory, and the theory which, in one form or another, is acquiesced in by the great majority of speculative jurists.

I have said that the Roman principle of Occupancy has determined the tenor of that chapter of International Law which is concerned with Capture in War. The Law of Warlike Capture derives its rules from the assumption that communities are remitted to a state of nature by the outbreak of hostilities, and that, in the artificial natural condition thus produced, the institution of private property falls into abeyance so far as concerns the belligerents. As the later writers on the Law of Nature have always been anxious to maintain that private property was in some sense sanctioned by the system which they were expounding, the hypothesis that an enemy's property is *res nullius* has seemed to them perverse and shocking, and they are careful to stigmatise it as a mere fiction of jurisprudence. But, as soon as the Law of Nature is traced to its source in the Jus Gentium, we see at once how the goods of an enemy came to be looked upon as nobody's property, and therefore as capable of being acquired by the first occupant. The idea would occur spontaneously to persons practising the ancient forms of Warfare, when victory dissolved the organisation of the conquering army and dismissed the soldiers to indiscriminate plunder. It is probable, however, that originally it was only movable property which was thus

permitted to be acquired by the Captor. We
know on independent authority that a very
different rule prevailed in ancient Italy as to
the acquisition of ownership in the soil of a
conquered country, and we may therefore suspect
that the application of the principle of occupancy
to land (always a matter of difficulty) dates from
the period when the Jus Gentium was becoming
the Code of Nature, and that it is the result of
a generalisation effected by the jurisconsults of
the golden age. Their dogmas on the point are
preserved in the Pandects of Justinian, and
amount to an unqualified assertion that enemy's
property of every sort is *res nullius* to the other
belligerent, and that Occupancy, by which the
Captor makes it his own, is an institution of
Natural Law. The rules which International
jurisprudence derives from these positions have
sometimes been stigmatised as needlessly indulgent
to the ferocity and cupidity of combatants, but
the charge has been made, I think, by persons
who are unacquainted with the history of wars,
and who are consequently ignorant how great
an exploit it is to command obedience for a rule
of any kind. The Roman principle of Occupancy,
when it was admitted into the modern law of
Capture in War, drew with it a number of subordinate canons, limiting and giving precision
to its operation, and if the contests which have
been waged since the treatise of Grotius became
an authority, are compared with those of an
earlier date, it will be seen that, as soon as the
Roman maxims were received, Warfare instantly
assumed a more tolerable complexion. If the

Roman law of Occupancy is to be taxed with having had pernicious influence on any part of the modern Law of Nations, there is another chapter in it which may be said, with some reason, to have been injuriously affected. In applying to the discovery of new countries the same principles which the Romans had applied to the finding of a jewel, the Publicists forced into their service a doctrine altogether unequal to the task expected from it. Elevated into extreme importance by the discoveries of the great navigators of the fifteenth and sixteenth centuries, it raised more disputes than it solved. The greatest uncertainty was very shortly found to exist on the very two points on which certainty was most required, the extent of the territory which was acquired for his sovereign by the discoverer, and the nature of the acts which were necessary to complete the *adprehensio* or assumption of sovereign possession. Moreover, the principle itself, conferring as it did such enormous advantages as the consequence of a piece of good luck, was instinctively mutinied against by some of the most adventurous nations in Europe, the Dutch, the English, and the Portuguese. Our own countrymen, without expressly denying the rule of International Law, never did, in practice, admit the claim of the Spaniards to engross the whole of America south of the Gulf of Mexico, or that of the King of France to monopolise the valleys of the Ohio and the Mississippi. From the accession of Elizabeth to the accession of Charles the Second, it cannot be said that there was at any time thorough peace in the American waters, and the encroachments of the New England Colonists on the territory of the French King continued for almost a century longer. Bentham was so struck with the confusion attending the application of the legal principle, that he went out of his way to eulogise the famous Bull of Pope Alexander the Sixth, dividing the undiscovered countries of the world between the Spaniards and Portuguese by a line drawn one hundred leagues West of the Azores ; and, grotesque as his praises may appear at first sight, it may be doubted whether the arrangement of Pope Alexander is absurder in principle than the rule of Public Law which gave half a continent to the monarch whose servants had fulfilled the conditions required by Roman jurisprudence for the acquisition of property in a valuable object which could be covered by the hand.

To all who pursue the inquiries which are the subject of this volume, Occupancy is pre-eminently interesting on the score of the service it has been made to perform for speculative jurisprudence, in furnishing a supposed explanation of the origin of private property. It was once universally believed that the proceeding implied in Occupancy was identical with the process by which the earth and its fruits, which were at first in common, became the allowed property of individuals. The course of thought which led to this assumption is not difficult to understand, if we seize the shade of difference which separates the ancient from the modern conception of Natural Law. The Roman lawyers had laid down that Occupancy was one of the Natural modes of acquiring pro-

perty, and they undoubtedly believed that, were
mankind living under the institutions of Nature,
Occupancy would be one of their practices.   How
far they persuaded themselves that such a condition of the race had ever existed, is a point,
as I have already stated, which their language
leaves in much uncertainty ; but they certainly
do seem to have made the conjecture, which has
at all times possessed much plausibility, that
the institution of property was not so old as
the existence of mankind.   Modern jurisprudence,
accepting all their dogmas without reservation,
went far beyond them in the eager curiosity with
which it dwelt on the supposed state of Nature.
Since then it had received the position that the
earth and its fruits were once *res nullius*, and
since its peculiar view of Nature led it to assume
without hesitation that the human race had
actually practised the Occupancy of *res nullius*
long before the organisation of civil societies,
the inference immediately suggested itself that
Occupancy was the process by which the " no
man's goods " of the primitive world became the
private property of individuals in the world of
history.   It would be wearisome to enumerate
the jurists who have subscribed to this theory in
one shape or another, and it is the less necessary
to attempt it because Blackstone, who is always
a faithful index of the average opinions of his
day, has summed them up in his 2nd book and
1st chapter.

   " The earth," he writes, " and all things therein
were the general property of mankind from the
immediate gift of the Creator.   Not that the

communion of goods seems ever to have been applicable, even in the earliest ages, to aught but the substance of the thing ; nor could be extended to the use of it. For, by the law of nature and reason, he who first began to use it acquired therein a kind of transient property that lasted so long as he was using it, and no longer ; or to speak with greater precision, the right of possession continued for the same time only that the act of possession lasted. Thus the ground was in common, and no part was the permanent property of any man in particular ; yet whoever was in the occupation of any determined spot of it, for rest, for shade, or the like, acquired for the time a sort of ownership, from which it would have been unjust and contrary to the law of nature to have driven him by force, but the instant that he quitted the use or occupation of it, another might seize it without injustice." He then proceeds to argue that " when mankind increased in number, it became necessary to entertain conceptions of more permanent dominion, and to appropriate to individuals not the immediate use only, but the very substance of the thing to be used."

Some ambiguities of expression in this passage lead to the suspicion that Blackstone did not quite understand the meaning of the proposition which he found in his authorities, that property in the earth's surface was first acquired, under the law of Nature, by the *occupant* ; but the limitation which designedly or through misapprehension he has imposed on the theory brings it into a form which it has not infrequently assumed. Many writers more famous than Blackstone for precision of language have laid down that, in the beginning of things, Occupancy first gave a right against the world to an exclusive but temporary enjoyment, and that afterwards this right, while it remained exclusive, became perpetual. Their object in so stating their theory was to reconcile the doctrine that in the state of Nature *res nullius* became property through Occupancy, with the inference which they drew from the Scriptural history that the Patriarchs did not at first permanently appropriate the soil which had been grazed over by their flocks and herds.

The only criticism which could be directly applied to the theory of Blackstone would consist in inquiring whether the circumstances which make up his picture of a primitive society are more or less probable than other incidents which could be imagined with equal readiness. Pursuing this method of examination, we might fairly ask whether the man who had *occupied* (Blackstone evidently uses this word with its ordinary English meaning) a particular spot of ground for rest or shade would be permitted to retain it without disturbance. The chances surely are that his right to possession would be exactly co-extensive with his power to keep it, and that he would be constantly liable to disturbance by the first comer who coveted the spot and thought himself strong enough to drive away the possessor. But the truth is that all such cavil at these positions is perfectly idle from the very baselessness of the positions themselves. What mankind did in the primitive state may not be a hopeless subject of inquiry, but of their motives for doing it it is impossible to know anything. These sketches of the plight of human beings in the first ages of the world are effected by first supposing mankind to be divested of a great part of the circumstances by which they are now surrounded, and by then assuming that, in the condition thus imagined, they would preserve the same sentiments and prejudices by which they are now actuated,— although, in fact, these sentiments may have been created and engendered by those very circumstances of which, by the hypothesis, they are to be stripped.

There is an aphorism of Savigny which has been sometimes thought to countenance a view of the origin of property somewhat similar to the theories epitomised by Blackstone. The great German jurist has laid down that all property is founded on Adverse Possession ripened by Prescription. It is only with respect to Roman law that Savigny makes this statement, and before it can fully be appreciated much labour must be expended in explaining and defining the expressions employed. His meaning will, however, be indicated with sufficient accuracy if we consider him to assert that, how far soever we carry our inquiry into the ideas of property received among the Romans, however closely we approach in tracing them to the infancy of law, we can get no farther than a conception of ownership involving the three elements in the canon—Possession, Adverseness of Possession, that is, a holding not permissive or subordinate, but exclusive against the world, and Prescription, or a period of time during which the Adverse Possession has unin-

terruptedly continued.   It is exceedingly probable
that this maxim might be enunciated with more
generality than was allowed to it by its author,
and that no sound or safe conclusion can be looked
for from investigations into any system of laws
which are pushed farther back than the point at
which these combined ideas constitute the notion
of proprietary right.   Meantime, so far from
bearing out the popular theory of the origin of
property, Savigny's canon is particularly valuable
as directing our attention to its weakest point.
In the view of Blackstone and those whom he
follows, it was the mode of assuming the exclusive
enjoyment which mysteriously affected the minds
of the fathers of our race.   But the mystery does
not reside here.   It is not wonderful that property
began in adverse possession.   It is not surprising
that the first proprietor should have been the
strong man armed who kept his goods in peace.
But why it was that lapse of time created a sentiment of respect for his possession—which is the
exact source of the universal reverence of mankind
for that which has for a long period *de facto* existed
—are questions really deserving the profoundest
examination, but lying far beyond the boundary
of our present inquiries.

Before pointing out the quarter in which we
may hope to glean some information, scanty and
uncertain at best, concerning the early history of
proprietary right, I venture to state my opinion
that the popular impression in reference to the
part played by Occupancy in the first stages of
civilisation directly reverses the truth.   Occupancy
is the advised assumption of physical possession ;

and the notion that an act of this description confers a title to "res nullius," so far from being characteristic of very early societies, is in all probability the growth of a refined jurisprudence and of a settled condition of the laws. It is only when the rights of property have gained a sanction from long practical inviolability, and when the vast majority of the objects of enjoyment have been subjected to private ownership, that mere possession is allowed to invest the first possessor with dominion over commodities in which no prior proprietorship has been asserted. The sentiment in which this doctrine originated is absolutely irreconcilable with that infrequency and uncertainty of proprietary rights which distinguish the beginnings of civilisation. Its true basis seems to be, not an instinctive bias towards the institution of Property, but a presumption, arising out of the long continuance of that institution, that *everything ought to have an owner*. When possession is taken of a "res nullius," that is, of an object which *is* not, or has *never* been, reduced to dominion, the possessor is permitted to become proprietor from a feeling that all valuable things are naturally the subjects of an exclusive enjoyment, and that in the given case there is no one to invest with the right of property except the Occupant. The Occupant, in short, becomes the owner, because all things are presumed to be somebody's property and because no one can be pointed out as having a better right than he to the proprietorship of this particular thing.

Even were there no other objection to the descriptions of mankind in their natural state which we have been discussing, there is one particular in which they are fatally at variance with the authentic evidence possessed by us. It will be observed, that the acts and motives which these theories suppose are the acts and motives of Individuals. It is each Individual who for himself subscribes the Social Compact. It is some shifting sandbank in which the grains are Individual men, that according to the theory of Hobbes is hardened into the social rock by the wholesome discipline of force. It is an Individual who, in the picture drawn by Blackstone, " is in the occupation of a determined spot of ground for rest, for shade, or the like." The vice is one which necessarily afflicts all the theories descended from the Natural Law of the Romans, which differed principally from their Civil Law in the account which it took of Individuals, and which has rendered precisely its greatest service to civilisation in enfranchising the individual from the authority of archaic society. But Ancient Law, it must again be repeated, knows next to nothing of Individuals. It is concerned not with Individuals, but with Families, not with single human beings, but groups. Even when the law of the State has succeeded in penetrating the small circles of kindred into which it had originally no means of penetrating, the view it takes of Individuals is curiously different from that taken by jurisprudence in its maturest stage. The life of each citizen is not regarded as limited by birth and death ; it is but a continuation of the existence of his forefathers, and it will be prolonged in the existence of his descendants.

The Roman distinction between the Law of Persons and the Law of Things, which though extremely convenient is entirely artificial, has evidently done much to divert inquiry on the subject before us from the true direction. The lessons learned in discussing the Jus Personarum have been forgotten where the Jus Rerum is reached, and Property, Contract, and Delict, have been considered as if no hints concerning their original nature were to be gained from the facts ascertained respecting the original condition of Persons. The futility of this method would be manifest if a system of pure archaic law could be brought before us, and if the experiment could be tried of applying to it the Roman classifications. It would soon be seen that the separation of the Law of Persons from that of Things has no meaning in the infancy of the law, that the rules belonging to the two departments are inextricably mingled together, and that the distinctions of the later jurists are appropriate only to the later jurisprudence. From what has been said in the earlier portions of this treatise, it will be gathered that there is a strong *à priori* improbability of our obtaining any clue to the early history of property, if we confine our notice to the proprietary rights of individuals. It is more than likely that joint-ownership, and not separate ownership, is the really archaic institution, and that the forms of property which will afford us instruction will be those which are associated with the rights of families and of groups of kindred. The Roman jurisprudence will not here assist in enlightening us, for it is exactly the Roman jurisprudence which, transformed by the theory of Natural Law, has bequeathed to the moderns the impression that individual ownership is the normal state of proprietary right, and that ownership in common by groups of men is only the exception to a general rule. There is, however, one community which will always be carefully examined by the inquirer who is in quest of any lost institution of primeval society. How far soever any such institution may have undergone change among the branch of the Indo-European family which has been settled for ages in India, it will seldom be found to have entirely cast aside the shell in which it was originally reared. It happens that, among the Hindoos, we do find a form of ownership which ought at once to rivet our attention from its exactly fitting in with the ideas which our studies in the Law of Persons would lead us to entertain respecting the original condition of property. The Village Community of India is at once an organised patriarchal society and an assemblage of co-proprietors. The personal relations to each other of the men who compose it are indistinguishably confounded with their proprietary rights, and to the attempts of English functionaries to separate the two may be assigned some of the most formidable miscarriages of Anglo-Indian administration. The Village Community is known to be of immense antiquity. In whatever direction research has been pushed into Indian history, general or local, it has always found the Community in existence at the farthest point of its progress. A great number of intelligent and observant writers, most of whom had no theory of any sort to support concerning its nature and

origin, agree in considering it the least destructible
institution of a society which never willingly sur-
renders any one of its usages to innovation.
Conquests and revolutions seem to have swept
over it without disturbing or displacing it, and
the most beneficent systems of government in
India have always been those which have recognised it as the basis of administration.

The mature Roman law, and modern jurisprudence following in its wake, look upon co-ownership
as an exceptional and momentary condition of the
rights of property. This view is clearly indicated
in the maxim which obtains universally in Western
Europe, *Nemo in communione potest invitus detineri*
(" No one can be kept in co-proprietorship against
his will "). But in India this order of ideas
is reversed, and it may be said that separate
proprietorship is always on its way to become
proprietorship in common. The process has been
adverted to already. As soon as a son is born, he
acquires a vested interest in his father's substance,
and on attaining years of discretion he is even, in
certain contingencies, permitted by the letter of
the law to call for a partition of the family estate.
As a fact, however, a division rarely takes place
even at the death of the father, and the property
constantly remains undivided for several generations, though every member of every generation
has a legal right to an undivided share in it.
The domain thus held in common is sometimes
administered by an elected manager, but more
generally, and in some provinces always, it is
managed by the eldest agnate, by the eldest representative of the eldest line of the stock. Such

18

an assemblage of joint proprietors, a body of
kindred holding domain in common, is the simplest
form of an Indian Village Community, but the
Community is more than a brotherhood of relatives
and more than an association of partners. It is
an organised society, and besides providing for
the management of the common fund, it seldom
fails to provide, by a complete staff of functionaries, for internal government, for police, for the
administration of justice, and for the apportionment of taxes and public duties.

The process which I have described as that
under which a Village Community is formed, may
be regarded as typical. Yet it is not to be supposed that every Village Community in India drew
together in so simple a manner. Although, in the
North of India, the archives, as I am informed,
almost invariably show that the Community was
founded by a single assemblage of blood-relations,
they also supply information that men of alien
extraction have always, from time to time, been
engrafted on it, and a mere purchaser of a share
may generally, under certain conditions, be admitted to the brotherhood. In the South of the
Peninsula there are often Communities which
appear to have sprung not from one but from two
or more families : and there are some whose composition is known to be entirely artificial ; indeed,
the occasional aggregation of men of different
castes in the same society is fatal to the hypothesis
of a common descent. Yet in all these brotherhoods either the tradition is preserved, or the
assumption made, of an original common parentage. Mountstuart Elphinstone, who writes more

particularly of the Southern Village Communities, observes of them (History of India, p. 71, 1905 edn.): " The popular notion is that the Village landholders are all descended from one or more individuals who settled the Village ; and that the only exceptions are formed by persons who have derived their rights by purchase or otherwise from members of the original stock. The supposition is confirmed by the fact that, to this day, there are only single families of landholders in small villages and not many in large ones ; but each has branched out into so many members that it is not uncommon for the whole agricultural labour to be done by the landholders, without the aid either of tenants or of labourers. The rights of the landholders are theirs collectively, and, though they almost always have a more or less perfect partition of them, they never have an entire separation. A landholder, for instance, can sell or mortgage his rights ; but he must first have the consent of the Village, and the purchaser steps exactly into his place and takes up all his obligations. If a family becomes extinct, its share returns to the common stock."

Some considerations which have been offered in the fifth chapter of this volume will assist the reader, I trust, in appreciating the significance of Elphinstone's language. No institution of the primitive world is likely to have been preserved to our day, unless it has acquired an elasticity foreign to its original nature through some vivifying legal fiction. The Village Community then is not necessarily an assemblage of blood-relations, but it is *either* such an assemblage *or* a body of co-proprietors formed on the model of an association of kinsmen. The type with which it should be compared is evidently not the Roman Family, but the Roman Gens or House. The Gens was also a group on the model of the family ; it was the family extended by a variety of fictions of which the exact nature was lost in antiquity. In historical times, its leading characteristics were the very two which Elphinstone remarks in the Village Community. There was always the assumption of a common origin, an assumption sometimes notoriously at variance with fact : and, to repeat the historian's words, " if a family became extinct, its share returned to the common stock." In old Roman law, unclaimed inherit-ances escheated to the Gentiles. It is further suspected by all who have examined their history that the Communities, like the Gentes, have been very generally adulterated by the admission of strangers, but the exact mode of absorption cannot now be ascertained. At present, they are recruited, as Elphinstone tells us, by the admission of purchasers, with the consent of the brotherhood. The acquisition of the adopted member is, however, of the nature of a universal succession ; together with the share he has bought, he succeeds to the liabilities which the vendor had incurred towards the aggregate group. He is an Emptor Familiæ, and inherits the legal clothing of the person whose place he begins to fill. The consent of the whole brotherhood re-quired for his admission may remind us of the consent which the Comitia Curiata, the Parliament of that larger brotherhood of self-styled kinsmen, the ancient Roman commonwealth, so strenuously insisted on as essential to the legalisation of an Adoption or the confirmation of a Will.

The tokens of an extreme antiquity are discoverable in almost every single feature of the Indian Village Communities. We have so many independent reasons for suspecting that the infancy of law is distinguished by the prevalence of co-ownership, by the intermixture of personal with proprietary rights, and by the confusion of public with private duties, that we should be justified in deducing many important conclusions from our observation of these proprietary brotherhoods, even if no similarly compounded societies could be detected in any other part of the world. It happens, however, that much earnest curiosity has been very recently attracted to a similar set of phenomena in those parts of Europe which have been most slightly affected by the feudal transformation of property, and which in many important particulars have as close an affinity with the Eastern as with the Western world. The researches of M. de Haxthausen, M. Tengoborski, and others, have shown us that the Russian villages are not fortuitous assemblages of men, nor are they unions founded on contract; they are naturally organised communities like those of India. It is true that these villages are always in theory the patrimony of some noble proprietor, and the peasants have within historical times been converted into the predial, and to a great extent into the personal, serfs of the seignior. But the pressure of this superior ownership has never crushed the ancient organisation of the village, and it is probable that the enactment

of the Czar of Russia, who is supposed to have
introduced serfdom, was really intended to prevent
the peasants from abandoning that co-operation
without which the old social order could not
long be maintained. In the assumption of an
agnatic connection between the villagers, in the
blending of personal rights with privileges of
ownership, and in a variety of spontaneous provisions for internal administration, the Russian
village appears to be a nearly exact repetition of
the Indian Community; but there is one important difference which we note with the greatest
interest. The co-owners of an Indian village,
though their property is blended, have their
rights distinct, and this separation of rights is
complete and continues indefinitely. The severance of rights is also theoretically complete in a
Russian village, but there it is only temporary.
After the expiration of a given, but not in all
cases of the same, period, separate ownerships
are extinguished, the land of the village is thrown
into a mass, and then it is redistributed among
the families composing the community, according
to their number. This repartition having been
effected, the rights of families and of individuals
are again allowed to branch out into various
lines, which they continue to follow till another
period of division comes round. An even more
curious variation from this type of ownership
occurs in some of those countries which long
formed a debatable land between the Turkish
Empire and the possessions of the House of
Austria. In Servia, in Croatia, and the Austrian
Sclavonia, the villages are also brotherhoods of

persons who are at once co-owners and kinsmen ; but there the internal arrangements of the community differ from those adverted to in the last two examples. The substance of the common property is in this case neither divided in practice nor considered in theory as divisible, but the entire land is cultivated by the combined labour of all the villagers, and the produce is annually distributed among the households, sometimes according to their supposed wants, sometimes according to rules which give to particular persons a fixed share of the usufruct. All these practices are traced by the jurists of the East of Europe to a principle which is asserted to be found in the earliest Sclavonian laws, the principle that the property of families cannot be divided for a perpetuity.

The great interest of these phenomena in an inquiry like the present arises from the light they throw on the development of distinct proprietary rights *inside* the groups by which property seems to have been originally held. We have the strongest reason for thinking that property once belonged not to individuals nor even to isolated families, but to larger societies composed on the patriarchal model ; but the mode of transition from ancient to modern ownerships, obscure at best, would have been infinitely obscurer if several distinguishable forms of Village Communities had not been discovered and examined. It is worth while to attend to the varieties of internal arrangement within the patriarchal groups which are, or were till recently, observable among races of Indo-European blood. The chiefs of the

ruder Highland clans used, it is said, to dole out
food to the heads of the households under their
jurisdiction at the very shortest intervals, and
sometimes day by day. A periodical distribution
is also made to the Sclavonian villagers of the
Austrian and Turkish provinces by the elders
of their body, but then it is a distribution once
for all of the total produce of the year. In the
Russian villages, however, the substance of the
property ceases to be looked upon as indivisible,
and separate proprietary claims are allowed freely
to grow up, but then the progress of separation
is peremptorily arrested after it has continued
a certain time. In India, not only is there no
indivisibility of the common fund, but separate
proprietorship in parts of it may be indefinitely
prolonged and may branch out into any number
of derivative ownerships, the *de facto* partition of
the stock being, however, checked by inveterate
usage, and by the rule against the admission of
strangers without the consent of the brotherhood.
It is not of course intended to insist that these
different forms of the Village Community represent distinct stages in a process of transmutation
which has been everywhere accomplished in the
same manner. But, though the evidence does not
warrant our going so far as this, it renders less
presumptuous the conjecture that private property, in the shape in which we know it, was
chiefly formed by the gradual disentanglement
of the separate rights of individuals from the
blended rights of a community. Our studies in
the Law of Persons seemed to show us the Family
expanding into the Agnatic group of kinsmen

then the Agnatic group dissolving into separate households ; lastly, the household supplanted by the individual ; and it is now suggested that each step in the change corresponds to an analogous alteration in the nature of Ownership. If there be any truth in the suggestion, it is to be observed that it materially affects the problem which theorists on the origin of Property have generally proposed to themselves. The question—perhaps an insoluble one—which they have mostly agitated is, what were the motives which first induced men to respect each other's possessions ? It may still be put, without much hope of finding an answer to it, in the form of an inquiry into the reasons which led one composite group to keep aloof from the domain of another. But, if it be true that far the most important passage in the history of Private Property is its gradual separation from the co-ownership of kinsmen, then the great point of inquiry is identical with that which lies on the threshold of all historical law—what were the motives which originally prompted men to hold together in the family union ? To such a question, Jurisprudence, unassisted by other sciences, is not competent to give a reply. The fact can only be noted.

The undivided state of property in ancient societies is consistent with a peculiar sharpness of division, which shows itself as soon as any single share is completely separated from the patrimony of the group. This phenomenon springs, doubtless, from the circumstance that the property is supposed to become the domain of a new group, so that any dealing with it, in

its divided state, is a transaction between two
highly complex bodies.   I have already compared
Ancient Law to Modern International Law, in
respect of the size and complexity of the corporate
associations, whose rights and duties it settles.
As the contracts and conveyances known to
ancient law are contracts and conveyances to
which not single individuals, but organised com-
panies of men, are parties, they are in the highest
degree ceremonious ; they require a variety of
symbolical acts and words intended to impress
the business on the memory of all who take
part in it ; and they demand the presence of
an inordinate number of witnesses.   From these
peculiarities, and others allied to them, springs
the universally unmalleable character of the
ancient forms of property.   Sometimes the patrimony of the family is absolutely inalienable, as
was the case with the Sclavonians, and still oftener,
though alienations may not be entirely illegiti-
mate, they are virtually impracticable, as among
most of the Germanic tribes, from the necessity
of having the consent of a large number of persons
to the transfer.   Where these impediments do
not exist, or can be surmounted, the act of conveyance itself is generally burdened with a perfect
load of ceremony, in which not one iota can be
safely neglected.   Ancient law uniformly refuses to
dispense with a single gesture, however grotesque ;
with a single syllable, however its meaning may
have been forgotten ; with a single witness, however superfluous may be his testimony.   The
entire solemnities must be scrupulously completed
by persons legally entitled to take part in it,

or else the conveyance is null, and the seller is re-established in the rights of which he had vainly attempted to divest himself.

These various obstacles to the free circulation of the objects of use and enjoyment, begin of course to make themselves felt as soon as society has acquired even a slight degree of activity, and the expedients by which advancing communities endeavour to overcome them form the staple of the history of Property. Of such expedients there is one which takes precedence of the rest from its antiquity and universality. The idea seems to have spontaneously suggested itself to a great number of early societies, to classify property into kinds. One kind or sort of property is placed on a lower footing of dignity than the others, but at the same time is relieved from the fetters which antiquity has imposed on them. Subsequently, the superior convenience of the rules governing the transfer and descent of the lower order of property becomes generally recognised, and by a gradual course of innovation the plasticity of the less dignified class of valuable objects is communicated to the classes which stand conventionally higher. The history of Roman Property Law is the history of the assimilation of Res Mancipi to Res Nec Mancipi. The history of Property on the European continent is the history of the subversion of the feudalised law of land by the Romanised law of movables; and though the history of ownership in England is not nearly completed, it is visibly the law of personalty which threatens to absorb and annihilate the law of realty.

The only *natural* classification of the objects

of enjoyment, the only classification which corresponds with an essential difference in the subject-
matter, is that which divides them into Movables
and Immovables. Familiar as is this classification to jurisprudence, it was very slowly developed
by Roman law, from which we inherit it, and was
only finally adopted by it in its latest stage. The
classifications of Ancient Law have sometimes a
superficial resemblance to this. They occasionally
divide property into categories, and place immovables in one of them ; but then it is found
that they either class along with immovables a
number of objects which have no sort of relation
with them, or else divorce them from various
rights to which they have a close affinity. Thus,
the Res Mancipi of Roman Law included not only
land but slaves, horses, and oxen. Scottish law
ranks with land a certain class of securities, and
Hindoo law associates it with slaves. English law,
on the other hand, parts leases of land for years
from other interests in the soil, and joins them
to personalty under the name of chattels real.
Moreover, the classifications of Ancient Law are
classifications implying superiority and inferiority ;
while the distinction between movables and immovables, so long at least as it was confined to
Roman jurisprudence, carried with it no suggestion
whatever of a difference in dignity. The Res
Mancipi, however, did certainly at first enjoy a
precedence over the Res Nec Mancipi, as did
heritable property in Scotland, and realty in
England, over the personalty to which they were
opposed. The lawyers of all systems have spared
no pains in striving to refer these classifications to

some intelligible principle ; but the reasons of the severance must ever be vainly sought for in the philosophy of law : they belong not to its philosophy, but to its history.   The explanation which appears to cover the greatest number of instances is, that the objects of enjoyment honoured above the rest were the forms of property known first and earliest to each particular community, and dignified therefore emphatically with the designation of *Property*.   On the other hand, the articles not enumerated among the favoured objects seem to have been placed on a lower standing, because the knowledge of their value was posterior to the epoch at which the catalogue of superior property was settled.   They were at first unknown, rare, limited in their uses, or else regarded as mere appendages to the privileged objects.   Thus, though the Roman Res Mancipi included a number of movable articles of great value, still the most costly jewels were never allowed to take rank as Res Mancipi, because they were unknown to the early Romans.   In the same way chattels real in England are said to have been degraded to the footing of personalty, from the infrequency and valuelessness of such estates under the feudal land-law.   But the grand point of interest is the continued degradation of these commodities when their importance had increased and their number had multiplied.   Why were they not successively included among the favoured objects of enjoyment ?   One reason is found in the stubbornness with which Ancient Law adheres to its classifications.   It is a characteristic both of uneducated minds and of early societies, that they are little able to conceive a general rule apart from the particular applications of it with which they are practically familiar. They cannot dissociate a general term or maxim from the special examples which meet them in daily experience ; and in this way the designation covering the best-known forms of property is denied to articles which exactly resemble them in being objects of enjoyment and subjects of right. But to these influences, which exert peculiar force in a subject-matter so stable as that of law, are afterwards added others more consistent with progress in enlightenment and in the conceptions of general expediency. Courts and lawyers become at last alive to the inconvenience of the embarrassing formalities required for the transfer, recovery, or devolution of the favoured commodities, and grow unwilling to fetter the newer descriptions of property with the technical trammels which characterised the infancy of law. Hence arises a disposition to keep these last on a lower grade in the arrangements of Jurisprudence, and to permit their transfer by simpler processes than those which, in archaic conveyances, serve as stumbling-blocks to good faith and stepping-stones to fraud. We are perhaps in some danger of under-rating the inconveniences of the ancient modes of transfer. Our instruments of conveyance are written, so that their language, well pondered by the professional draftsman, is rarely defective in accuracy. But an ancient conveyance was not written, but *acted*. Gestures and words took the place of written technical phraseology, and any formula mispronounced, or symbolical act omitted, would have vitiated the proceeding as fatally as a material mistake in stating the uses or setting out the remainders would, two hundred years ago, have vitiated an English deed. Indeed, the mischiefs of the archaic ceremonial are even thus only half stated. So long as elaborate conveyances, written or acted, are required for the alienation of *land* alone, the chances of mistake are not considerable in the transfer of a description of property which is seldom got rid of with much precipitation. But the higher class of property in the ancient world comprised not only land but several of the commonest and several of the most valuable movables. When once the wheels of society had begun to move quickly, there must have been immense inconvenience in demanding a highly intricate form of transfer for a horse or an ox, or for the most costly chattel of the old world—the Slave. Such commodities must have been constantly and even ordinarily conveyed with incomplete forms, and held, therefore, under imperfect titles.

The Res Mancipi of old Roman law were, land,—in historical times, land on Italian soil,—slaves and beasts of burden, such as horses and oxen. It is impossible to doubt that the objects which make up the class are the instruments of agricultural labour, the commodities of first consequence to a primitive people. Such commodities were at first, I imagine, called emphatically Things or Property, and the mode of conveyance by which they were transferred was called a Mancipium or Mancipation ; but it was not probably till much later that they received the distinctive appellation of Res Mancipi, " Things which require a Mancipation." By their side there may have existed or grown up a class of objects, for which it was not worth while to insist upon the full ceremony of Mancipation. If would be enough if, in transferring these last from owner to owner, a part only of the ordinary formalities were proceeded with, namely, that actual delivery, physical transfer, or *tradition*, which is the most obvious index of a change of proprietorship. Such commodities were the Res Nec Mancipi of the ancient jurisprudence, "things which did not require a Mancipation," little prized probably at first, and not often passed from one group of proprietors to another. While, however, the list of the Res Mancipi was irrevocably closed, that of the Res Nec Mancipi admitted of indefinite expansion; and hence every fresh conquest of man over material nature added an item to the Res Nec Mancipi, or effected an improvement in those already recognised. Insensibly, therefore, they mounted to an equality with the Res Mancipi, and the impression of an intrinsic inferiority being thus dissipated, men began to observe the manifold advantages of the simple formality which accompanied their transfer over the more intricate and more venerable ceremonial. Two of the agents of legal amelioration, Fictions and Equity, were assiduously employed by the Roman lawyers to give the practical effects of a Mancipation to a Tradition; and, though Roman legislators long shrank from enacting that the right of property in a Res Mancipi should be immediately transferred by bare delivery of the article, yet even this step was at last ventured upon by Justinian, in whose jurisprudence the

difference between Res Mancipi and Res Nec
Mancipi disappears, and Tradition or Delivery
becomes the one great conveyance known to the
law.   The marked preference which the Roman
lawyers very early gave to Tradition caused them
to assign it a place in their theory which has helped
to blind their modern disciples to its true history.
It was classed among the " natural " modes of
acquisition, both because it was generally practised
among the Italian tribes, and because it was a
process which attained its object by the simplest
mechanism. If the expressions of the jurisconsults
be pressed, they undoubtedly imply that Tradition,
which belongs to the Law Natural, is more ancient
than Mancipation, which is an institution of Civil
Society ; and this, I need not say, is the exact
reverse of the truth.

The distinction between Res Mancipi and Res
Nec Mancipi is the type of a class of distinctions
to which civilisation is much indebted, distinctions
which run through the whole mass of commodities,
placing a few of them in a class by themselves,
and relegating the others to a lower category.
The inferior kinds of property are first, from disdain and disregard, released from the perplexed
ceremonies in which primitive law delights, and
then afterwards, in another state of intellectual
progress, the simple methods of transfer and recovery which have been allowed to come into
use serve as a model which condemns by its convenience and simplicity the cumbrous solemnities
inherited from ancient days. But in some societies,
the trammels in which Property is tied up are
much too complicated and stringent to be relaxed

19

in so easy a manner. Whenever male children have been born to a Hindoo, the law of India, as I have stated, gives them all an interest in his property, and makes their consent a necessary condition of its alienation. In the same spirit, the general usage of the old Germanic peoples—it is remarkable that the Anglo-Saxon customs seem to have been an exception—forbade alienations without the consent of the male children; and the primitive law of the Sclavonians even prohibited them altogether. It is evident that such impediments as these cannot be overcome by a distinction between kinds of property, inasmuch as the difficulty extends to commodities of all sorts; and accordingly, Ancient Law, when once launched on a course of improvement, encounters them with a distinction of another character, a distinction classifying property, not according to its nature but according to its origin. In India, where there are traces of both systems of classification, the one which we are considering is exemplified in the difference which Hindoo law establishes between Inheritances and Acquisitions. The inherited property of the father is shared by the children as soon as they are born; but according to the custom of most provinces, the acquisitions made by him during his lifetime are wholly his own, and can be transferred by him at pleasure. A similar distinction was not unknown to Roman Law, in which the earliest innovation on the Parental Powers took the form of a permission given to the son to keep for himself whatever he might have acquired in military service. But the most extensive use ever made of this mode of

classification appears to have been among the
Germans. I have repeatedly stated that the *allod*,
though not inalienable, was commonly transferable
with the greatest difficulty ; and moreover, it
descended exclusively to the agnatic kindred.
Hence an extraordinary variety of distinctions
came to be recognised, all intended to diminish the
inconveniences inseparable from allodial property.
The *wehrgeld*, for example, or composition for the
homicide of a relative, which occupies so large a
space in German jurisprudence, formed no part of
the family domain, and descended according to
rules of succession altogether different. Similarly,
the *reipus*, or fine leviable on the re-marriage of a
widow, did not enter into the *allod* of the person
to whom it was paid, and followed a line of devolution in which the privileges of the agnates were
neglected. The law, too, as among the Hindoos,
distinguished the Acquisitions of the chief of the
household from his Inherited property, and permitted him to deal with them under much more
liberal conditions. Classifications of the other sort
were also admitted, and the familiar distinction
drawn between land and movables ; but movable
property was divided into several subordinate
categories, to each of which different rules applied.
This exuberance of classification, which may strike
us as strange in so rude a people as the German
conquerors of the Empire, is doubtless to be explained by the presence in their systems of a
considerable element of Roman Law, absorbed by
them during their long sojourn on the confines of
the Roman dominion. It is not difficult to trace
a great number of the rules governing the transfer

and devolution of the commodities which lay outside the *allod*, to their source in Roman jurisprudence, from which they were probably borrowed
at widely distant epochs, and in fragmentary
importations. How far the obstacles to the free
circulation of property were surmounted by such
contrivances, we have not the means even of
conjecturing, for the distinctions adverted to have
no modern history. As I before explained, the
allodial form of property was entirely lost in the
feudal, and when the consolidation of feudalism
was once completed, there was practically but one
distinction left standing of all those which had
been known to the western world—the distinction
between land and goods, immovables and movables. Externally this distinction was the same
with that which Roman law had finally accepted,
but the law of the middle ages differed from that
of Rome in distinctly considering immovable
property to be more dignified than movable.
Yet this one sample is enough to show the importance of the class of expedients to which it
belongs. In all the countries governed by systems
based on the French codes, that is, through much
the greatest part of the Continent of Europe, the
law of movables, which was always Roman law,
has superseded and annulled the feudal law of
land. England is the only country of importance
in which this transmutation, though it has gone
some way, is not nearly accomplished. Our own,
too, it may be added, is the only considerable
European country in which the separation of
movables from immovables has been somewhat
disturbed by the same influences which caused

the ancient classifications to depart from the only
one which is countenanced by nature. In the
main, the English distinction has been between
land and goods ; but a certain class of goods have
gone as heir-looms with the land, and a certain
description of interests in land have from historical
causes been ranked with personalty. This is not
the only instance in which English jurisprudence,
standing apart from the main current of legal
modification, has reproduced phenomena of archaic
law.

I proceed to notice one or two more contrivances by which the ancient trammels of
proprietary right were more or less successfully
relaxed, premising that the scheme of this treatise
only permits me to mention those which are of
great antiquity. On one of them in particular
it is necessary to dwell for a moment or two,
because persons unacquainted with the early
history of law will not be easily persuaded that
a principle, of which modern jurisprudence has
very slowly and with the greatest difficulty
obtained the recognition, was really familiar to
the very infancy of legal science. There is no
principle in all law which the moderns, in spite
of its beneficial character, have been so loath to
adopt and to carry to its legitimate consequences
as that which was known to the Romans as
Usucapion, and which has descended to modern
jurisprudence under the name of Prescription.
It was a positive rule of the oldest Roman law,
a rule older than the Twelve Tables, that commodities which had been uninterruptedly possessed for a certain period became the property of

the possessor. The period of possession was exceedingly short—one or two years, according to the nature of the commodities—and in historical times Usucapion was only allowed to operate when possession had commenced in a particular way ; but I think it likely that at a less advanced epoch possession was converted into ownership under conditions even less severe than we read of in our authorities. As I have said before, I am far from asserting that the respect of men for *de facto* possession is a phenomenon which jurisprudence can account for by itself, but it is very necessary to remark that primitive societies, in adopting the principle of Usucapion, were not beset with any of the speculative doubts and hesitations which have impeded its reception among the moderns. Prescriptions were viewed by the modern lawyers, first with repugnance, afterwards with reluctant approval. In several countries, including our own, legislation long declined to advance beyond the rude device of barring all actions based on a wrong whch had been suffered earlier than a fixed point of time in the past, generally the first year of some preceding reign ; nor was it till the middle ages had finally closed, and James the First had ascended the throne of England, that we obtained a true statute of limitation of a very imperfect kind. This tardiness in copying one of the most famous chapters of Roman law, which was no doubt constantly read by the majority of European lawyers, the modern world owes to the influence of the Canon Law. The ecclesiastical customs out of which the Canon Law grew, concerned as

they were with sacred or quasi-sacred interests,
very naturally regarded the privileges which they
conferred as incapable of being lost through disuse
however prolonged ; and in accordance with this
view, the spiritual jurisprudence, when afterwards
consolidated, was distinguished by a marked
leaning against Prescriptions. It was the fate
of the Canon Law, when held up by the clerical
lawyers as a pattern to secular legislation, to have
a peculiar influence on first principles. It gave
to the bodies of custom which were formed
throughout Europe far fewer express rules than
did the Roman law, but then it seems to have
communicated a bias to professional opinion on
a surprising number of fundamental points, and
the tendencies thus produced progressively gained
strength as each system was developed. One of
the dispositions it produced was a disrelish for
Prescriptions ; but I do not know that this prejudice would have operated as powerfully as it
has done, if it had not fallen in with the doctrine
of the scholastic jurists of the realist sect, who
taught that, whatever turn actual legislation
might take, a *right*, how long soever neglected,
was in point of fact indestructible. The remains
of this state of feeling still exist. Wherever the
philosophy of law is earnestly discussed, questions
respecting the speculative basis of Prescription
are always hotly disputed ; and it is still a point
of the greatest interest in France and Germany.
whether a person who has been out of possession
for a series of years is deprived of his ownership
as a penalty for his neglect, or loses it through the
summary interposition of the law in its desire

to have a *finis litium*. But no such scruples
troubled the mind of early Roman society. Their
ancient usages directly took away the ownership
of everybody who had been out of possession,
under certain circumstances, during one or two
years. What was the exact tenor of the rule of
Usucapion in its earliest shape, it is not easy to
say; but, taken with the limitations which we
find attending it in the books, it was a most useful
security against the mischiefs of a too cumbrous
system of conveyance. In order to have the
benefit of Usucapion, it was necessary that the
adverse possession should have begun in good
faith, that is, with belief on the part of the possessor
that he was lawfully acquiring the property,
and it was further required that the commodity
should have been transferred to him by some
mode of alienation which, however unequal to
conferring a complete title in the particular case,
was at least recognised by the law. In the case
therefore of a Mancipation, however slovenly the
performance might have been, yet if it had been
carried so far as to involve a Tradition or Delivery,
the vice of the title would be cured by Usucapion
in two years at most. I know nothing in the
practice of the Romans which testifies so strongly
to their legal genius as the use which they made
of Usucapion. The difficulties which beset them
were nearly the same with those which embarrassed
and still embarrass the lawyers of England.
Owing to the complexity of their system, which
as yet they had neither the courage nor the power
to reconstruct, actual right was constantly getting
divorced from technical right, the equitable

ownership from the legal. But Usucapion, as manipulated by the jurisconsults, supplied a self-acting machinery, by which the defects ol titles to property were always in course of being cured, and by which the ownerships that were temporarily separated were again rapidly cemented together with the briefest possible delay. Usucapion did not lose its advantages till the reforms of Justinian. But as soon as law and equity had been completely fused, and when Mancipation ceased to be the Roman conveyance, there was no further necessity for the ancient contrivance, and Usucapion, with its periods of time considerably lengthened, became the Prescription which has at length been adopted by nearly all systems of modern law.

I pass by with brief mention another expedient having the same object with the last, which, though it did not immediately make its appearance in English legal history, was of immemorial antiquity in Roman law; such indeed is its apparent age that some German civilians, not sufficiently aware of the light thrown on the subject by the analogies of English law, have thought it even older than the Mancipation. I speak of the Cessio in Jure, a collusive recovery, in a Court of Law, of property sought to be conveyed. The plaintiff claimed the subject of this proceeding with the ordinary forms of a litigation; the defendant made default; and the commodity was of course adjudged to the plaintiff. I need scarcely remind the English lawyer that this expedient suggested itself to our forefathers, and produced those famous Fines and Recoveries

which did so much to undo the harshest trammels
of the feudal land-law. The Roman and English
contrivances have very much in common and
illustrate each other most instructively, but there
is this difference between them, that the object
of the English lawyers was to remove complications
already introduced into the title, while the Roman
jurisconsults sought to prevent them by sub-
stituting a mode of transfer necessarily unim-
peachable for one which too often miscarried.
The device is in fact one which suggests itself
as soon as Courts of Law are in steady operation,
but are nevertheless still under the empire of
primitive notions. In an advanced state of legal
opinion, tribunals regard collusive litigation as
an abuse of their procedure ; but there has always
been a time when, if their forms were scrupulously
complied with, they never dreamed of looking
further.

The influence of Courts of Law and of their
procedure upon Property has been most extensive,
but the subject is too large for the dimensions of
this treatise, and would carry us further down
the course of legal history than is consistent with
its scheme. It is desirable, however, to mention,
that to this influence we must attribute the importance of the distinction between Property and
Possession—not, indeed, the distinction itself,
which (in the language of an eminent English
civilian) is the same thing as the distinction
between the legal right to act upon a thing and
the physical power to do so—but the extraordinary
importance which the distinction has obtained
in the philosophy of law. Few educated persons

are so little versed in legal literature as not to
have heard that the language of the Roman jurisconsults on the subject of Possession long occasioned the greatest possible perplexity, and that
the genius of Savigny is supposed to have chiefly
proved itself by the solution which he discovered
for the enigma.   Possession, in fact, when employed by the Roman lawyers, appears to have
contracted a shade of meaning not easily accounted
for.   The word, as appears from its etymology,
must have originally denoted physical contact
or physical contact resumable at pleasure ; but
as actually used, without any qualifying epithet,
it signifies not simply physical detention, but
physical detention coupled with the intention to
hold the thing detained as one's own.   Savigny,
following Niebuhr, perceived that for this anomaly
there could only be a historical origin.   He
pointed out that the Patrician burghers of Rome,
who had become tenants of the greatest part
of the public domain at nominal rents, were, in
the view of the old Roman law, mere possessors,
but then they were possessors intending to keep
their land against all comers.   They, in truth,
put forward a claim almost identical with that
which has recently been advanced in England
by the lessees of Church lands.   Admitting that
in theory they were the tenants-at-will of the
State, they contended that time and undisturbed
enjoyment had ripened their holding into a species
of ownership, and that it would be unjust to eject
them for the purpose of redistributing the domain.
The association of this claim with the Patrician
tenancies, permanently influenced the sense of

" possession." Meanwhile the only legal remedies of which the tenants could avail themselves, if ejected or threatened with disturbance, were the Possessory Interdicts, summary processes of Roman law which were either expressly devised by the Prætor for their protection, or else, according to another theory, had in olden times been employed for the provisional maintenance of possessions pending the settlement of questions of legal right. It came, therefore, to be understood that everybody who possessed property *as his own* had the power of demanding the Interdicts, and, by a system of highly artificial pleading, the Interdictal process was moulded into a shape fitted for the trial of conflicting claims to a disputed possession. Then commenced a movement which, as Mr. John Austin pointed out, exactly reproduced itself in English law. Proprietors, *domini*, began to prefer the simpler forms or speedier course of the Interdict to the lagging and intricate formalities of the Real Action, and for the purpose of availing themselves of the possessory remedy fell back upon the possession which was supposed to be involved in their proprietorship. The liberty conceded to persons who were not true Possessors, but Owners, to vindicate their rights by possessory remedies, though it may have been at first a boon, had ultimately the effect of seriously deteriorating both English and Roman jurisprudence. The Roman law owes to it those subtleties on the subject of Possession which have done so much to discredit it, while English law, after the actions which it appropriated to the recovery of real property had fallen into the most hopeless confusion, got rid at last of the whole tangled mass by a heroic remedy. No one can doubt that the virtual abolition of the English real actions which took place nearly thirty years since was a public benefit, but still persons sensitive to the harmonies of jurisprudence will lament that, instead of cleansing, improving, and simplifying the true proprietary actions, we sacrificed them all to the possessory action of ejectment, thus basing our whole system of land recovery upon a legal fiction.

Legal tribunals have also powerfully assisted to shape and modify conceptions of proprietary right by means of the distinction between Law and Equity, which always makes its first appearance as a distinction between jurisdictions. Equitable property in England is simply property held under the jurisdiction of the Court of Chancery. At Rome, the Prætor's Edict introduced its novel principles in the guise of a promise that under certain circumstances a particular action or a particular plea would be granted ; and, accordingly, the property *in bonis*, or Equitable Property, of Roman Law was property exclusively protected by remedies which had their source in the Edict. The mechanism by which equitable rights were saved from being overridden by the claims of the legal owner was somewhat different in the two systems. With us their independence is secured by the Injunction of the Court of Chancery. Since, however, Law and Equity, while not as yet consolidated, were administered under the Roman system by the same Court,

nothing like the Injunction was required, and
the Magistrate took the simpler course of refusing
to grant to the Civil Law Owner those actions
and pleas by which alone he could obtain the
property that belonged in equity to another.
But the practical operation of both systems was
nearly the same. Both, by means of a distinction
in procedure, were able to preserve new forms
of property in a sort of provisional existence,
until the time should come when they were
recognised by the whole law. In this way, the
Roman Prætor gave an immediate right of property
to the person who had acquired a Res Mancipi
by mere delivery, without waiting for the ripening
of Usucapion. Similarly he in time recognised
an ownership in the Mortgagee, who had at first
been a mere "bailee" or depositary, and in the
Emphyteuta, or tenant of land which was subject
to a fixed perpetual rent. Following a parallel
line of progress, the English Court of Chancery
created a special proprietorship for the Mortgagor,
for the Cestui que Trust, for the Married Woman
who had the advantage of a particular kind of
settlement, and for the Purchaser who had not
yet acquired a complete legal ownership. All
these are examples in which forms of proprietary
right, distinctly new, were recognised and preserved. But indirectly Property has been affected
in a thousand ways by equity, both in England
and at Rome. Into whatever corner of jurisprudence its authors pushed the powerful instrument in their command, they were sure to meet,
and touch, and more or less materially modify the
law of property. When in the preceding pages

I have spoken of certain ancient legal distinctions and expedients as having powerfully affected the history of ownership, I must be understood to mean that the greatest part of their influence has arisen from the hints and suggestions of improvement infused by them into the mental atmosphere which was breathed by the fabricators of equitable systems.

But to describe the influence of Equity on Ownership would be to write its history down to our own days. I have alluded to it principally because several esteemed contemporary writers have thought that in the Roman severance of Equitable from Legal property we have the clue to that difference in the conception of Ownership, which apparently distinguishes the law of the middle ages from the law of the Roman Empire. The leading characteristic of the feudal conception is its recognition of a double proprietorship, the superior ownership of the lord of the fief co-existing with the inferior property or estate of the tenant. Now, this duplication of proprietary right looks, it is urged, extremely like a generalised form of the Roman distribution of rights over property into *Quiritarian* or legal, and (to use a word of late origin) *Bonitarian* or equitable. Gaius himself observes upon the splitting of *dominion* into two parts as a singularity of Roman law, and expressly contrasts it with the entire or allodial ownership to which other nations were accustomed. Justinian, it is true, reconsolidàted dominion into one, but then it was the partially reformed system of the Western Empire, and not Justinian's jurisprudence, with which the barbarians were in contact during so many centuries. While they remained poised on the edge of the Empire, it may well be that they learned this distinction, which afterwards bore remarkable fruit. In favour of this theory, it must at all events be admitted that the element of Roman law in the various bodies of barbarian custom has been very imperfectly examined. The erroneous or insufficient theories which have served to explain Feudalism resemble each other in their tendency to draw off attention from this particular ingredient in its texture. The older investigators, who have been mostly followed in this country, attached an exclusive importance to the circumstances of the turbulent period during which the Feudal system grew to maturity ; and in later times a new source of error has been added to those already existing, in that pride of nationality which has led German writers to exaggerate the completeness of the social fabric which their forefathers had built up before their appearance in the Roman world. One or two English inquirers who looked in the right quarter for the foundations of the feudal system, failed nevertheless to conduct their investigations to any satisfactory result, either from searching too exclusively for analogies in the compilations of Justinian, or from confining their attention to the compendia of Roman law which are found appended to some of the extant barbarian codes. But, if Roman jurisprudence had any influence on the barbarous societies, it had probably produced the greatest part of its effects before the legislation of Justinian, and before the preparation of these compendia. It was not the reformed and purified jurisprudence of Justinian, but the undigested system which prevailed in the Western Empire, and which the Eastern *Corpus Juris* never succeeded in displacing, that I conceive to have clothed with flesh and muscle the scanty skeleton of barbarous usage. The change must be supposed to have taken place before the Germanic tribes had distinctly appropriated, as conquerors, any portion of the Roman dominions, and therefore long before Germanic monarchs had ordered breviaries of Roman law to be drawn up for the use of their Roman subjects. The necessity for some such hypothesis will be felt by everybody who can appreciate the difference between archaic and developed law. Rude as are the *Leges Barbarorum* which remain to us, they are not rude enough to satisfy the theory of their purely barbarous origin ; nor have we any reason for believing that we have received, in written records, more than a fraction of the fixed rules which were practised among themselves by the members of the conquering tribes. If we can once persuade ourselves that a considerable element of debased Roman law already existed in the barbarian systems, we shall have done something to remove a grave difficulty. The German Law of the conquerors and the Roman law of their subjects would not have combined if they had not possessed more affinity for each other than refined jurisprudence has usually for the customs of savages. It is extremely likely that the codes of the barbarians, archaic as they seem, are only a compound of true primitive usage with half-understood

20

Roman rules, and that it was the foreign ingredient which enabled them to coalesce with a
Roman jurisprudence that had already receded
somewhat from the comparative finish which it
had acquired under the Western Emperors.

But, though all this must be allowed, there are
several considerations which render it unlikely
that the feudal form of ownership was directly
suggested by the Roman duplication of domainial
rights. The distinction between legal and equitable property strikes one as a subtlety little likely
to be appreciated by barbarians; and, moreover,
it can scarcely be understood unless Courts of Law
are contemplated in regular operation. But the
strongest reason against this theory is the existence
in Roman law of a form of property—a creation
of Equity, it is true—which supplies a much
simpler explanation of the transition from one set
of ideas to the other. This is the Emphyteusis,
upon which the Fief of the middle ages has often
been fathered, though without much knowledge
of the exact share which it had in bringing feudal
ownership into the world. The truth is that the
Emphyteusis, not probably as yet known by its
Greek designation, marks one stage in a current
of ideas which led ultimately to feudalism. The
first mention in Roman history of estates larger
than could be farmed by a Paterfamilias, with his
household of sons and slaves, occurs when we come
to the holdings of the Roman patricians. These
great proprietors appear to have had no idea of
any system of farming by free tenants. Their
latifundia seem to have been universally cultivated
by slave-gangs, under bailiffs who were themselves

slaves or freedmen ; and the only organisation
attempted appears to have consisted in dividing
the inferior slaves into small bodies, and making
them the *peculium* of the better and trustier sort,
who thus acquired a kind of interest in the efficiency of their labour.   This system was, however,
especially disadvantageous to one class of estated
proprietors, the Municipalities.   Functionaries in
Italy were changed with the rapidity which often
surprises us in the administration of Rome herself ;
so that the superintendence of a large landed
domain by an Italian corporation must have been
excessively imperfect.   Accordingly, we are told
that with the municipalities began the practice of
letting out *agri vectigales*, that is, of leasing land
for a perpetuity to a free tenant, at a fixed rent,
and under certain conditions.   The plan was
afterwards extensively imitated by individual
proprietors, and the tenant, whose relation to
the owner had originally been determined by his
contract, was subsequently recognised by the
Prætor as having himself a qualified proprietorship,
which in time became known as an Emphyteusis.
From this point the history of tenure parts into
two branches.   In the course of that long period
during which our records of the Roman Empire
are most incomplete, the slave-gangs of the great
Roman families became transformed into the
coloni, whose origin and situation constitute one
of the obscurest questions in all history.   We may
suspect that they were formed partly by the
elevation of the slaves, and partly by the degradation of the free farmers ; and that they prove
the richer classes of the Roman Empire to have

become aware of the increased value which
landed property obtains when the cultivator has
an interest in the produce of the land. We know
that their servitude was predial ; that it wanted
many of the characteristics of absolute slavery,
and that they acquitted their service to the
landlord in rendering to him a fixed portion of
the annual crop. We know further that they
survived all the mutations of society in the ancient
and modern worlds. Though included in the
lower courses of the feudal structure, they continued in many countries to render to the landlord
precisely the same dues which they had paid to
the Roman *dominus*, and from a particular class
among them, the *coloni medietarii*, who reserved
half the produce for the owner, are descended
the *metayer* tenantry, who still conduct the
cultivation of the soil in almost all the South of
Europe. On the other hand, the Emphyteusis,
if we may so interpret the allusions to it in the
Corpus Juris, became a favourite and beneficial
modification of property ; and it may be conjectured that wherever free farmers existed, it was
this tenure which regulated their interest in the
land. The Prætor, as has been said, treated the
Emphyteuta as a true proprietor. When ejected,
he was allowed to reinstate himself by a Real
Action, the distinctive badge of proprietary right,
and he was protected from disturbance by the
author of his lease so long as the *canon*, or quit-rent,
was punctually paid. But at the same time it
must not be supposed that the ownership of the
author of the lease was either extinct or dormant.
It was kept alive by a power of re-entry on non-

payment of the rent, a right of pre-emption in case of sale, and a certain control over the mode of cultivation.   We have, therefore, in the Emphyteusis a striking example of the double ownership which characterised feudal property, and one, moreover, which is much simpler and much more easily imitated than the juxtaposition of legal and equitable rights.   The history of the Roman tenure does not end, however, at this point.   We have clear evidence that between the great fortresses which, disposed along the line of the Rhine and Danube, long secured the frontier of the Empire against its barbarian neighbours, there extended a succession of strips of land, the *agri limitrophi*, which were occupied by veteran soldiers of the Roman army on the terms of an Emphyteusis.   There was a double ownership. The Roman State was landlord of the soil, but the soldiers cultivated it without disturbance so long as they held themselves ready to be called out for military service whenever the state of the border should require it.   In fact, a sort of garrison-duty, under a system closely resembling that of the military colonies on the Austro-Turkish border, had taken the place of the quit-rent which was the service of the ordinary Emphyteuta. It seems impossible to doubt that this was the precedent copied by the barbarian monarchs who founded feudalism.   It had been within their view for some hundred years, and many of the veterans who guarded the border were, it is to be remembered, themselves of barbarian extraction, who probably spoke the Germanic tongues.   Not only does the proximity of so easily followed a model explain whence the Frankish and Lombard Sovereigns got the idea of securing the military service of their followers by granting away portions of their public domain ; but it perhaps explains the tendency which immediately showed itself in the Benefices to become hereditary, for an Emphyteusis, though capable of being moulded to the terms of the original contract, nevertheless descended as a general rule to the heirs of the grantee. It is true that the holder of a benefice, and more recently the lord of one of those fiefs into which the benefices were transformed, appears to have owed certain services which were not likely to have been rendered by the military colonist, and were certainly not rendered by the Emphyteuta. The duty of respect and gratitude to the feudal superior, the obligation to assist in endowing his daughter and equipping his son, the liability to his guardianship in minority, and many other similar incidents of tenure, must have been literally borrowed from the relations of Patron and Freedman under Roman law, that is, of quondam-master and quondam-slave. But then it is known that the earliest beneficiaries were the personal companions of the sovereign, and it is indisputable that this position, brilliant as it seems, was at first attended by some shade of servile debasement. The person who ministered to the Sovereign in his Court had given up something of that absolute personal freedom which was the proudest privilege of the allodial proprietor.

NOTE O

CAPTURE, OCCUPATION, POSSESSION

THE statements made in the early part of this chapter about the Roman doctrine of capture in war, its relation to the ordinary rules of *occupatio,* and the relation of both to the modern law of nations, are not easy to follow. Maine's general results do not depend on the accuracy of these statements, but it is necessary to indicate the points on which a reader unacquainted with Roman and international law might find the text misleading. First, there is really no authority for attributing to the Roman jurists the unqualified opinion that all spoil of war belonged to the individual captor, nor for deducing the rule of war from the law of *occupatio* in time of peace. Next, it is by no means clear that the Roman law of *occupatio* was more than one of many elements which went to form the modern rules as to belligerent rights. It is necessary to examine the authorities in some detail.

Maine seems to have relied on a passage of Gaius in the title of the Digest " de adquirendo rerum dominio " (41, 1, ll. 5, §7, 7. §1 ; l. 6 is clumsily interpolated by the compilers from another writer, and is not to our purpose). Gaius has spoken of the " occupation " of *res nullius,* such as wild animals, and goes on to other classes of cases in which occupation or something like it confers ownership (and not merely possession) *iure gentium.* This last term would seem, in relation to hostile capture, to point to the actual usage of war rather than to the ideal law of nature, which at all events would not justify treating captives of free condition as slaves. "Item quae ex hostibus capiuntur iure gentium statim capientium finat . . . adeo quidem ut et liberi homines in servitutem deducantur." Then Paulus says, at the head of the next title, " de adquirenda vel amittenda possessione " : "Item bello capta et insula in mari enata et gemmae lapilli margaritae in litoribus inventae eius fiunt, qui primus eorum possessionem nanctus est." Obviously no proof or authority was needed to show that a public enemy in arms could have no civil rights. The point is not that spoil of war ceases to belong to the enemy, but that capture, when it occurs, makes the captor an owner and not merely a possessor as between himself and his fellow-citizens. This does not tell us what is lawful spoil of war according to any specially Roman usage, nor does it exclude the restrictions of military discipline. Under the Empire, in fact, the commanding officer might distribute booty if he pleased, but plunder for the individual soldier's benefit or any kind of subsequent private appropriation was distinctly forbidden. " Is, qui praedam ab hostibus captam subripuit, lege peculatus tenetur et in quadruplum damnatur " : Modestinus in D. 48, 13, *ad legem Iuliam peculatus,*

15 (ed. Mommsen, *vulg.* 13). Indeed, it may well be that the
dicta of Gaius and Paulus contemplate only the case of enemy
property found on Roman ground at the outbreak of a war:
"quae res hostiles *apud nos* sunt non publicae sed occupantium
fiunt": Celsus, D. 41, 1, 51. Grotius comments on this dictum
of Celsus, understanding it in this sense, and holds the right of
private capture to be confined to acts not in the course of service,
"extra ministerium publicum": De Iure Belli ac Pacis, III. vi.
xii. § 1; and so Girard, "Manuel," p. 314. There is no doubt that
land seized in war was acquired and distributed by the State:
Pomponius in D. 49, 15, *de captivis*, 20, §1. In considering these
passages it is just as well to remember that problems arising out
of a state of war between Rome and a civilized or wealthy enemy
must have seemed a mere archaic curiosity to the jurists who
flourished under the Antonines.

Then as to Grotius's use of the Roman law, he certainly quotes
the words of Gaius already set out; but almost in the same breath
he quotes the Old Testament, Plato, Xenophon, and Aristotle
(*op. cit.* III. vi. ii. § 4). He denies (iv. § 1) that enemy's land can be
acquired by mere invasion short of permanent occupation in force.
He seems to think private plundering admissible in strict right,
but elsewhere, under the head of *temperaments*—a kind of counsels
of perfection to mitigate the rigour of war, most of which have
since been adopted as rules—he suggests that captured property
should be restored on the conclusion of peace, so far as practicable
(III. xiii., "temperamentum circa res captas"). Again, an early
trait of Grotius, "De Iure Praedae," published only in our own time
(ed. Hamaker, Hag. Com. 1868), altogether repudiates the occupation theory of the right to spoil of war. He likens it to the right
of judicial execution, and explains away the dictum of Gaius by
holding that the captor takes only as the servant and in the
name of the State; and he fortifies his doctrine, after the manner
of the time, which he continued to follow in his own later work,
with Hebrew, Homeric, and other Greek examples. It is difficult
to find here much adoption of the Roman law of Occupancy.
Perhaps other publicists of the seventeenth or eighteenth century
may have been less discriminating than Grotius. If this is to
be verified, it must be by some one more familiar with their
writings than myself. No further light is thrown on the point
in Maine's Cambridge lectures on international law, which he did
not live to revise finally for publication. These questions, however,
have long been antiquarian; modern practice has abrogated the
old harsh customs of war, and the seizure of movables or other
personal property in its bare form has, except in a very few cases,
become illegal (Hall, "Intern. Law," 5th ed. p. 427: the whole
chapter should be consulted).

Maine observes at p. 262 that the Roman law of Occupancy was altogether unequal to the task of settling disputes of title between different nations claiming new territories in right of their respective subjects who had discovered and more or less taken possession of them. Undoubtedly this is true, and it could not be otherwise. The difficulties have arisen in almost every case, down to the recent boundary question between Venezuela and British Guiana, from attempts to treat isolated, slight, and partial acts of dominion as equivalent to effective possession. Roman law knows nothing of any "occupation" which does not amount to full and actual control. Hence the learning of occupation had to be supplemented by that of possession. Roman law, like the Common Law, recognises the fact that a man cannot physically hold or control at the same time every square foot of a parcel of land, and therefore it allows legal possession to be acquired by entry on a part in the name of the whole and with intent to possess everything included in the boundaries. "Quod autem diximus et corpore et animo adquirere nos debere possessionem, non utique ita accipiendum est, ut qui fundum possidere velit omnes glebas circumambulet : sed sufficit quamlibet partem eius fundi introire, dum mente et cogitatione hac sit, uti totum fundum usque ad terminum velit possidere" (Paulus in D. 41, 2, *de adq. vel amitt. poss.* 3, §1). In order to apply this rule, however, we have to assume that the boundaries are known or ascertainable, and also that there is no effective opposition ; and when the facts to which the application is to be made are those alleged to amount to a national occupation of unsettled territory, it is often far from easy to say whether these conditions are satisfied. In case of dispute whether possession has been established, we must resort to the rule of common sense, which is expressly adopted by the authorities of the Common Law, and does not contradict anything in the Roman Law, namely that regard must be had to the kind of use and control of which the subject-matter is capable (authorities collected in Pollock and Wright on Possession, pp. 31-5). On the question what is the "terminus" in the occupation of unsettled territory, certain conventional rules, which must be sought in the regular text-books of international law, have been more or less generally adopted by the custom of nations, and in some cases express agreements have been made (Hall, *op. cit.* p. 114). The doctrine that occupancy produces ownership is of course not of the highest antiquity. Besides the reasons given by Maine, the conception of individual ownership as a legal right, the *dominium* of Roman law, is itself relatively modern. How and why Roman law developed that conception as early as it did is a historical problem which, so far as I have learnt, we cannot solve with our materials. We only know that Roman property law, for whatever reason, was already quite individualist at the time of the Twelve Tables. I am not sure that I fully understand Maine's passing remark about the influence of Natural Law in this point (p. 270).

At all events the transformation of the Hindu Joint Family to its modern type can hardly be set down to any such influence, and, so far as it has gone, the example appears fairly parallel.

Blackstone's account of the origin of property is loose enough to deserve nearly all of Maine's criticism. He wholly fails to distinguish between physical control or " detention," possession in law, and ownership, and he talks as if our refined legal conceptions had come to primeval man ready made, and in exactly the form and language of eighteenth-century publicists. But perhaps it was needless cruelty to suggest that Blackstone either did not understand the technical meaning of Occupation or intended to impose on his readers by playing with a verbal ambiguity. The word *occupare* is, after all, not purely technical in Latin ; it certainly has no technical meaning in the passage of Cicero which Blackstone quotes ("Comm." ii. 4 ; Cic. "de Fin." iii. 20, § 67). Cicero was neither an original philosopher nor a great jurist ; but no one would charge him with supposing that the right of a spectator in a theatre to the place he has taken ("eum locum quem quisque occuparit") had anything to do with the permanent acquisition of *dominium*. It would be more plausible to credit him with an inkling of the historical truth pointed out by Maine in these pages, that the notion of absolute legal ownership, and still more the presumption that everything ought to have an owner, or that, as our own books say, "the law must needs reduce the properties of all goods to some man," are rather modern than primitive. Blackstone's neglect to observe that the detached individual man whom he postulates is a kind of person altogether unknown to archaic institutions is the common and fatal fault, as Maine has in effect said, of all individualist theories of society : of Hobbes's, which Locke's was intended to refute, no less than of Blackstone's, which is a slight modification of Locke's.

Incidentally, but with provoking brevity, Maine speaks of Savigny's aphorism that property is founded on adverse possession ripened by prescription. This aphorism is certainly true for English law. Property in goods is, in the terms and process of the Common Law, not distinguishable from a right, present or deferred, to possess them ; and it is only under statutory provisions of very recent introduction and partial application that we know any means of proving title to English land other than showing continuous undisturbed possession, under a consistent claim of title, for a time long enough to exclude any reasonable fear of adverse claims. The conventional fixing of that time first by the usage of conveyancers and latterly by positive law makes no difference to the principle, nor do the elaborate rules which have been developed in various matters of detail. Title-deeds, as I have said elsewhere, are nothing but the written history of the possession and of the right in which it has been exercised. This is essentially

a Germanic institution, as any one who pursues the subject will
find; and when we consider the ideas of early Germanic law, we
shall perhaps be less apt to find any problem in the fact of a
possessor's rights being recognised by Roman law than to wonder
how Roman law came so early by the full and clear conception
of an owner's rights as distinct from possession. As to the
historical origin of the Roman doctrine of Possession there are
now several theories in the field, and none of them can be said
to be generally accepted, certainly not Savigny's, which was
dominant when Maine wrote.

NOTE P

THE INDIAN VILLAGE COMMUNITY

AFTER Maine had acquired official knowledge of Indian affairs,
he gave a hint in his lecture on "Village Communities" that the
local customs of India are neither so simple nor so uniform in type
as an ordinary European reader of "Ancient Law" might infer.
"I shall have hereafter to explain," he said,[1] "that, though there
are strong general resemblances between the Indian village
communities wherever they are found in anything like completeness,
they prove on close inspection to be not simple but composite
bodies, including a number of classes with very various rights and
claims." The publication in more than one form (most conveniently in "The Indian Village Community," Lond. 1896) of
B. H. Baden-Powell's authoritative researches on the Land Systems
of British India has since made it common or at least easily
accessible[2] knowledge that Indian villages are divisible into
two principal and widely different types, of which the "assemblage
of co-proprietors," formerly assumed to be the only normal one,
is not the more ancient. Sir Alfred Lyall (L.Q.R. ix. 27) has
approved Baden-Powell's "conclusion that the oldest form of
village was *not*, as is usually supposed, a group of cultivators
having joint or communistic interests, but a disconnected set
of families who severally owned their separate holdings." There
is a headman and there are village officers; we may say there is
administrative unity for many purposes; but there is not communal
ownership or tenure. There is no evidence that in villages of this
kind, usually called *raiyatwārī*, and prevalent in Central and
Southern India, the holdings were ever otherwise than separate
and independent; "the so-called joint village followed, and did

---

[1] I cannot find any fulfilment of this intention in Maine's published work. See
the Preface to the first edition of "Village Communities" for the probable
explanation.

[2] Baden-Powell's work appears to have been wholly unknown to a learned
gentleman resident at Madras, who published some notes on "Ancient Law" a
few years ago.

not precede, the village of separate holdings." In the joint or "landlord" villages of Oudh, the United (formerly North-West) Provinces, and the Panjāb, we find a dominant family or clan, oligarchs and in fact landlords as regards the inferior majority of inhabitants, and more or less democratic (for the shares are not always equal) among themselves. This type of village, which is in some ways curiously like a smaller reproduction of a Greek city-state, may be due to several causes. Conquest may produce it, or a deliberate new settlement, or joint inheritance among descendants of a single founder. In the case of conquest it may be superimposed on a former *raiyatwārī* village. Baden-Powell points out that all writers on the subject down to a time later than the publication not only of "Ancient Law" but of "Village Communities" had to generalise on incomplete materials.

" It can hardly be doubted that the information available when Sir H. S. Maine wrote was very far from being what it has since become. None of the reports on the Panjāb frontier tribal-villages were written—or at least were available in print; and the greater part of the best Settlement Reports of the North-West Provinces, Oudh and the Panjāb, are dated in years subsequent to the publication of 'Village Communities.' Further, the Settlement Reports of the Central Provinces, the District Manuals of Southern India, and the Survey Reports and Gazetteers of the Bombay districts were many of them not written, and the others were hardly known beyond the confines of their presidencies. In this fact I find the explanation of the total omission in Sir H. S. Maine's pages of any specific mention of the *raiyatwārī* form of village, and the little notice he takes of the tribal or clan constitution of Indian races in general, and of the frontier tribal villages in the Panjāb " ("The Indian Village Community," p. 4).

It will be quite a mistake, however, as we may learn at large from Baden-Powell, to assume that the family tenure or property which is the unit of the *raiyatwārī* village system is equivalent to individual ownership or any kind of ownership as understood in modern Western law. What is certain is that there is no such thing as *the* village community of Hindu times, any more than there is any such thing as *the* village community of the Middle Ages in Europe. But there remains much profit to be derived from comparing the effects of more or less similar causes in fixing the customs of land tenure in the East and the West, whether those effects are, as they sometimes are, closely similar, or varied by the presence of other and different conditions. We no longer expect to find complete and parallel survivals of a common prehistoric stock of institutions, but it is not less interesting to find how easily parallel types may be developed at very distant times and places ; and we are free to hold as a pious opinion that the Indian village council still known as the Five (*panchāyat*)—though that has long ceased to be the usual number in practice, and the institution belongs only to the "landlord" type of village—may go back to the same origin as our own reeve and four men, who flourish in Canada to this day. Robuster faith might be needed to find more than accident in the number of five hearths and five lawful men on Horace's estate ("habitatum quinque focis et Quinque bonos solitum Variam dimittere patres," Ep. i. 14). A system of dividing land so as to give every man a share of every quality, which resembles our medieval common-field system even in minute detail, is described by Baden-Powell (*op. cit.* pp. 191, 414).

With regard to the supposed corporate or quasi-corporate ownership of European and especially English village communities, Professor Maitland's section thereon in "Domesday Book and Beyond," pp. 340-56, gives a sound and much needed criticism of the loose language which was current among historical writers a generation ago.

NOTE Q

RES MANCIPI; ALIENATION IN EARLY LAW

MAINE'S opinion that the *res mancipi* of ancient Roman law were the instruments of agricultural labour, the commodities of first consequence to a primitive people" is entirely confirmed by the best recent authors. Professor Girard, agreeing with Ihering, Sohm, and Cuq, considers the soundest explanation ("la doctrine la moins aventureuse.") to be that the category consists of the necessary elements of the original Roman farmer's goods, to which alone, therefore, the early "Roman forms of alienation" were applicable. It is further suggested that at first only *res mancipi* were the subjects of full ownership, and that, at a time before individual property in land was alienable, the distinction *mancipi—nec mancipi* coincided with that of *familia* and *pecunia*, which had become obsolete at the date of the Twelve Tables (Girard, "Manuel," p. 247). Muirhead's explanation ("Private Law of Rome," p. 63) is similar, adding that the things constituting the *familia* were those which determined a Roman citizen's political qualification after the Servian reforms. Alienation of such things might affect the owner's political standing, and was therefore of public importance; but I am not clear that this reason is not superfluous. Muirhead observes, deliberately not following Gaius, that the fundamental notion of *mancipium* is *manum*—not *manu—capere*, the acquirement of *manus* in the sense of legal dominion (*op. cit.* p. 61), which seems highly probable.

As to the fetters on alienation usually found in early systems of property law, Maine set it down as "remarkable that the Anglo-Saxon customs seem to have been an exception" to the prevailing Germanic usage which forbade alienation of land without the

consent of the family or at least the sons of the grantor. Maine's
insight is now justified. The freedom which he thought anomalous,
though it was accepted as a fact by the best authorities then
accessible on Anglo-Saxon law, was really very partial indeed,
being confined to land, or rather lordship over land, held by
privileged persons and bodies under the privileged instruments
known to contemporaries as " books " and to us as charters. Only
after the Norman Conquest did the charter become a " common
assurance." As I tried not long ago to sum up in the simplest
form practicable what is known and not known about customary
land tenure before the Conquest, I may as well repeat my words :—

" We know next to nothing of the rules under which free men,
whether of greater or lesser substance, held ' folk-land,' that is,
estates governed by the old customary law. Probably there was
not much buying and selling of such land. There is no reason to
suppose that alienation was easier than in other archaic societies,
and some local customs found surviving long after the Conquest
point to the conclusion that often the consent of the village as
well as of the family was a necessary condition of a sale. Indeed,
it is not certain that folk-land, generally speaking, could be sold
at all. There is equally no reason to think that ordinary free
landholders could dispose of their land by will, or were in the
habit of making wills for any purpose. Anglo-Saxon wills (or
rather documents more like a modern will than a modern deed)
exist, but they are the wills of great folk, such as were accustomed
to witness the king's charters, had their own wills witnessed or
confirmed by bishops and kings, and held charters of their own ;
and it is by no means clear that the lands dealt with in these wills
were held as ordinary folk-land. In some cases it looks as if a
special licence or consent had been required ; we also hear of
persistent attempts by the heirs to dispute even gifts to great
churches " (" The Expansion of the Common Law," pp. 156-7).

The analogy which Maine points out (p. 297) between the Roman
cessio in iure and the Fines and Recoveries of medieval English
law is of course genuine ; but much earlier Germanic examples
of a like device may be found, though not in England. *Auflassung*
is the modern German term. Methods of this kind, when once
ascertained to be efficient, are often used merely by way of abundant
caution in spite of the additional trouble and expense involved.
But in the classical real -property law of the fifteenth century Fine
and Recovery were already taking their places as regular specialised
parts of a technical machinery.

CHAPTER IX

THE EARLY HISTORY OF CONTRACT

THERE are few general propositions concerning the age to which we belong which seem at first sight likely to be received with readier concurrence than the assertion that the society of our day is mainly distinguished from that of preceding generations by the largeness of the sphere which is occupied in it by Contract. Some of the phenomena on which this proposition rests are among those most frequently singled out for notice, for comment, and for eulogy. Not many of us are so unobservant as not to perceive that in innumerable cases where old law fixed a man's social position irreversibly at his birth, modern law allows him to create it for himself by convention ; and indeed several of the few exceptions which remain to this rule are constantly denounced with passionate indignation. The point, for instance, which is really debated in the vigorous controversy still carried on upon the subject of negro servitude, is whether the status of the slave does not belong to by-gone institutions, and whether the only relation between employer and labourer which commends itself to modern morality be not a relation determined exclusively by contract. The recognition of this difference between past ages and the present enters into the very essence of the most famous contemporary speculations. It is certain that the science of Political Economy, the only department of moral inquiry which has made any considerable progress in our day, would fail to correspond with the facts of life if it were not true that Imperative Law had abandoned the largest part of the field which it once occupied, and had left men to settle rules of conduct for themselves with a liberty never allowed to them till recently. The bias indeed of most persons trained in political economy is to consider the general truth on which their science reposes as entitled to become universal, and, when they apply it as an art, their efforts are ordinarily directed to enlarging the province of Contract and to curtailing that of Imperative Law, except so far as law is necessary to enforce the performance of Contracts. The impulse given by thinkers who are under the influence of these ideas is beginning to be very strongly felt in the Western world. Legislation has nearly confessed its inability to keep pace with the activity of man in discovery, in invention, and in the manipulation of accumulated wealth ; and the law even of the least advanced communities tends more and more to become a mere surface-stratum, having under it an ever-changing assemblage of contractual rules with which it rarely interferes except to compel compliance with a few fundamental principles, or unless it be called in to punish the violation of good faith.

Social inquiries, so far as they depend on the consideration of legal phenomena, are in so backward a condition that we need not be surprised at not finding these truths recognised in the commonplaces which pass current concerning the progress of society. These commonplaces answer much more to our prejudices than to our convictions. The strong disinclination of most men to regard morality as advancing seems to be especially powerful when the virtues on which Contract depends are in question, and many of us have an almost instinctive reluctance to admitting that good faith and trust in our fellows are more widely diffused than of old, or that there is anything in contemporary manners which parallels the loyalty of the antique world. From time to time, these prepossessions are greatly strengthened by the spectacle of frauds, unheard of before the period at which they were observed, and astonishing from their complication as well as shocking from their criminality. But the very character of these frauds shows clearly that, before they became possible, the moral obligations of which they are the breach must have been more than proportionately developed. It is the confidence reposed and deserved by the many which affords facilities for the bad faith of the few, so that, if colossal examples of dishonesty occur, there is no surer conclusion than that scrupulous honesty is displayed in the average of the transactions which, in the particular case, have supplied the delinquent with his opportunity. If we insist on reading the history of morality as reflected in jurisprudence, by turning our eyes not on the law of Contract but on the law of Crime, we must be careful that we read it aright. The only form of dishonesty treated of in the most ancient

Roman law is Theft. At the moment at which I write, the newest chapter in the English criminal law is one which attempts to prescribe punishment for the frauds of Trustees. The proper inference from this contrast is not that the primitive Romans practised a higher morality than ourselves. We should rather say that, in the interval between their days and ours, morality has advanced from a very rude to a highly refined conception—from viewing the rights of property as exclusively sacred, to looking upon the rights growing out of the mere unilateral reposal of confidence as entitled to the protection of the penal law.

The definite theories of jurists are scarcely nearer the truth in this point than the opinions of the multitude. To begin with the views of the Roman lawyers, we find them inconsistent with the true history of moral and legal progress. One class of contracts, in which the plighted faith of the contracting parties was the only material ingredient, they specifically denominated Contracts *juris gentium*, and though these contracts were undoubtedly the latest born into the Roman system, the expression employed implies, if a definite meaning be extracted from it, that they were more ancient than certain other forms of engagement treated of in Roman law, in which the neglect of a mere technical formality was as fatal to the obligation as misunderstanding or deceit. But then the antiquity to which they were referred was vague, shadowy, and only capable of being understood through the Present ; nor was it until the language of the Roman lawyers became the language of an age which had lost the key to their mode of thought that a "Contract of the Law of Nations" came to be distinctly looked upon as a contract known to man in a state of Nature. Rousseau adopted both the juridical and the popular error. In the Dissertation on the effects of Art and Science upon Morals, the first of his works which attracted attention and the one in which he states most unreservedly the opinions which made him the founder of a sect, the veracity and good faith attributed to the ancient Persians are repeatedly pointed out as traits of primitive innocence which have been gradually obliterated by civilisation; and at a later period he found a basis for all his speculations in the doctrine of an original Social Contract. The Social Contract or Compact is the most systematic form which has ever been assumed by the error we are discussing. It is a theory which, though nursed into importance by political passions, derived all its sap from the speculations of lawyers. True it certainly is that the famous Englishmen, for whom it had first had attraction, valued it chiefly for its political serviceableness, but, as I shall presently attempt to explain, they would never have arrived at it, if politicians had not long conducted their controversies in legal phraseology. Nor were the English authors of the theory blind to that speculative amplitude which recommended it so strongly to the Frenchmen who inherited it from them. Their writings show they perceived that it could be made to account for all social, quite as well as for all political phenomena. They had observed the fact, already striking in their day, that of the positive rules obeyed by men, the greater part were created by Contract, the lesser by Imperative Law. But they were ignorant or careless of the historical relation of these two constituents of jurisprudence. It was for the purpose, therefore, of gratifying their speculative tastes by attributing all jurisprudence to a uniform source, as much as with the view of eluding the doctrines which claimed a divine parentage for Imperative Law, that they devised the theory that all Law had its origin in Contract. In another stage of thought, they would have been satisfied to leave their theory in the condition of an ingenious hypothesis or a convenient verbal formula. But that age was under the dominion of legal superstitions. The State of Nature had been talked about till it had ceased to be regarded as paradoxical, and hence it seemed easy to give a fallacious reality and definiteness to the contractual origin of Law by insisting on the Social Compact as a historical fact.

Our own generation has got rid of these erroneous juridical theories, partly by outgrowing the intellectual state to which they belong, and partly by almost ceasing to theorise on such subjects altogether. The favourite occupation of active minds at the present moment, and the one which answers to the speculations of our fore-fathers on the origin of the social state, is the analysis of society as it exists and moves before our eyes ; but, through omitting to call in the assistance of history, this analysis too often degenerates into an idle exercise of curiosity, and is especially apt to incapacitate the inquirer for comprehending states of society which differ considerably from that to which he is accustomed. The mistake of judging the men of other periods by the morality of our own day has its parallel in the mistake of supposing that every wheel and bolt in the modern social machine had its counterpart in more rudimentary societies. Such impressions ramify very widely, and masque themselves very subtly, in historical works written in the modern fashion; but I find the trace of their presence in the domain of jurisprudence in the praise which is frequently bestowed on the little apologue of Montesquieu concerning the Troglodytes, inserted in the "Lettres Persanes." The Troglodytes were a people who systematically violated their Contracts, and so perished utterly. If the story bears the moral which its author intended, and is employed to expose an anti-social heresy by which this century and the last have been threatened, it is most unexceptionable; but if the inference be obtained from it that society could not possibly hold together without attaching a sacredness to promises and agreements which should be on something like a par with the respect that is paid to them by a mature civilisation, it involves an error so grave as to be fatal to all sound understanding of legal history. The fact is that the Troglodytes have flourished and founded powerful states with very small attention to the obligations of Contract. The point which before all others has to be apprehended in the constitution of primitive societies is that the individual creates for himself few or no rights, and few or no duties. The rules which he obeys are derived first from the

station into which he is born, and next from the
imperative commands addressed to him by the
chief of the household of which he forms part.
Such a system leaves the very smallest room for
Contract. The members of the same family (for
so we may interpret the evidence) are wholly
incapable of contracting with each other, and the
family is entitled to disregard the engagements
by which any one of its subordinate members has
attempted to bind it. Family, it is true, may
contract with family, chieftain with chieftain, but
the transaction is one of the same nature, and
encumbered by as many formalities, as the
alienation of property, and the disregard of one
iota of the performance is fatal to the obligation.
The positive duty resulting from one man's
reliance on the word of another is among the
slowest conquests of advancing civilisation.

Neither Ancient Law nor any other source of
evidence discloses to us society entirely destitute
of the conception of Contract. But the conception, when it first shows itself, is obviously rudimentary. No trustworthy primitive record can
be read without perceiving that the habit of mind
which induces us to make good a promise is as yet
imperfectly developed, and that acts of flagrant
perfidy are often mentioned without blame and
sometimes described with approbation. In the
Homeric literature, for instance, the deceitful
cunning of Ulysses appears as a virtue of the same
rank with the prudence of Nestor, the constancy
of Hector, and the gallantry of Achilles. Ancient
law is still more suggestive of the distance which
separates the crude form of Contract from its

maturity. At first, nothing is seen like the interposition of law to compel the performance of
a promise. That which the law arms with its
sanctions is not a promise, but a promise accompanied with a solemn ceremonial. Not only are
the formalities of equal importance with the
promise itself, but they are, if anything, of greater
importance; for that delicate analysis which
mature jurisprudence applies to the conditions of
mind under which a particular verbal assent is
given appears, in ancient law, to be transferred
to the words and gestures of the accompanying
performance. No pledge is enforced if a single
form be omitted or misplaced, but, on the other
hand, if the forms can be shown to have been
accurately proceeded with, it is of no avail to
plead that the promise was made under duress
or deception. The transmutation of this ancient
view into the familiar notion of a Contract is
plainly seen in the history of jurisprudence. First
one or two steps in the ceremonial are dispensed
with; then the others are simplified or permitted
to be neglected on certain conditions; lastly, a
few specific contracts are separated from the rest
and allowed to be entered into without form,
the selected contracts being those on which the
activity and energy of social intercourse depend.
Slowly, but most distinctly, the mental engagement isolates itself amid the technicalities, and
gradually becomes the sole ingredient on which
the interest of the jurisconsult is concentrated.
Such a mental engagement, signified through
external acts, the Romans called a Pact or Convention; and when the Convention has once been

conceived as the nucleus of a Contract, it soon becomes the tendency of advancing jurisprudence to break away the external shell of form and ceremony. Forms are thenceforward only retained so far as they are guarantees of authenticity and securities for caution and deliberation. The idea of a Contract is fully developed, or, to employ the Roman phrase, Contracts are absorbed in Pacts.

The history of this course of change in Roman law is exceedingly instructive. At the earliest dawn of the jurisprudence, the term in use for a Contract was one which is very familiar to the students of historical Latinity. It was *nexum*, and the parties to the contract were said to be *nexi*, expressions which must be carefully attended to on account of the singular durableness of the metaphor on which they are founded. The notion that persons under a contractual engagement are connected together by a strong *bond* or *chain*, continued till the last to influence the Roman jurisprudence of Contract; and flowing thence it has mixed itself with modern ideas. What then was involved in this nexum or bond? A definition which has descended to us from one of the Latin antiquarians describes *nexum* as *omne quod geritur per æs et libram*, " every transaction with the copper and the balance," and these words have occasioned a good deal of perplexity. The copper and the balance are the well-known accompaniments of the Mancipation, the ancient solemnity described in a former chapter, by which the right of ownership in the highest form of Roman Property was transferred from one person to another. Mancipation was a *conveyance*, and

hence has arisen the difficulty, for the definition
thus cited appears to confound Contracts and
Conveyances, which in the philosophy of jurisprudence are not simply kept apart, but are
actually opposed to each other. The *jus in re*,
right *in rem*, right " availing against all the world,"
or Proprietary Right, is sharply distinguished by
the analyst of mature jurisprudence from the *jus
ad rem*, right *in personam*, right " availing against
a single individual or group," or Obligation. Now
Conveyances transfer Proprietary Rights, Contracts create Obligations—how then can the two
be included under the same name or same general
conception ? This, like many similar embarrass-
ments, has been occasioned by the error of ascrib-
ing to the mental condition of an unformed society
a faculty which pre-eminently belongs to an
advanced stage of intellectual development, the
faculty of distinguishing in speculation ideas
which are blended in practice. We have indications not to be mistaken of a state of social affairs
in which Conveyances and Contracts were practically confounded ; nor did the discrepance of the
conceptions become perceptible till men had begun
to adopt a distinct practice in contracting and
conveying.

It may here be observed that we know enough
of ancient Roman law to give some idea of the
mode of transformation followed by legal conceptions and by legal phraseology in the infancy
of Jurisprudence. The change which they under-
go appears to be a change from general to special ;
or, as we might otherwise express it, the ancient
conceptions and the ancient terms are subjected

to a process of gradual specialisation. An ancient legal conception corresponds not to one but to several modern conceptions. An ancient technical expression serves to indicate a variety of things which in modern law have separate names allotted to them. If, however, we take up the history of Jurisprudence at the next stage, we find that the subordinate conceptions have gradually disengaged themselves, and that the old general names are giving way to special appellations. The old general conception is not obliterated, but it has ceased to cover more than one or a few of the notions which it first included. So too the old technical name remains, but it discharges only one of the functions which it once performed. We may exemplify this phenomenon in various ways. Patriarchal Power of all sorts appears, for instance, to have been once conceived as identical in character, and it was doubtless distinguished by one name. The Power exercised by the ancestor was the same whether it was exercised over the family or the material property—over flocks, herds, slaves, children, or wife. We cannot be absolutely certain of its old Roman name, but there is very strong reason for believing, from the number of expressions indicating shades of the notion of *power* into which the word *manus* enters, that the ancient general term was *manus*. But, when Roman law has advanced a little, both the name and the idea have become specialised. Power is discriminated, both in word and in conception, according to the object over which it is exerted. Exercised over material commodities or slaves, it has become *dominium*—over children, it is *Potestas*—over free persons whose services have been made away to another by their own ancestor, it is *mancipium*—over a wife, it is still *manus*. The old word, it will be perceived, has not altogether fallen into desuetude, but is confined to one very special exercise of the authority it had formerly denoted. This example will enable us to comprehend the nature of the historical alliance between Contracts and Conveyances. There seems to have been one solemn ceremonial at first for all solemn transactions, and its name at Rome appears to have been *nexum*. Precisely the same forms which were in use when a conveyance of property was effected seem to have been employed in the making of a contract. But we have not very far to move onwards before we come to a period at which the notion of a Contract has disengaged itself from the notion of a Conveyance. A double change has thus taken place. The transaction " with the copper and the balance," when intended to have for its office the transfer of property, is known by the new and special name of Mancipation. The ancient Nexum still designates the same ceremony, but only when it is employed for the special purpose of solemnising a contract.

When two or three legal conceptions are spoken of as anciently blended in one, it is not intended to imply that some one of the included notions may not be older than the others, or, when those others have been formed, may not greatly predominate over and take precedence of them. The reason why one legal conception continues so long to cover several conceptions, and one technical phrase to do instead of several, is doubtless that practical changes are accomplished in the law of primitive societies long before men see occasion to notice or name them.   Though I have said that Patriarchal Power was not at first distinguished according to the objects over which it was exercised, I feel sure that Power over Children was the root of the old conception of Power ; and I cannot doubt that the earliest use of the Nexum, and the one primarily regarded by those who resorted to it, was to give proper solemnity to the alienation of property.   It is likely that a very slight perversion of the Nexum from its original functions first gave rise to its employment in Contracts, and that the very slightness of the change long prevented its being appreciated or noticed.   The old name remained because men had not become conscious that they wanted a new one ; the old notion clung to the mind because nobody had seen reason to be at the pains of examining it. We have had the process clearly exemplified in the history of Testaments.   A Will was at first a simple conveyance of Property.   It was only the enormous practical difference that gradually showed itself between this particular conveyance and all others which caused it to be regarded separately, and even as it was, centuries elapsed before the ameliorators of law cleared away the useless encumbrance of the nominal mancipation, and consented to care for nothing in the Will but the expressed intentions of the Testator.   It is unfortunate that we cannot track the early history of Contracts with the same absolute confidence as the early history of Wills, but we are not quite without hints that contracts first showed

themselves through the *nexum* being put to a new
use and afterwards obtained recognition as distinct transactions through the important practical
consequences of the experiment. There is some,
but not very violent, conjecture in the following
delineation of the process. Let us conceive a sale
for ready money as the normal type of the Nexum.
The seller brought the property of which he
intended to dispose—a slave, for example—the
purchaser attended with the rough ingots of copper
which served for money—and an indispensable
assistant, the *libripens*, presented himself with
a pair of scales. The slave with certain fixed
formalities was handed over to the vendee—the
copper was weighed by the *libripens* and passed
to the vendor. So long as the business lasted it
was a *nexum*, and the parties were *nexi* ; but the
moment it was completed, the *nexum* ended, and
the vendor and purchaser ceased to bear the name
derived from their momentary relation. But
now, let us move a step onward in commercial
history. Suppose the slave transferred, but the
money not paid. In *that* case, the *nexum* is
finished, so far as the seller is concerned, and when
he has once handed over his property, he is no
longer *nexus* ; but, in regard to the purchaser, the
nexum continues. The transaction, as to his part
of it, is incomplete, and he is still considered to be
nexus. It follows, therefore, that the same term
described the conveyance by which the right of
property was transmitted, and the personal obligation of the debtor for the unpaid purchase-money.
We may still go forward, and picture to ourselves
a proceeding wholly formal, in which *nothing* is

handed over and *nothing* paid ; we are brought at once to a transaction indicative of much higher commercial activity, an *executory Contract of Sale.*

If it be true that, both in the popular and in the professional view, a *Contract* was long regarded as an *incomplete Conveyance,* the truth has importance for many reasons. The speculations of the last century concerning mankind in a state of nature, are not unfairly summed up in the doctrine that " in the primitive society property was nothing, and obligation everything " ; and it will now be seen that, if the proposition were reversed, it would be nearer the reality. On the other hand, considered historically, the primitive association of Conveyances and Contracts explains something which often strikes the scholar and jurist as singularly enigmatical, I mean the extraordinary and uniform severity of very ancient systems of law to *debtors,* and the extravagant powers which they lodge with *creditors.* When once we understand that the *nexum* was artificially prolonged to give time to the debtor, we can better comprehend his position in the eye of the public and of the law. His indebtedness was doubtless regarded as an anomaly, and suspense of payment in general as an artifice and a distortion of strict rule. The person who had duly consummated his part in the transaction must, on the contrary, have stood in peculiar favour ; and nothing would seem more natural than to arm him with stringent facilities for enforcing the completion of a proceeding which, of strict right, ought never to have been extended or deferred.

Nexum, therefore, which originally signified a Conveyance of property, came insensibly to denote a Contract also, and ultimately so constant became the association between this word and the notion of a Contract, that a' special term, Mancipium or Mancipatio, had to be used for the purpose of designating the true nexum or transaction in which the property was really transferred.   Contracts are therefore now severed from Conveyances, and the first stage in their history is accomplished, but still they are far enough from that epoch of their development when the promise of the contractor has a higher sacredness than the formalities with which it is coupled.   In attempting to indicate the character of the changes passed through in this interval, it is necessary to trespass a little on a subject which lies properly beyond the range of these pages, the analysis of Agreement effected by the Roman jurisconsults.   Of this analysis, the most beautiful monument of their sagacity, I need not say more than that it is based on the theoretical separation of the Obligation from the Convention or Pact.   Bentham and Mr. Austin have laid down that the " two main essentials of a contract are these : first, a signification by the promising party of his *intention* to do the acts or to observe the forbearances which he promises to do or to observe. Secondly, a signification by the promisee that he *expects* the promising party will fulfil the proffered promise." This is virtually identical with the doctrine of the Roman lawyers, but then, in their view, the result of these " significations " was not a Contract, but a Convention or Pact.   A Pact was the utmost product of the engagements of individuals agreeing among themselves, and it distinctly fell short of a Contract. Whether it ultimately became a Contract depended on the question whether the law annexed an Obligation to it. A Contract was a Pact (or Convention) *plus* an Obligation. So long as the Pact remained unclothed with the Obligation, it was called *nude* or *naked*.

What was an Obligation ? It is defined by the Roman lawyers as " Juris vinculum, quo necessitate adstringimur alicujus solvendæ rei." This definition connects the Obligation with the Nexum through the common metaphor on which they are founded, and shows us with much clearness the pedigree of a peculiar conception. The Obligation is the " bond " or " chain," with which the law joins together persons or groups of persons, in consequence of certain voluntary acts. The acts which have the effect of attracting an Obligation are chiefly those classed under the heads of Contract and Delict, of Agreement and Wrong ; but a variety of other acts have a similar consequence which are not capable of being comprised in an exact classification. It is to be remarked, however, that the Pact does not draw to itself the Obligation in consequence of any moral necessity ; it is the law which annexes it in the plenitude of its power, a point the more necessary to be noted, because a different doctrine has sometimes been propounded by modern interpreters of the Civil Law who had moral or metaphysical theories of their own to support. The image of a *vinculum juris* colours and pervades every part of the Roman law of Contract and Delict. The law bound the parties together, and the *chain* could only be undone by the process called *solutio,* an expression still figurative, to which our word " payment " is only occasionally and incidentally equivalent. The consistency with which the figurative image was allowed to present itself, explains an otherwise puzzling peculiarity of Roman legal phraseology, the fact that " Obligation " signifies rights as well as duties, the right, for example, to have a debt paid as well as the duty of paying it. The Romans kept, in fact, the entire picture of the " legal chain " before their eyes, and regarded one end of it no more and no less than the other.

In the developed Roman law, the Convention, as soon as it was completed, was, in almost all cases, at once crowned with the Obligation, and so became a Contract ; and this was the result to which contract-law was surely tending. But for the purpose of this inquiry, we must attend particularly to the intermediate stage—that in which something more than a perfect agreement was required to attract the obligation. This epoch is synchronous with the period at which the famous Roman classification of Contracts into four sorts—the Verbal, the Literal, the Real, and the Consensual—had come into use, and during which these four orders of contract constituted the only descriptions of engagement which the law would enforce. The meaning of the fourfold distribution is readily understood as soon as we apprehend the theory which severed the Obligation from the Convention. Each class of contracts was in fact named from certain formalities which were required over and above the mere agreement of the

22

contracting parties. In the Verbal Contract, as soon as the Convention was effected, a form of words had to be gone through before the " vinculum juris " was attached to it. In the Literal Contract, an entry in a ledger or table-book had the effect of clothing the Convention with the Obligation, and the same result followed, in the case of the Real Contract, from the delivery of the Res or Thing which was the subject of the preliminary engagement. The contracting parties came, in short, to an understanding in each case ; but, if they went no further, they were not *obliged* to one another, and could not compel performance or ask redress for a breach of faith. But let them comply with certain prescribed formalities, and the Contract was immediately complete, taking its name from the particular form which it had suited them to adopt. The exceptions to this practice will be noticed presently.

I have enumerated the four Contracts in their historical order, which order, however, the Roman Institutional writers did not invariably follow. There can be no doubt that the Verbal Contract was the most ancient of the four, and that it is the eldest known descendant of the primitive Nexum. Several species of Verbal Contract were anciently in use, but the most important of all, and the only one treated of by our authorities, was effected by means of a *stipulation*, that is, a Question and Answer ; a question addressed by the person who exacted the promise, and an answer given by the person who made it. This question and answer constituted the additional ingredient which, as I have just explained, was

demanded by the primitive notion over and above
the mere agreement of the persons interested.
They formed the agency by which the Obligation
was annexed. The old Nexum has now bequeathed to maturer jurisprudence first of all
the conception of a chain uniting the contracting
parties, and this has become the Obligation. It
has further transmitted the notion of a ceremonial
accompanying and consecrating the engagement,
and this ceremonial has been transmuted into the
Stipulation. The conversion of the solemn conveyance, which was the prominent feature of the
original Nexum, into a mere question and answer,
would be more of a mystery than it is if we had
not the analogous history of Roman Testaments
to enlighten us. Looking at that history, we
can understand how the formal conveyance was
first separated from the part of the proceeding
which had immediate reference to the business
in hand, and how afterwards it was omitted
altogether. As then the question and answer of
the Stipulation were unquestionably the Nexum
in a simplified shape, we are prepared to find
that they long partook of the nature of a technical
form. It would be a mistake to consider them
as exclusively recommending themselves to the
older Roman lawyers through their usefulness
in furnishing persons meditating an agreement
with an opportunity for consideration and reflection. It is not to be disputed that they had
a value of this kind, which was gradually recognised; but there is proof that their function
in respect to Contracts was at first formal and
ceremonial in the statement of our authorities,

that not every question and answer was of old sufficient to constitute a Stipulation, but only a question and answer couched in technical phraseology specially appropriated to the particular occasion.

But although it is essential for the proper appreciation of the history of contract-law that the Stipulation should be understood to have been looked upon as a solemn form before it was recognised as a useful security, it would be wrong on the other hand to shut our eyes to its real usefulness. The Verbal Contract, though it had lost much of its ancient importance, survived to the latest period of Roman jurisprudence; and we may take it for granted that no institution of Roman law had so extended a longevity unless it served some practical advantage. I observe in an English writer some expressions of surprise that the Romans even of the earliest times were content with so meagre a protection against haste and irreflection. But on examining the Stipulation closely, and remembering that we have to do with a state of society in which written evidence was not easily procurable, I think we must admit that this Question and Answer, had it been expressly devised to answer the purpose which it served, would have been justly designated a highly ingenious expedient. It was the *promisee* who, in the character of stipulator, put all the terms of the contract into the form of a question, and the answer was given by the *promisor*. " Do you promise that you will deliver me such and such a slave, at such and such a place, on such and such a day ? " " I do promise." Now, if we reflect for a moment, we shall see that this obligation to put the promise interrogatively inverts the natural position of the parties, and, by effectually breaking the tenor of the conversation, prevents the attention from gliding over a dangerous pledge. With us, a verbal promise is, generally speaking, to be gathered exclusively from the words of the promisor. In old Roman law, another step was absolutely required; it was necessary for the promisee, after the agreement had been made, to sum up all its terms in a solemn interrogation; and it was of this interrogation, of course, and of the assent to it, that proof had to be given at the trial—*not* of the promise, which was not in itself binding. How great a difference this seemingly insignificant peculiarity may make in the phraseology of contract-law is speedily realised by the beginner in Roman jurisprudence, one of whose first stumbling-blocks is almost universally created by it. When we in English have occasion, in mentioning a contract, to connect it for convenience' sake with one of the parties,—for example, if we wished to speak generally of a contractor,—it is always the promis*or* at whom our words are pointing. But the general language of Roman law takes a different turn; it always regards the contract, if we may so speak, from the point of view of the promis*ee*; in speaking of a party to a contract, it is always the Stipulator, the person who asks the question, who is primarily alluded to. But the serviceableness of the stipulation is most vividly illustrated by referring to the actual examples in the pages of the Latin comic dramatists. If the entire scenes are read down in which these passages occur (ex. gra. Plautus, *Pseudolus*, Act I. sc. 1 ; Act IV. sc. 6 ; *Trinummus*, Act V. sc. 2), it will be perceived how effectually the attention of the person meditating the promise must have been arrested by the question, and how ample was the opportunity for withdrawal from an improvident undertaking.

In the Literal or Written Contract, the formal act by which an Obligation was superinduced on the Convention, was an entry of the sum due, where it could be specifically ascertained, on the debit side of a ledger. The explanation of this contract turns on a point of Roman domestic manners, the systematic character and exceeding regularity of book-keeping in ancient times. There are several minor difficulties of old Roman law, as, for example, the nature of the Slave's Peculium, which are only cleared up when we recollect that a Roman household consisted of a number of persons strictly accountable to its head, and that every single item of domestic receipt and expenditure, after being entered in waste books, was transferred at stated periods to a general household ledger. There are some obscurities, however, in the descriptions we have received of the Literal Contract, the fact being that the habit of keeping books ceased to be universal in later times, and the expression " Literal Contract " came to signify a form of engagement entirely different from that originally understood. We are not, therefore, in a position to say, with respect to the primitive Literal Contract, whether the obligation was created by a simple entry on the part of the creditor, or whether the consent of the debtor or a correspondent entry in his own books was necessary to give it legal effect. The essential point is however established, that, in the case of this Contract, all formalities were dispensed with on a condition being complied with. This is another step downwards in the history of contract-law.

The Contract which stands next in historical succession, the Real Contract, shows a great advance in ethical conceptions. Whenever any agreement had for its object the delivery of a specific thing—and this is the case with the large majority of simple engagements—the Obligation was drawn down as soon as the delivery had actually taken place. Such a result must have involved a serious innovation on the oldest ideas of Contract ; for doubtless, in the primitive times, when a contracting party had neglected to clothe his agreement in a stipulation, nothing done in pursuance of the agreement would be recognised by the law. A person who had paid over money on loan would be unable to sue for its repayment unless he had formally *stipulated* for it. But, in the Real Contract, performance on one side is allowed to impose a legal duty on the other—evidently on ethical grounds. For the first time then moral considerations appear as an ingredient in Contract-law, and the Real Contract differs from its two predecessors in being founded on these, rather than on respect for technical forms or on deference to Roman domestic habits.

We now reach the fourth class, or Consensual Contracts, the most interesting and important of

all. Four specified Contracts were distinguished
by this name : Mandatum, *i.e.* Commission or
Agency ; Societas or Partnership ; Emtio Ven-
ditio or Sale ; and Locatio Conductio or Letting
and Hiring. A few pages back, after stating that
a Contract consisted of a Pact or Convention to
which an Obligation had been superadded, I spoke
of certain acts or formalities by which the law
permitted the Obligation to be attracted to the
Pact. I used this language on account of the
advantage of a general expression, but it is not
strictly correct unless it be understood to include
the negative as well as the positive. For, in truth,
the peculiarity of these Consensual Contracts is
that *no* formalities are required to create them out
of the Pact. Much that is indefensible, and much
more that is obscure, has been written about the
Consensual Contracts, and it has even been asserted
that in them the *consent* of the Parties is more
emphatically given than in any other species of
agreement. But the term Consensual merely
indicates that the Obligation is here annexed
at once to the *Consensus*. The Consensus, or
mutual assent of the parties, is the final and
crowning ingredient in the Convention, and it
is the special characteristic of agreements falling
under one of the four heads of Sale, Partnership,
Agency, and Hiring, that, as soon as the assent
of the parties has supplied this ingredient, there
is *at once* a Contract. The Consensus draws
with it the Obligation, performing, in transactions
of the sort specified, the exact functions which
are discharged, in the other contracts, by the
Res or Thing, by the *Verba* stipulationis, and by

the *Literæ* or written entry in a ledger.   Consensual
is therefore a term which does not involve the
slightest anomaly, but is exactly analogous to
Real, Verbal, and Literal.

In the intercourse of life the commonest and
most important of all the contracts are unquestionably the four styled Consensual.   The larger part
of the collective existence of every community
is consumed in transactions of buying and selling,
of letting and hiring, of alliances between men
for purposes of business, of delegation of business
from one man to another ; and this is no doubt the
consideration which led the Romans, as it has led
most societies, to relieve these transactions from
technical incumbrance, to abstain as much as
possible from clogging the most efficient springs
of social movement.   Such motives were not of
course confined to Rome, and the commerce of the
Romans with their neighbours must have given
them abundant opportunities for observing that
the contracts before us tended everywhere to
become *Consensual*, obligatory on the mere signification of mutual assent.   Hence, following their
usual practice, they distinguished these contracts
as contracts *Juris Gentium*.   Yet I do not think
that they were so named at a very early period.
The first notions of a Jus Gentium may have been
deposited in the minds of the Roman lawyers
long before the appointment of a Prætor Peregrinus, but it would only be through extensive
and regular trade that they would be familiarised
with the contractual system of other Italian
communities, and such a trade would scarcely
attain considerable proportions before Italy had

been thoroughly pacified, and the supremacy of Rome conclusively assured. Although, however, there is strong probability that the Consensual Contracts were the latest born into the Roman system, and though it is likely that the qualification, *Juris Gentium*, stamps the recency of their origin, yet this very expression, which attributes them to the " Law of Nations," has in modern times produced the notion of their extreme antiquity. For, when the " Law of Nations " had been converted into the " Law of Nature," it seemed to be implied that the Consensual Contracts were the type of the agreements most congenial to the natural state ; and hence arose the singular belief that the younger the civilisation, the simpler must be its forms of contract.

The Consensual Contracts, it will be observed, were extremely limited in number. But it cannot be doubted that they constituted the stage in the history of Contract-law from which all modern conceptions of contract took their start. The motion of the will which constitutes agreement was now completely insulated, and became the subject of separate contemplation ; forms were entirely eliminated from the notion of contract, and external acts were only regarded as symbols of the internal act of volition. The Consensual Contracts had, moreover, been classed in the Jus Gentium, and it was not long before this classification drew with it the inference that they were the species of agreement which represented the engagements approved of by Nature and included in her code. This point once reached, we are prepared for several celebrated doctrines and distinctions of the Roman lawyers. One of them is the distinction between Natural and Civil Obligations. When a person of full intellectual maturity had deliberately bound himself by an engagement, he was said to be under a *natural obligation*, even though he had omitted some necessary formality, and even though through some technical impediment he was devoid of the formal capacity for making a valid contract. The law (and this is what the distinction implies) would not enforce the obligation, but it did not absolutely refuse to recognise it; and *natural obligations* differed in many respects from obligations which were merely null and void, more particularly in the circumstance that they could be civilly confirmed, if the capacity for contract were subsequently acquired. Another very peculiar doctrine of the jurisconsults could not have had its origin earlier than the period at which the Convention was severed from the technical ingredients of Contract. They taught that though nothing but a Contract could be the foundation of an *action*, a mere Pact or Convention could be the basis of a *plea*. It followed from this, that though nobody could sue upon an agreement which he had not taken the precaution to mature into a Contract by complying with the proper forms, nevertheless a claim arising out of a valid contract could be rebutted by proving a counter-agreement which had never got beyond the state of a simple convention. An action for the recovery of a debt could be met by showing a mere informal agreement to waive or postpone the payment.

The doctrine just stated indicates the hesitation of the Prætors in making their advances towards the greatest of their innovations. Their theory of Natural law must have led them to look with especial favour on the Consensual Contracts and on those Pacts or Conventions of which the Consensual Contracts were only particular instances ; but they did not at once venture on extending to all Conventions the liberty of the Consensual Contracts. They took advantage of that special superintendence over procedure which had been confided to them since the first beginnings of Roman law, and, while they still declined to permit a suit to be launched which was not based on a formal contract, they gave full play to their new theory of agreement in directing the ulterior stages of the proceeding. But, when they had proceeded thus far, it was inevitable that they should proceed farther. The revolution of the ancient law of Contract was consummated when the Prætor of some one year announced in his Edict that he would grant equitable actions upon Pacts which had never been matured at all into Contracts, provided only that the Pacts in question had been founded on a consideration (*causa*). Pacts of this sort are always enforced under the advanced Roman jurisprudence. The principle is merely the principle of the Consensual Contract carried to its proper consequence ; and, in fact, if the technical language of the Romans had been as plastic as their legal theories, these Pacts enforced by the Prætor would have been styled new Contracts, new Consensual Contracts. Legal phraseology is, however, the part of the law which is the last to alter, and the Pacts equitably enforced continued to be designated simply Præ-torian Pacts. It will be remarked that unless there were consideration for the Pact, it would continue *nude* so far as the new jurisprudence was concerned ; in order to give it effect, it would be necessary to convert it by a stipulation into a Verbal Contract.

The extreme importance of this history of Contract, as a safeguard against almost innumerable delusions, must be my justification for discussing it at so considerable a length. It gives a complete account of the march of ideas from one great landmark of jurisprudence to another. We begin with the Nexum, in which a Contract and a Conveyance are blended, and in which the formalities which accompany the agreement are even more important than the agreement itself. From the Nexum we pass to the Stipulation, which is a simplified form of the older ceremonial. The Literal Contract comes next, and here all formalities are waived, if proof of the agreement can be supplied from the rigid observances of a Roman household. In the Real Contract a moral duty is for the first time recognised, and persons who have joined or acquiesced in the partial performance of an engagement are forbidden to repudiate it on account of defects in form. Lastly, the Consensual Contracts emerge, in which the mental attitude of the contractors is solely regarded, and external circumstances have no title to notice except as evidence of the inward undertaking. It is of course uncertain how far this progress of Roman ideas from a gross to a refined conception exemplifies the necessary progress of human thought on the subject of Contract. The Contract-law of all other ancient societies but the Roman is either too scanty to furnish information, or else is entirely lost ; and modern jurisprudence is so thoroughly leavened with the Roman notions that it furnishes us with no contrasts or parallels from which instruction can be gleaned. From the absence, however, of everything violent, marvellous, or unintelligible in the changes I have described, it may be reasonably believed that the history of Ancient Roman Contracts is, up to a certain point, typical of the history of this class of legal conceptions in other ancient societies. But it is only up to a certain point that the progress of Roman law can be taken to represent the progress of other systems of jurisprudence. The theory of Natural law is exclusively Roman. The notion of the *vinculum juris*, so far as my knowledge extends, is exclusively Roman. The many peculiarities of the mature Roman Law of Contract and Delict which are traceable to these two ideas, whether singly or in combination, are therefore among the exclusive products of one particular society. These later legal conceptions are important, not because they typify the necessary results of advancing thought under all conditions, but because they have exercised perfectly enormous influence on the intellectual diathesis of the modern world.

I know nothing more wonderful than the variety of sciences to which Roman law, Roman Contract-law more particularly, has contributed modes of thought, courses of reasoning, and a technical language. Of the subjects which have whetted the intellectual appetite of the moderns, there is scarcely one, except Physics, which has not been filtered through Roman jurisprudence. The science of pure Metaphysics had, indeed, rather a Greek than a Roman parentage, but Politics, Moral Philosophy, and even Theology, found in Roman law not only a vehicle of expression, but a nidus in which some of their profoundest inquiries were nourished into maturity. For the purpose of accounting for this phenomenon, it is not absolutely necessary to discuss the mysterious relation between words and ideas, or to explain how it is that the human mind has never grappled with any subject of thought, unless it has been provided beforehand with a proper store of language and with an apparatus of appropriate logical methods. It is enough to remark, that, when the philosophical interests of the Eastern and Western worlds were separated, the founders of Western thought belonged to a society which spoke Latin and reflected in Latin. But in the Western provinces the only language which retained sufficient precision for philosophical purposes was the language of Roman law, which by a singular fortune had preserved nearly all the purity of the Augustan age, while vernacular Latin was degenerating into a dialect of portentous barbarism. And if Roman jurisprudence supplied the only means of exactness in speech, still more emphatically did it furnish the only means of exactness, subtlety, or depth in thought. For at least three centuries philosophy and science were without a home in the West and though metaphysics and metaphysical theology were engrossing the mental energies of multitudes of Roman subjects, the phraseology employed in these ardent inquiries was exclusively Greek, and their theatre was the Eastern half of the Empire. Sometimes, indeed, the conclusions of the Eastern disputants became so important that every man's assent to them, or dissent from them, had to be recorded, and then the West was introduced to the results of Eastern controversy, which it generally acquiesced in without interest and without resistance. Meanwhile, one department of inquiry, difficult enough for the most laborious, deep enough for the most subtile, delicate enough for the most refined, had never lost its attractions for the educated classes of the Western provinces. To the cultivated citizen of Africa, of Spain, of Gaul, and of Northern Italy, it was jurisprudence, and jurisprudence only, which stood in the place of poetry and history, of philosophy and science. So far then from there being anything mysterious in the palpably legal complexion of the earliest efforts of Western thought, it would rather be astonishing if it had assumed any other hue. I can only express my surprise at the scantiness of the attention which has been given to the difference between Western ideas and Eastern, between Western theology and Eastern, caused by the presence of a new ingredient. It is precisely because the influence of jurisprudence begins to be powerful that the foundation of Constantinople and the subsequent separation of the Western empire from the Eastern are epochs in philosophical history. But Con-

tinental thinkers are doubtless less capable of
appreciating the importance of this crisis by the
very intimacy with which notions derived from
Roman law are mingled up with their everyday
ideas. Englishmen, on the other hand, are blind
to it through the monstrous ignorance to which
they condemn themselves of the most plentiful
source of the stream of modern knowledge, of the
one intellectual result of the Roman civilisation.
At the same time, an Englishman who will be at
the pains to familiarise himself with the classical
Roman law, is perhaps, from the very slightness
of the interest which his countrymen have hitherto
taken in the subject, a better judge than a Frenchman or a German of the value of the assertions
I have ventured to make. Anybody who knows
what Roman jurisprudence is, as actually practised
by the Romans, and who will observe in what
characteristics the earliest Western theology and
philosophy differ from the phases of thought
which preceded them, may be safely left to pronounce what was the new element which had
begun to pervade and govern speculation.

The part of Roman law which has had most
extensive influence on foreign subjects of inquiry
has been the law of Obligation, or, what comes
nearly to the same thing, of Contract and Delict.
The Romans themselves were not unaware of
the offices which the copious and malleable
terminology belonging to this part of their system
might be made to discharge, and this is proved by
their employment of the peculiar adjunct *quasi*
in such expressions as Quasi-Contract and Quasi-
Delict. " Quasi," so used, is exclusively a term

of classification. It has been usual with English critics to identify the Quasi-Contracts with *implied* contracts, but this is an error, for implied contracts are true contracts, which quasi-contracts are not. In implied contracts, acts and circumstances are the symbols of the same ingredients which are symbolised, in express contracts, by words ; and whether a man employs one set of symbols or the other must be a matter of indifference so far as concerns the theory of agreement. But a Quasi-Contract is not a contract at all. The commonest sample of the class is the relation subsisting between two persons, one of whom has paid money to the other through mistake. The law, consulting the interests of morality, imposes an obligation on the receiver to refund, but the very nature of the transaction indicates that it is not a contract, inasmuch as the Convention, the most essential ingredient of Contract, is wanting. This word " quasi," prefixed to a term of Roman law, implies that the conception to which it serves as an index is connected with the conception with which the comparison is instituted by a strong superficial analogy or resemblance. It does not denote that the two conceptions are the same, or that they belong to the same genus. On the contrary, it negatives the notion of an identity between them ; but it points out that they are sufficiently similar for one to be classed as the sequel to the other, and that the phraseology taken from one department of law may be transferred to the other, and employed without violent straining in the statement of rules which would otherwise be imperfectly expressed.

It has been shrewdly remarked, that the confusion between Implied Contracts, which are true contracts, and Quasi-Contracts, which are not contracts at all, has much in common with the famous error which attributed political rights and duties to an Original Compact between the governed and the governor. Long before this theory had clothed itself in definite shape, the phraseology of Roman contract-law had been largely drawn upon to describe that reciprocity of rights and duties which men had always conceived as existing between sovereigns and subjects. While the world was full of maxims setting forth with the utmost positiveness the claims of kings to implicit obedience—maxims which pretended to have had their origin in the New Testament, but which were really derived from indelible recollections of the Cæsarian despotism—the consciousness of correlative rights possessed by the governed would have been entirely without the means of expression if the Roman law of Obligation had not supplied a language capable of shadowing forth an idea which was as yet imperfectly developed. The antagonism between the privileges of kings and their duties to their subjects was never, I believe, lost sight of since Western history began, but it had interest for few except speculative writers so long as feudalism continued in vigour, for feudalism effectually controlled by express customs the exorbitant theoretical pretensions of most European sovereigns. It is notorious, however, that as soon as the decay of the Feudal System had thrown the mediæval constitutions out of working order, and when the Reformation had discredited the authority of the Pope, the doctrine of the divine right of Kings rose immediately into an importance which had never before attended it. The vogue which it obtained entailed still more constant resort to the phraseology of Roman law, and a controversy which had originally worn a theological aspect assumed more and more the air of a legal disputation. A phenomenon then appeared which has repeatedly shown itself in the history of opinion. Just when the argument for monarchical authority rounded itself into the definite doctrine of Filmer, the phraseology, borrowed from the Law of Contract, which had been used in defence of the rights of subjects, crystallised into the theory of an actual original compact between king and people, a theory which, first in English and afterwards, and more particularly, in French hands, expanded into a comprehensive explanation of all the phenomena of society and law. But the only real connection between political and legal science had consisted in the last giving to the first the benefit of its peculiarly plastic terminology. The Roman jurisprudence of Contract had performed for the relation of sovereign and subject precisely the same service which, in a humbler sphere, it rendered to the relation of persons bound together by an obligation of " quasi-contract." It had furnished a body of words and phrases which approximated with sufficient accuracy to the ideas which then were from time to time forming on the subject of political obligation. The doctrine of an Original Compact can never be put higher than it is placed by Dr. Whewell, when he suggests that, though unsound, "it may be a *convenient* form for the expression of moral truths."

The extensive employment of legal language on political subjects previously to the invention of the Original Compact, and the powerful influence which that assumption has exercised subsequently, amply account for the plentifulness in political science of words and conceptions, which were the exclusive creation of Roman jurisprudence. Of their plentifulness in Moral Philosophy a rather different explanation must be given, inasmuch as ethical writings have laid Roman law under contribution much more directly than political speculations, and their authors have been much more conscious of the extent of their obligation. In speaking of moral philosophy as extraordinarily indebted to Roman jurisprudence, I must be understood to intend moral philosophy as understood previously to the break in its history effected by Kant, that is, as the science of the rules governing human conduct, of their proper interpretation, and of the limitations to which they are subject. Since the rise of the Critical Philosophy, moral science has almost wholly lost its older meaning, and, except where it is preserved under a debased form in the casuistry still cultivated by Roman Catholic theologians, it seems to be regarded nearly universally as a branch of ontological inquiry. I do not know that there is a single contemporary English writer, with the exception of Dr. Whewell, who understands moral philosophy as it was understood before it was absorbed by metaphysics and before the groundwork of its rules came to be a more

important consideration than the rules themselves.
So long, however, as ethical science had to do with
the practical regimen of conduct, it was more or
less saturated with Roman law. Like all the
great subjects of modern thought, it was originally
incorporated with theology.   The science of Moral
Theology, as it was at first called, and as it is still
designated by the Roman Catholic divines, was
undoubtedly constructed, to the full knowledge
of its authors, by taking principles of conduct
from the system of the Church, and by using
the language and methods of jurisprudence for
their expression and expansion. While this process went on, it was inevitable that jurisprudence,
though merely intended to be the vehicle of
thought, should communicate its colour to the
thought itself.   The tinge received through contact
with legal conceptions is perfectly perceptible in
the earliest ethical literature of the modern world,
and it is evident, I think, that the Law of Contract,
based as it is on the complete reciprocity and
indissoluble connection of rights and duties, has
acted as a wholesome corrective to the predis-
positions of writers who, if left to themselves,
might have exclusively viewed a moral obligation
as the public duty of a citizen in the Civitas Dei.
But the amount of Roman Law in moral theology
becomes sensibly smaller at the time of its cultivation by the great Spanish moralists. Moral
theology, developed by the juridical method of
doctor commenting on doctor, provided itself
with a phraseology of its own ; and Aristotelian
peculiarities of reasoning and expression, imbibed
doubtless in great part from the Disputations on

Morals in the academical schools, take the place of that special turn of thought and speech which can never be mistaken by any person conversant with the Roman law. If the credit of the Spanish school of moral theologians had continued, the juridical ingredient in ethical science would have been insignificant, but the use made of their conclusions by the next generation of Roman Catholic writers on these subjects almost entirely destroyed their influence. Moral Theology, degraded into Casuistry, lost all interest for the leaders of European speculation; and the new science of Moral Philosophy, which was entirely in the hands of the Protestants, swerved greatly aside from the path which the moral theologians had followed. The effect was vastly to increase the influence of Roman law on ethical inquiry.

" Shortly * after the Reformation, we find two great schools of thought dividing this class of subjects between them. The most influential of the two was at first the sect or school known to us as the Casuists, all of them in spiritual communion with the Roman Catholic Church, and nearly all of them affiliated to one or other of her religious orders. On the other side were a body of writers connected with each other by a common intellectual descent from the great author of the treatise ' De Jure Belli et Pacis,' Hugo Grotius. Almost all of the latter were adherents of the Reformation; and though it cannot be said that they were formally and avowedly at conflict

* The passage quoted is transcribed, with slight alterations, from a paper contributed by the author to the " Cambridge Essays " for 1856.

with the Casuists, the origin and objects of their
system were nevertheless essentially different from
those of Casuistry.   It is necessary to call attention
to this difference, because it involves the question
of the influence of Roman law on that department
of thought with which both systems are concerned.
The book of Grotius, though it touches questions
of pure Ethics in every page, and though it is
the parent immediate or remote of innumerable
volumes of formal morality, is not, as is well
known, a professed treatise on Moral Philosophy ;
it is an attempt to determine the Law of Nature,
or Natural Law. Now, without entering upon
the question whether the conception of a Law
Natural be not exclusively a creation of the
Roman jurisconsults, we may lay down that,
even on the admission of Grotius himself, the
dicta of the Roman jurisprudence as to what
parts of known positive law must be taken to
be parts of the Law of Nature, are, if not infallible,
to be received at all events with the profoundest
respect. Hence the system of Grotius is impli-
cated with Roman law at its very foundation,
and this connection rendered inevitable—what
the legal training of the writer would perhaps
have entailed without it—the free employment
in every paragraph of technical phraseology, and
of modes of reasoning, defining, and illustrating,
which must sometimes conceal the sense, and
almost always the force and cogency, of the argument from the reader who is unfamiliar with the
sources whence they have been derived. On the
other hand, Casuistry borrows little from Roman
law, and the views of morality contended for

have nothing whatever in common with the undertaking of Grotius. All that philosophy of right and wrong which has become famous, or infamous, under the name of Casuistry, had its origin in the distinction between Mortal and Venial sin. A natural anxiety to escape the awful consequences of determining a particular act to be mortally sinful, and a desire, equally intelligible, to assist the Roman Catholic Church in its conflict with Protestantism by disburthening it of an inconvenient theory, were the motives which impelled the authors of the Casuistical philosophy to the invention of an elaborate system of criteria, intended to remove immoral actions, in as many cases as possible, out of the category of mortal offences, and to stamp them as venial sins. The fate of this experiment is matter of ordinary history. We know that the distinctions of Casuistry, by enabling the priesthood to adjust spiritual control to all the varieties of human character, did really confer on it an influence with princes, statesmen, and generals, unheard of in the ages before the Reformation, and did really contribute largely to that great reaction which checked and narrowed the first successes of Protestantism. But beginning in the attempt, not to establish, but to evade—not to discover a principle, but to escape a postulate—not to settle the nature of right and wrong, but to determine what was not wrong of a particular nature,— Casuistry went on with its dexterous refinements till it ended in so attenuating the moral features of actions, and so belying the moral instincts of our being, that at length the conscience of mankind rose suddenly in revolt against it, and consigned to one common ruin the system and its doctors. The blow, long pending, was finally struck in the 'Provincial Letters' of Pascal, and since the appearance of those memorable Papers, no moralist of the smallest influence or credit has ever avowedly conducted his speculations in the footsteps of the Casuists. The whole field of ethical science was thus left at the exclusive command of the writers who followed Grotius; and it still exhibits in an extraordinary degree the traces of that entanglement with Roman law which is sometimes imputed as a fault, and sometimes the highest of its recommendations, to the Grotian theory. Many inquiriers since Grotius's day have modified his principles, and many, of course, since the rise of the Critical Philosophy, have quite deserted them; but even those who have departed most widely from his fundamental assumptions have inherited much of his method of statement, of his train of thought, and of his mode of illustration; and these have little meaning and no point to the person ignorant of Roman jurisprudence."

I have already said that, with the exception of the physical sciences, there is no walk of knowledge which has been so slightly affected by Roman law as Metaphysics. The reason is that discussion on metaphysical subjects has always been conducted in Greek, first in pure Greek, and afterwards in a dialect of Latin expressly constructed to give expression to Greek conceptions. The modern languages have only been fitted to metaphysical inquiries by adopting this Latin dialect, or by imitating the process which was originally followed in its formation. The source of the phraseology which has been always employed for metaphysical discussion in modern times was the Latin translations of Aristotle, in which, whether derived or not from Arabic versions, the plan of the translator was not to seek for analogous expressions in any part of Latin literature, but to construct anew from Latin roots a set of phrases equal to the expression of Greek philosophical ideas. Over such a process the terminology of Roman law can have exercised little influence ; at most, a few Latin law terms in a transmuted shape have made their way into metaphysical language. At the same time it is worthy of remark that whenever the problems of metaphysics are those which have been most strongly agitated in Western Europe, the thought, if not the language, betrays a legal parentage. Few things in the history of speculation are more impressive than the fact that no Greek-speaking people has ever felt itself seriously perplexed by the great question of Free-will and Necessity. I do not pretend to offer any summary explanation of this, but it does not seem an irrelevant suggestion that neither the Greeks, nor any society speaking and thinking in their language, ever showed the smallest capacity for producing a philosophy of law. Legal science is a Roman creation, and the problem of Free-will arises when we contemplate a metaphysical conception under a legal aspect. How came it to be a question whether invariable sequence was identical with necessary connection ? I can only say that the tendency of Roman law, which became stronger as it advanced, was to look upon legal consequences as united to legal causes by an inexorable necessity, a tendency most markedly exemplified in the definition of Obligation which I have repeatedly cited, " Juris vinculum quo necessitate adstringimur alicujus solvendæ rei."

But the problem of Free-will was theological before it became philosophical, and, if its terms have been affected by jurisprudence, it will be because Jurisprudence has made itself felt in Theology. The great point of inquiry which is here suggested has never been satisfactorily elucidated. What has to be determined, is whether jurisprudence has ever served as the medium through which theological principles have been viewed ; whether, by supplying a peculiar language, a peculiar mode of reasoning, and a peculiar solution of many of the problems of life, it has ever opened new channels in which theological speculation could flow out and expand itself. For the purpose of giving an answer it is necessary to recollect what is already agreed upon by the best writers as to the intellectual food which theology first assimilated. It is conceded on all sides that the earliest language of the Christian Church was Greek, and that the problems to which it first addressed itself were those for which Greek philosophy in its later forms had prepared the way. Greek metaphysical literature contained the sole stock of words and ideas out of which the human mind could provide itself with the means of engaging in the profound controversies as to the Divine Persons, the Divine Substance, and the Divine Natures. The Latin language and the meagre Latin philosophy were quite unequal to the undertaking, and accordingly the Western or Latin-speaking provinces of the Empire adopted the conclusions of the East without disputing or reviewing them. " Latin Christianity," says Dean Milman, " accepted the creed which its narrow and barren vocabulary could hardly express in adequate terms. Yet, throughout, the adhesion of Rome and the West was a passive acquiescence in the dogmatic system which had been wrought out by the profounder theology of the Eastern divines, rather than a vigorous and original examination on her part of those mysteries. The Latin Church was the scholar as well as the loyal partisan of Athanasius." But when the separation of East and West became wider, and the Latin-speaking Western Empire began to live with an intellectual life of its own, its deference to the East was all at once exchanged for the agitation of a number of questions entirely foreign to Eastern speculation. " While Greek theology (Milman, ' Latin Christianity,' Preface, 5) went on defining with still more exquisite subtlety the Godhead and the nature of Christ " —" while the interminable controversy still lengthened out and cast forth sect after sect from the enfeebled community "—the Western Church threw itself with passionate ardour into a new order of disputes, the same which from those days to this have never lost their interest for any family of mankind at any time included in the Latin communion. The nature of Sin and its transmission by inheritance—the debt owed by

man and its vicarious satisfaction—the necessity
and sufficiency of the Atonement—above all the
apparent antagonism between Free-will and the
Divine Providence—these were the points which
the West began to debate as ardently as ever
the East had discussed the articles of its more
special creed. Why is it then that on the two
sides of the line which divides the Greek-speaking
from the Latin-speaking provinces there lie two
classes of theological problems so strikingly different from one another ? The historians of the
Church have come close upon the solution when
they remark that the new problems were more
" practical," less absolutely speculative, than
those which had torn Eastern Christianity asunder,
but none of them, so far as I am aware, has quite
reached it. I affirm without hesitation that the
difference between the two theological systems
is accounted for by the fact that, in passing from
the East to the West, theological speculation had
passed from a climate of Greek metaphysics to
a climate of Roman law. For some centuries
before these controversies rose into overwhelming
importance, all the intellectual activity of the
Western Romans had been expended on jurisprudence exclusively. They had been occupied
in applying a peculiar set of principles to all the
combinations in which the circumstances of life
are capable of being arranged. No foreign pursuit
or taste called off their attention from this engrossing occupation, and for carrying it on they
possessed a vocabulary as accurate as it was
copious, a strict method of reasoning, a stock of
general propositions on conduct more or less

verified by experience, and a rigid moral philosophy. It was impossible that they should not select from the questions indicated by the Christian records those which had some affinity with the order of speculations to which they were accustomed, and that their manner of dealing with them should not borrow something from their forensic habits. Almost everybody who has knowledge enough of Roman law to appreciate the Roman penal system, the Roman theory of the obligations established by Contract or Delict, the Roman view of Debts and of the modes of incurring, extinguishing, and transmitting them, the Roman notion of the continuance of individual existence by Universal Succession, may be trusted to say whence arose the frame of mind to which the problems of Western theology proved so congenial, whence came the phraseology in which these problems were stated, and whence the description of reasoning employed in their solution. It must only be recollected that the Roman law which had worked itself into Western thought was neither the archaic system of the ancient city, nor the pruned and curtailed jurisprudence of the Byzantine Emperors ; still less, of course, was it the mass of rules, nearly buried in a parasitical overgrowth of modern speculative doctrine, which passes by the name of Modern Civil Law. I speak only of that philosophy of jurisprudence, wrought out by the great juridical thinkers of the Antonine age, which may still be partially reproduced from the Pandects of Justinian, a system to which few faults can be attributed except perhaps that it aimed at a higher degree of

elegance, certainty, and precision than human
affairs will permit to the limits within which
human law seeks to confine them.

It is a singular result of that ignorance of
Roman law which Englishmen readily confess, and
of which they are sometimes not ashamed to boast,
that many English writers of note and credit
have been led by it to put forward the most untenable of paradoxes concerning the condition
of human intellect during the Roman empire.
It has been constantly asserted, as unhesitatingly
as if there were no temerity in advancing the
proposition, that from the close of the Augustan
era to the general awakening of interest on the
points of the Christian faith, the mental energies
of the civilised world were smitten with a paralysis.
Now there are two subjects of thought—the only
two perhaps with the exception of physical science
—which are able to give employment to all the
powers and capacities which the mind possesses.
One of them is Metaphysical inquiry, which knows
no limits so long as the mind is satisfied to work
on itself ; the other is Law, which is as extensive
as the concerns of mankind. It happens that,
during the very period indicated, the Greek-
speaking provinces were devoted to one, the Latin-
speaking provinces to the other of these studies.
I say nothing of the fruits of speculation in
Alexandria and the East, but I confidently affirm
that Rome and the West had an occupation in
hand fully capable of compensating them for the
absence of every other mental exercise, and I
add that the results achieved, so far as we know
them, were not unworthy of the continuous and

exclusive labour bestowed on producing them. Nobody except a professional lawyer is perhaps in a position completely to understand how much of the intellectual strength of individuals Law is capable of absorbing, but a layman has no difficulty in comprehending why it was that an unusual share of the collective intellect of Rome was engrossed by jurisprudence. " The proficiency * of a given community in jurisprudence depends in the long run on the same conditions as its progress in any other line of inquiry ; and the chief of these are the proportion of the national intellect devoted to it, and the length of time during which it is so devoted. Now, a combination of all the causes, direct and indirect, which contribute to the advancing and perfecting of a science, continued to operate on the jurisprudence of Rome through the entire space between the Twelve Tables and the severance of the two Empires,—and that not irregularly or at intervals, but in steadily increasing force and constantly augmenting number. We should reflect that the earliest intellectual exercise to which a young nation devotes itself is the study of its laws. As soon as the mind makes its first conscious efforts towards generalisation, the concerns of every-day life are the first to press for inclusion within general rules and comprehensive formulas. The popularity of the pursuit on which all the energies of the young commonwealth are bent is at the outset unbounded ; but it ceases in time. The monopoly of mind by law is broken down. The crowd at the morning audience of the great

* "Cambridge Essays," 1856.

24

Roman jurisconsult lessens. The students are counted by hundreds instead of thousands in the English Inns of Court. Art, Literature, Science, and Politics claim their share of the national intellect; and the practice of jurisprudence is confined within the circle of a profession, never indeed limited or insignificant, but attracted as much by the rewards as by the intrinsic recommendations of their science. This succession of changes exhibited itself even more strikingly at Rome than in England. To the close of the Republic the law was the sole field for all ability except the special talent of a capacity for generalship. But a new stage of intellectual progress began with the Augustan age, as it did with our own Elizabethan era. We all know what were its achievements in poetry and prose; but there are some indications, it should be remarked, that, besides its efflorescence in ornamental literature, it was on the eve of throwing out new aptitudes for conquest in physical science. Here, however, is the point at which the history of mind in the Roman States ceases to be parallel to the routes which mental progress has since then pursued. The brief span of Roman literature, strictly so called, was suddenly closed under a variety of influences, which, though they may partially be traced, it would be improper in this place to analyse. Ancient intellect was forcibly thrust back into its old courses, and law again became no less exclusively the proper sphere for talent than it had been in the days when the Romans despised philosophy and poetry as the toys of a childish race. Of what nature were the external inducements which, during the Imperial period, tended to draw a man of inherent capacity to the pursuits of the jurisconsult may best be understood by considering the option which was practically before him in his choice of a profession. He might become a teacher of rhetoric, a commander of frontier-posts, or a professional writer of panegyrics. The only other walk of active life which was open to him was the practice of the law. Through *that* lay the approach to wealth, to fame, to office, to the council-chamber of the monarch—it may be to the very throne itself."

The premium on the study of jurisprudence was so enormous that there were schools of law in every part of the Empire, even in the very domain of Metaphysics. But, though the transfer of the seat of empire to Byzantium gave a perceptible impetus to its cultivation in the East, jurisprudence never dethroned the pursuits which there competed with it. Its language was Latin, an exotic dialect in the Eastern half of the Empire. It is only of the West that we can lay down that law was not only the mental food of the ambitious and aspiring, but the sole aliment of all intellectual activity. Greek philosophy had never been more than a transient fashionable taste with the educated class of Rome itself, and when the new Eastern capital had been created, and the Empire subsequently divided into two, the divorce of the Western provinces from Greek speculation, and their exclusive devotion to jurisprudence, became more decided than ever. As soon then as they ceased to sit at the feet of the Greeks and began to ponder out a theology of their own, the theology proved to be permeated with forensic ideas and couched in a forensic phraseology. It is certain that this substratum of law in Western theology lies exceedingly deep. A new set of Greek theories, the Aristotelian philosophy, made their way afterwards into the West, and almost entirely buried its indigenous doctrines. But when at the Reformation it partially shook itself free from their influence, it instantly supplied their place with Law. It is difficult to say whether the religious system of Calvin or the religious system of the Arminians has the more markedly legal character.

The vast influence of this specific jurisprudence of Contract produced by the Romans upon the corresponding department of modern Law belongs rather to the history of mature jurisprudence than to a treatise like the present. It did not make itself felt till the school of Bologna founded the legal science of modern Europe. But the fact that the Romans, before their Empire fell, had so fully developed the conception of Contract becomes of importance at a much earlier period than this. Feudalism, I have repeatedly asserted, was a compound of archaic barbarian usage with Roman law; no other explanation of it is tenable, or even intelligible. The earliest social forms of the feudal period differ in little from the ordinary associations in which the men of primitive civilisations are everywhere seen united. A Fief was an organically complete brotherhood of associates whose proprietary and personal rights were inextricably blended together. It had much in common with an Indian Village Community and much in common with a Highland clan. But still it presents some phenomena which we never find in the associations which are spontaneously formed by beginners in civilisation. True archaic communities are held together not by express rules, but by sentiment, or, we should perhaps say, by instinct ; and new comers into the brotherhood are brought within the range of this instinct by falsely pretending to share in the blood-relationship from which it naturally springs. But the earliest feudal communities were neither bound together by mere sentiment nor recruited by a fiction. The tie which united them was Contract, and they obtained new associates by contracting with them. The relation of the lord to the vassals had originally been settled by express engagement, and a person wishing to engraft himself on the brotherhood by *commendation* or *infeudation* came to a distinct understanding as to the conditions on which he was to be admitted. It is therefore the sphere occupied in them by Contract which principally distinguishes the feudal institutions from the unadulterated usages of primitive races. The lord had many of the characteristics of a patriarchal chieftain, but his prerogative was limited by a variety of settled customs traceable to the express conditions which had been agreed upon when the infeudation took place. Hence flow the chief differences which forbid us to class the feudal societies with true archaic communities. They were much more durable and much more various ; more durable, because express rules are less destructible than instinctive habits, and more various, because the contracts on which they were founded were adjusted to the minutest circumstances and wishes of the persons who surrendered or granted away their lands. This last consideration may serve to indicate how greatly the vulgar opinions current among us as to the origin of modern society stand in need of revision. It is often said that the irregular and various contour of modern civilisation is due to the exuberant and erratic genius of the Germanic races, and it is often contrasted with the dull routine of the Roman Empire. The truth is that the Empire bequeathed to modern society the legal conception to which all this irregularity is attributable; if the customs and institutions of barbarians have one characteristic more striking than another, it is their extreme uniformity.

NOTE R

CONTRACT IN EARLY LAW

REMEMBERING that Maine did not profess to write a treatise on Roman law, we shall not follow this brilliant and suggestive chapter with a critical eye for details. But we must note that Savigny's explanation of the Stipulation as an "imperfect conveyance"—a truncated form of the Nexum (about which, by the way, little seems to be really known)—is not accepted by any recent author. The origin is now sought in an earlier religious obligation, probably by oath; opinions differ, as might be expected, as to the conjectural details (Muirhead, 22-7; Girard, 481, sqq.; Pacchioni, "Actio ex sponsu," Bologna, 1888; Zocco-Rosa in Annuario dello Istituto di storia di diritto Romano, vol. 8, Catania, 1902; Sohm's note, "Institutes," tr. Ledlie, 3rd ed., p. 64). To such an origin the fact that the words "spondes? spondeo" could be used only by Roman citizens appears to point, though Savigny strangely failed to see this; and in medieval English law we actually find the religious sanction of the spiritual courts interposed, in the name of correcting the sinful breach of plighted faith *(fidei læsio)*, to enforce promises which were still

mere words for temporal courts, bound as they were to the archaic
categories of forms of action.   English example also shows how
improbable it is that contract should be derived from an imperfect
conveyance.   In medieval English law a debt is constituted not
by the debtor's promise to repay, but by a supposed grant of the
sum to the creditor, and the creditor's action alleges no promise,
but is in exactly the same form as an action to recover land,
and is expressly called an action of property.   Here we have
conveyance enough.   But the action of debt was quite incompetent
to become the starting-point of any true law of contract, and when
a way was found to sue on informal promises outside its limits,
that way was altogether different.   All this is in no degree pre-
judicial to the substance of Maine's argument, which is to show
that the law of contract, or, to be exact, any comprehensive
doctrine of contract, appears everywhere only at an advanced
stage of legal development.   This is undoubtedly sound.   Even
the classical Roman law in its final form never attained a really
general theory of contracts.   Ultimately the want was supplied,
but it would hardly be too much to say of the canonists on the
Continent, certainly not too much to say of the common lawyers
in England, that they took the kingdom of heaven by violence (cp.
my "Oxford Lectures," 1890, pp. 59-62 ; details and references for
the English history in Pollock on Contract, 7th ed. 136, 170; the
use of the specially English term Consideration to represent
the Roman *causa* is too dangerous a liberty to be allowed to any
lesser man than Maine).

Maine censures unnamed English critics (p. 345) for identifying
the quasi-contracts of the Civil Law (the term is, of course, not
classical) with the implied contracts of the Common Law.   But
the truth is that this latter expression is, or very lately was,
ambiguous.   Real agreements manifested by acts and conduct,
and not by words, were constantly spoken of as "implied"
contracts in English books, as Maine says, at the time when he
wrote and long afterwards.   Thus the Indian Contract Act of 1872
declares that a promise made otherwise than in words is said to
be implied.   Here a real agreement is inferred as a fact.   But
also many "relations resembling those created by contract" (to
use again the language of the Indian Act) arise from facts which
in Roman law would produce an obligation *quasi ex contractu*.
Such facts, under the Common Law, may produce an obligation
ascribed in the old system of pleading to a fictitious promise,
which promise was said to be "implied" by the law.   There
are therefore so-called implied contracts in our law which may
quite properly be compared with the quasi-contracts of the Roman
law; they cover, indeed, much of the same ground.   Of late years
the term Quasi-contract has been fully naturalised in the American
law schools, and by this time it is fairly well known in England.

" Constructive contract" would have been correct and in harmony with the general usage of the Common Law, but no one seems ever to have used it.

One result, and a somewhat important one of observing how late and slow of growth any general doctrine of contract has been in any system of civilized law is to strengthen the conviction that a huge anachronism is involved in those political theories which seek to make contract the foundation of all positive law and even of government itself. It should be noted that the doctrine of the Social Contract is much earlier than appears in Maine's statement, and that the theory of the divine right of kings, to which Maine alludes very briefly, was in its origin directed not against popular liberty but against papal and ecclesiastical claims to supremacy in temporal as well as spiritual affairs, as Mr. J. Neville Figgis has shown at large in his learned and acute monograph (" The Theory of the Divine Right of Kings," Cambridge, 1896).

We have said that the classical Roman system of contracts was not theoretically complete ; but this did not prevent the discovery that rights could be freely and largely modified by contract (for a discovery this was to the men of the Middle Ages, when the revived study of Roman law made the fact prominent) from exercising a fascination which is not at all exaggerated in Maine's remarks at the end of this chapter. For a time there was a tendency to assume that estates and interests in land could be modified without limit at the will of parties, and this was not effectually checked in England until the latter part of the thirteenth century.

CHAPTER X

THE Teutonic Codes, including those of our Anglo-Saxon ancestors, are the only bodies of archaic secular law which have come down to us in such a state that we can form an exact notion of their original dimensions. Although the extant fragments of Roman and Hellenic codes suffice to prove to us their general character, there does not remain enough of them for us to be quite sure of their precise magnitude or of the proportion of their parts to each other. But still on the whole all the known collections of ancient law are characterised by a feature which broadly distinguishes them from systems of mature jurisprudence. The proportion of criminal to civil law is exceedingly different. In the German codes, the civil part of the law has trifling dimensions as compared with the criminal. The traditions which speak of the sanguinary penalties inflicted by the code of Draco seem to indicate that it had the same characteristic. In the Twelve Tables alone, produced by a society of greater legal genius and at first of gentler manners, the civil law has something like its modern precedence ; but the relative amount of space given to the modes of redressing wrong, though not enormous, appears to have been large. It

may be laid down, I think, that the more archaic
the code, the fuller and the minuter is its penal
legislation. The phenomenon has often been
observed, and has been explained, no doubt to
a great extent correctly, by the violence habitual
to the communities which for the first time reduced
their laws to writing. The legislator, it is said,
proportioned the divisions of his work to the
frequency of a certain class of incidents in barbarian life. I imagine, however, that this account
is not quite complete. It should be recollected
that the comparative barrenness of civil law in
archaic collections is consistent with those other
characteristics of ancient jurisprudence which
have been discussed in this treatise. Nine-tenths
of the civil part of the law practised by civilised
societies are made up of the Law of Persons, of
the Law of Property and of Inheritance, and of
the Law of Contract. But it is plain that all these
provinces of jurisprudence must shrink within
narrower boundaries, the nearer we make our
approaches to the infancy of social brotherhood.
The Law of Persons, which is nothing else than
the Law of Status, will be restricted to the scantiest
limits as long as all forms of status are merged
in common subjection to Paternal Power, as long
as the wife has no rights against her Husband,
the Son none against his Father, and the infant
Ward none against the Agnates who are his
Guardians. Similarly, the rules relating to Property and Succession can never be plentiful,
so long as land and goods devolve within the
family, and, if distributed at all, are distributed
inside its circle. But the greatest gap in ancient

civil law will always be caused by the absence of Contract, which some archaic codes do not mention at all, while others significantly attest the immaturity of the moral notions on which Contract depends by supplying its place with an elaborate jurisprudence of Oaths. There are no corresponding reasons for the poverty of penal law, and accordingly, even if it be hazardous to pronounce that the childhood of nations is always a period of ungoverned violence, we shall still be able to understand why the modern relation of criminal law to civil should be inverted in ancient codes.

I have spoken of primitive jurisprudence as giving to *criminal* law a priority unknown in a later age. The expression has been used for convenience' sake, but in fact the inspection of ancient codes shows that the law which they exhibit in unusual quantities is not true criminal law. All civilised systems agree in drawing a distinction between offences against the State or Community and offences against the Individual, and the two classes of injuries, thus kept apart, I may here, without pretending that the terms have always been employed consistently in jurisprudence, call Crimes and Wrongs, *crimina* and *delicta*. Now the penal Law of ancient communities is not the law of Crimes; it is the law of Wrongs, or, to use the English technical word, of Torts. The person injured proceeds against the wrong-doer by an ordinary civil action, and recovers compensation in the shape of money-damages if he succeeds. If the Commentaries of Gaius be opened at the place where the writer treats of the penal jurisprudence founded on the Twelve Tables, it will be seen that at the head of the civil wrongs recognised by the Roman law stood *Furtum* or *Theft*. Offences which we are accustomed to regard exclusively as *crimes* are exclusively treated as *torts*, and not theft only, but assault and violent robbery, are associated by the jurisconsult with trespass, libel, and slander. All alike gave rise to an Obligation or *vinculum juris*, and were all requited by a payment of money. This peculiarity, however, is most strongly brought out in the consolidated Laws of the Germanic tribes. Without an exception, they describe an immense system of money compensations for homicide, and with few exceptions, as large a scheme of compensation for minor injuries. "Under Anglo-Saxon law," writes Mr. Kemble ("Anglo-Saxons," i. 177), "a sum was placed on the life of every free man, according to his rank, and a corresponding sum on every wound that could be inflicted on his person, for nearly every injury that could be done to his civil rights, honour, or peace ; the sum being aggravated according to adventitious circumstances." These compositions are evidently regarded as a valuable source of income ; highly complex rules regulate the title to them and the responsibility for them ; and, as I have already had occasion to state, they often follow a very peculiar line of devolution, if they have not been acquitted at the decease of the person to whom they belong. If therefore the criterion of a *delict*, *wrong*, or *tort* be that the person who suffers it, and not the State, is conceived to be wronged,

it may be asserted that in the infancy of jurisprudence the citizen depends for protection against
violence or fraud not on the Law of Crime but on
the Law of Tort.

Torts then are copiously enlarged upon in
primitive jurisprudence. It must be added that
Sins are known to it also. Of the Teutonic codes
it is almost unnecessary to make this assertion,
because those codes, in the form in which we have
received them, were compiled or recast by Christian
legislators. But it is also true that non-Christian
bodies of archaic law entail penal consequences
on certain classes of acts and on certain classes
of omissions, as being violations of divine prescriptions and commands. The law administered
at Athens by the Senate of Areopagus was probably
a special religious code, and at Rome, apparently
from a very early period, the Pontifical jurisprudence punished adultery, sacrilege, and perhaps
murder. There were therefore in the Athenian
and in the Roman States laws punishing *sins*.
There were also laws punishing *torts*. The conception of offence against God produced the first
class of ordinances ; the conception of offence
against one's neighbour produced the second ;
but the idea of offence against the State or aggregate community did not at first produce a true
criminal jurisprudence.

Yet it is not to be supposed that a conception
so simple and elementary as that of wrong done
to the State was wanting in any primitive society.
It seems rather that the very distinctness with
which this conception is realised is the true cause
which at first prevents the growth of a criminal

law. At all events, when the Roman community
conceived itself to be injured, the analogy of a
personal wrong received was carried out to its
consequences with absolute literalness, and the
State avenged itself by a single act on the
individual wrong-doer. The result was that, in
the infancy of the commonwealth, every offence
vitally touching its security or its interests was
punished by a separate enactment of the legislature. And this is the earliest conception of a
·*crimen* or Crime—an act involving such high
issues that the State, instead of leaving its cognisance to the civil tribunal or the religious court,
directed a special law or *privilegium* against the
perpetrator. Every indictment therefore took
the form of a bill of pains and penalties, and the
trial of a *criminal* was a proceeding wholly extraordinary, wholly irregular, wholly independent
of settled rules and fixed conditions. Consequently, both for the reason that the tribunal
dispensing justice was the sovereign State itself
and also for the reason that no classification
of the acts prescribed or forbidden was possible,
there was not at this epoch any *Law* of Crimes,
any criminal jurisprudence. The procedure was
identical with the forms of passing an ordinary
statute ; it was set in motion by the same persons
and conducted with precisely the same solemnities.
And it is to be observed that, when a regular
criminal law with an apparatus of Courts and
officers for its administration had afterwards come
into being, the old procedure, as might be supposed
from its conformity with theory, still in strictness
remained practicable ; and, much as resort to

such an expedient was discredited, the people
of Rome always retained the power of punishing
by a special law offences against its majesty.
The classical scholar does not require to be
reminded that in exactly the same manner the
Athenian Bill of Pains and Penalties, or εἰσαγγελία,
survived the establishment of regular tribunals.
It is known too that when the freemen of the
Teutonic races assembled for legislation, they also
claimed authority to punish offences of peculiar
blackness or perpetrated by criminals of exalted
station. Of this nature was the criminal jurisdiction of the Anglo-Saxon Witenagemot.

It may be thought that the difference which I
have asserted to exist between the ancient and
modern view of penal law has only a verbal existence. The community, it may be said, besides
interposing to punish crimes legislatively, has from
the earliest times interfered by its tribunals to
compel the wrong-doer to compound for his wrong,
and if it does this, it must always have supposed
that in some way it was injured through his
offence. But, however rigorous this inference may
seem to us nowadays, it is very doubtful whether
it was actually drawn by the men of primitive
antiquity. How little the notion of injury to the
community had to do with the earliest interferences of the State *through its tribunals,* is shown
by the curious circumstances that in the original
administration of justice, the proceedings were a
close imitation of the series of acts which were
likely to be gone through in private life by persons
who were disputing, but who afterwards suffered
their quarrel to be appeased. The magistrate

carefully simulated the demeanour of a private arbitrator casually called in.

In order to show that this statement is not a mere fanciful conceit, I will produce the evidence on which it rests. Very far the most ancient judicial proceeding known to us is the Legis Actio Sacramenti of the Romans, out of which all the later Roman Law of Actions may be proved to have grown. Gaius carefully describes its ceremonial. Unmeaning and grotesque as it appears at first sight, a little attention enables us to decipher and interpret it.

The subject of litigation is supposed to be in Court. If it is movable, it is actually there. If it be immovable, a fragment or sample of it is brought in its place ; land, for instance, is represented by a clod, a house by a single brick. In the example selected by Gaius, the suit is for a slave. The proceeding begins by the plaintiff's advancing with a rod, which, as Gaius expressly tells, symbolised a spear. He lays hold of the slave and asserts a right to him with the words, " *Hunc ego hominem ex Jure Quiritium meum esse dico secundum suam causam sicut dixi* " ; and then saying, " *Ecce tibi Vindictam imposui*," he touches him with the spear. The defendant goes through the same series of acts and gestures. On this the Prætor intervenes, and bids the litigants relax their hold, " *Mittite ambo hominem*." They obey, and the plaintiff demands from the defendant the reason of his interference, " *Postulo anne dicas quâ ex causâ vindicaveris*," a question which is replied to by a fresh assertion of right, " *Jus peregi sicut vindictam imposui*." On this, the first claimant offers to stake a sum of money, called a Sacramentum, on the justice of his own case, " *Quando tu injuriâ provocasti, D æris Sacramento te provoco,*" and the defendant, in the phrase, " *Similiter ego te,*" accepts the wager. The subsequent proceedings were no longer of a formal kind, but it is to be observed that the Prætor took security for the Sacramentum, which always went into the coffers of the State.

Such was the necessary preface of every ancient Roman suit. It is impossible, I think, to refuse assent to the suggestion of those who see in it a dramatisation of the origin of Justice. Two armed men are wrangling about some disputed property. The Prætor, *vir pietate gravis*, happens to be going by and interposes to stop the contest. The disputants state their case to him, and agree that he shall arbitrate between them, it being arranged that the loser, besides resigning the subject of the quarrel, shall pay a sum of money to the umpire as remuneration for his trouble and loss of time. This interpretation would be less plausible than it is, were it not that, by a surprising coincidence, the ceremony described by Gaius as the imperative course of proceeding in a Legis Actio is substantially the same with one of the two subjects which the God Hephæstus is described by Homer as moulding into the First Compartment of the Shield of Achilles. In the Homeric trial-scene, the dispute, as if expressly intended to bring out the characteristics of primitive society, is not about property, but about the composition for a homicide. One person asserts that he has paid it, the other that he has

25

never received it. The point of detail, however, which stamps the picture as the counterpart of the archaic Roman practice is the reward designed for the judges. Two talents of gold lie in the middle, to be given to him who shall explain the grounds of the decision most to the satisfaction of the audience. The magnitude of this sum as compared with the trifling amount of the Sacramentum seems to me indicative of the difference between fluctuating usage and usage consolidated into law. The scene introduced by the poet as a striking and characteristic, but still only occasional, feature of city life in the heroic age has stiffened, at the opening of the history of civil process, into the regular, ordinary formalities of a lawsuit. It is natural therefore that in the Legis Actio the remuneration of the Judge should be reduced to a reasonable sum, and that, instead of being adjudged to one of a number of arbitrators by popular acclamation, it should be paid as a matter of course to the State which the Prætor represents. But that the incidents described so vividly by Homer, and by Gaius with even more than the usual crudity of technical language, have substantially the same meaning, I cannot doubt ; and in confirmation of this view it may be added that many observers of the earliest judicial usages of modern Europe have remarked that the fines inflicted by Courts on offenders were originally *sacramenta*. The State did not take from the defendant a composition for any wrong supposed to be done to itself, but claimed a share in the compensation awarded to the plaintiff simply as the fair price of its time and trouble. Mr. Kemble expressly assigns this character to the Anglo-Saxon *bannum* or *fredum*.

Ancient law furnishes other proofs that the earliest administrators of justice simulated the probable acts of persons engaged in a private quarrel. In settling the damages to be awarded, they took as their guide the measure of vengeance likely to be exacted by an aggrieved person under the circumstances of the case. This is the true explanation of the very different penalties imposed by ancient law on offenders caught in the act or soon after it and on offenders detected after considerable delay. Some strange exemplifications of this peculiarity are supplied by the old Roman law of Theft. The laws of the Twelve Tables seem to have divided Thefts into Manifest and Non-Manifest, and to have allotted extraordinarily different penalties to the offence according as it fell under one head or the other. The Manifest Thief was he who was caught within the house in which he had been pilfering, or who was taken while making off to a place of safety with the stolen goods ; the Twelve Tables condemned him to be put to death if he were already a slave, and if he were a freeman, they made him the bondsman of the owner of the property. The Non-Manifest Thief was he who was detected under any other circumstances than those described ; and the old code simply directed that an offender of this sort should refund double the value of what he had stolen. In Gaius's day the excessive severity of the Twelve Tables to the Manifest Thief had naturally been much mitigated, but the law still maintained the old principle by

mulcting him in fourfold the value of the stolen
goods, while the Non-Manifest Thief still continued
to pay merely the double. The ancient lawgiver
doubtless considered that the injured proprietor,
if left to himself, would inflict a very different
punishment when his blood was hot from that
with which he would be satisfied when the Thief
was detected after a considerable interval ; and to
this calculation the legal scale of penalties was
adjusted. The principle is precisely the same as
that followed in the Anglo-Saxon and other
Germanic codes, when they suffer a thief chased
down and caught with the booty to be hanged or
decapitated on the spot, while they exact the full
penalties of homicide from anybody who kills him
after the pursuit has been intermitted. These
archaic distinctions bring home to us very forcibly
the distance of a refined from a rude jurisprudence.
The modern administrator of justice has confessedly one of his hardest tasks before him when
he undertakes to discriminate between the degrees
of criminality which belong to offences falling
within the same technical description. It is
always easy to say that a man is guilty of man-
slaughter, larceny, or bigamy, but it is often most
difficult to pronounce what extent of moral guilt
he has incurred, and consequently what measure
of punishment he has deserved. There is hardly
any perplexity in casuistry, or in the analysis of
motive, which we may not be called upon to
confront, if we attempt to settle such a point with
precision ; and accordingly the law of our day
shows an increasing tendency to abstain as much
as possible from laying down positive rules on the

subject. In France, the jury is left to decide
whether the offence which it finds committed has
been attended by extenuating circumstances; in
England, a nearly unbounded latitude in the
selection of punishments is now allowed to the
judge; while all States have in reserve an ultimate
remedy for the miscarriages of law in the Prerogative of Pardon, universally lodged with the
Chief Magistrate. It is curious to observe how
little the men of primitive times were troubled
with these scruples, how completely they were
persuaded that the impulses of the injured person
were the proper measure of the vengeance he was
entitled to exact, and how literally they imitated
the probable rise and fall of his passions in fixing
their scale of punishment. I wish it could be said
that their method of legislation is quite extinct.
There are, however, several modern systems of law
which, in cases of graver wrong, admit the fact of
the wrong-doer having been taken in the act to
be pleaded in justification of inordinate punishment inflicted on him by the sufferer—an indul-
gence which, though superficially regarded it may
seem intelligible, is based, as it seems to me, on a
very low morality.

Nothing, I have said, can be simpler than the
considerations which ultimately led ancient societies to the formation of a true criminal jurisprudence. The State conceived itself to be wronged,
and the Popular Assembly struck straight at the
offender with the same movement which accompanied its legislative action. It is further true
of the ancient world—though not precisely of the
modern, as I shall have occasion to point out—

that the earliest criminal tribunals were merely
subdivisions, or committees, of the legislature.
This, at all events, is the conclusion pointed at by
the legal history of the two great states of antiquity
with tolerable clearness in one case, and with
absolute distinctness in the other.   The primitive
penal law of Athens intrusted the castigation of
offences partly to the Archons, who seem to have
punished them as *torts*, and partly to the Senate
of Areopagus, which punished them as *sins*.   Both
jurisdictions were substantially transferred in the
end to the Heliæa, the High Court of Popular
Justice, and the functions of the Archons and of
the Areopagus became either merely ministerial
or quite insignificant.   But " Heliæa " is only an
old word for assembly ; the Heliæa of classical
times was simply the Popular Assembly convened
for judicial purposes, and the famous Dikasteries
of Athens were only its subdivisions or panels.
The corresponding changes which occurred at
Rome are still more easily interpreted, because the
Romans confined their experiments to the penal
law, and did not, like the Athenians, construct
popular courts with a civil as well as a criminal
jurisdiction.   The history of Roman criminal
jurisprudence begins with the old Judicia Populi,
at which the Kings are said to have presided.
These were simply solemn trials of great offenders
under legislative forms.   It seems, however, that
from an early period the Comitia had occasionally
delegated its criminal jurisdiction to a Quæstio or
Commission, which bore much the same relation
to the Assembly which a Committee of the House
of Commons bears to the House itself, except that

the Roman Commissioners or Quæstores did not
merely *report* to the Comitia, but exercised all
powers which that body was itself in the habit of
exercising, even to the passing sentence on the
accused. A Quæstio of this sort was only appointed to try a particular offender, but there was
nothing to prevent two or three Quæstiones sitting
at the same time; and it is probable that several
of them were appointed simultaneously, when
several grave cases of wrong to the community
had occurred together. There are also indications
that now and then these Quæstiones approached
the character of our *Standing* Committees, in that
they were appointed periodically, and without
waiting for occasion to arise in the commission of
some serious crime. The old Quæstores Parricidii,
who are mentioned in connection with transactions
of very ancient date, as being deputed to try (or,
as some take it, to search out and try) all cases
of parricide and murder, seem to have been
appointed regularly every year; and the Duumviri Perduellionis, or Commission of Two for trial
of violent injury to the Commonwealth, are also
believed by most writers to have been named
periodically. The delegations of power to these
latter functionaries bring us some way forwards.
Instead of being appointed *when and as* state-
offences were committed, they had a general,
though a temporary jurisdiction over such as
might be perpetrated. Our proximity to a regular
criminal jurisprudence is also indicated by the
general terms " Parricidium " and " Perduellio,"
which mark the approach to something like a
classification of crimes.

The true criminal law did not however come into existence till the year B.C. 149, when L. Calpurnius Piso carried the statute known as the Lex Calpurnia de Repetundis. The law applied to cases Repetundarum Pecuniarum, that is, claims by Provincials to recover monies improperly received by a Governor-General, but the great and permanent importance of this statute arose from its establishing the first Quæstio Perpetua. A Quæstio Perpetua was a *Permanent* Commission as opposed to those which were occasional and to those which were temporary. It was a regular criminal tribunal, whose existence dated from the passing of the statute creating it and continued till another statute should pass abolishing it. Its members were not specially nominated, as were the members of the older Quæstiones, but provision was made in the law constituting it for selecting from particular classes the judges who were to officiate, and for renewing them in conformity with definite rules. The offences of which it took cognisance were also expressly named and defined in this statute, and the new Quæstio had authority to try and sentence all persons in future whose acts should fall under the definitions of crime supplied by the law. It was therefore a regular criminal judicature, administering a true criminal jurisprudence.

The primitive history of criminal law divides itself therefore into four stages. Understanding that the conception of *Crime*, as distinguished from that of *Wrong* or *Tort*, and from that of *Sin*, involves the idea of injury to the State or collective community, we first find that the commonwealth, in literal conformity with the conception, itself interposed directly, and by isolated acts, to avenge itself on the author of the evil which it had suffered. This is the point from which we start ; each indictment is now a bill of pains and penalties, a special law naming the criminal and prescribing his punishment. A *second* step is accomplished when the multiplicity of crimes compels the legislature to delegate its powers to particular Quæstiones or Commissions, each of which is deputed to investigate a particular accusation, and, if it be proved, to punish the particular offender. Yet *another* movement is made when the legislature, instead of waiting for the alleged commission of a crime as the occasion of appointing a Quæstio, periodically nominates Commissioners like the Quæstores Parricidii and the Duumviri Perduellionis, on the chance of certain classes of crimes being committed, and in the expectation that they *will* be perpetrated. The *last* stage is reached when the Quæstiones from being periodical or occasional become permanent Benches or Chambers—when the judges, instead of being named in the particular law nominating the Commission, are directed to be chosen through all future time in a particular way and from a particular class—and when certain acts are described in general language and declared to be crimes, to be visited, in the event of their perpetration, with specified penalties appropriated to each description.

If the Quæstiones Perpetuæ had had a longer history, they would doubtless have come to be regarded as a distinct institution, and their relation to the Comitia would have seemed no closer than the connection of our own Courts of Law with the Sovereign, who is theoretically the fountain of justice. But the Imperial despotism destroyed them before their origin had been completely forgotten, and so long as they lasted, these permanent Commissions were looked upon by the Romans as the mere depositaries of a delegated power. The cognisance of crimes was considered a natural attribute of the legislature, and the mind of the citizen never ceased to be carried back from the Quæstiones to the Comitia which had deputed them to put into exercise some of its own inalienable functions. The view which regarded the Quæstiones, even when they became permanent, as mere Committees of the Popular Assembly—as bodies which only ministered to a higher authority—had some important legal consequences which left their mark on the criminal law to the very latest period. One immediate result was that the Comitia continued to exercise criminal jurisdiction by way of bills of pains and penalties, long after the Quæstiones had been established. Though the legislature had consented to delegate its powers for the sake of convenience to bodies external to itself, it did not follow that it surrendered them. The Comitia and the Quæstiones went on trying and punishing offenders side by side ; and any unusual outburst of popular indignation was sure, until the extinction of the Republic, to call down upon its object an indictment before the Assembly of the Tribes.

One of the most remarkable peculiarities of the institutions of the Republic is also traceable to this dependence of the Quæstiones on the Comitia. The disappearance of the punishment of death from the penal system of Republican Rome used to be a very favourite topic with the writers of the last century, who were perpetually using it to point some theory of the Roman character or of modern social economy. The reason which can be confidently assigned for it stamps it as purely fortuitous. Of the three forms which the Roman legislature successively assumed, one, it is well known—the Comitia Centuriata—was exclusively taken to represent the State as embodied for military operations. The Assembly of the Centuries, therefore, had all powers which may be supposed to be properly lodged with a General commanding an army, and, among them, it had authority to subject all offenders to the same correction to which a soldier rendered himself liable by breaches of discipline. The Comitia Centuriata could therefore inflict capital punishment.   Not so, however, the Comitia Curiata or Comitia Tributa. They were fettered on this point by the sacredness with which the person of a Roman citizen, inside the walls of the city, was invested by religion and law ; and, with respect to the last of them, the Comitia Tributa, we know for certain that it became a fixed principle that the Assembly of the Tribes could at most impose a fine. So long as criminal jurisdiction was confined to the legislature, and so long as the assemblies of the Centuries and of the Tribes continued to exercise co-ordinate powers, it was easy to prefer indictments for graver crimes before the legislative body which dispensed the heavier penalties; but then it happened that the more democratic assembly, that of the Tribes, almost entirely superseded the others, and became the ordinary legislature of the later Republic. Now the decline of the Republic was exactly the period during which the Quæstiones Perpetuæ were established, so that the statutes creating them were all passed by a legislative assembly which itself could not, at its ordinary sittings, punish a criminal with death. It followed that the Permanent Judicial Commissions, holding a delegated authority, were circumscribed in their attributes and capacities by the limits of the powers residing with the body which deputed them. They could do nothing which the Assembly of the Tribes could not have done; and, as the Assembly could not sentence to death, the Quæstiones were equally incompetent to award capital punishment. The anomaly thus resulting was not viewed in ancient times with anything like the favour which it has attracted among the moderns, and indeed, while it is questionable whether the Roman character was at all the better for it, it is certain that the Roman Constitution was a great deal the worse. Like every other institution which has accompanied the human race down the current of its history, the punishment of death is a necessity of society in certain stages of the civilising process. There is a time when the attempt to dispense with it baulks both of the two great instincts which lie at the root of all penal law. Without it, the community neither feels that it is sufficiently revenged on the criminal, nor thinks that the example of his punishment is adequate to deter others from imitating him. The incompetence of the Roman Tribunals to pass sentence of death led distinctly and directly to those frightful Revolutionary intervals, known as the Proscriptions, during which all law was formally suspended simply because party violence could find no other avenue to the vengeance for which it was thirsting. No cause contributed so powerfully to the decay of political capacity in the Roman people as this periodical abeyance of the laws ; and, when it had once been resorted to, we need not hesitate to assert that the ruin of Roman liberty became merely a question of time. If the practice of the Tribunals had afforded an adequate vent for popular passion, the forms of judicial procedure would no doubt have been as flagrantly perverted as with us in the reigns of the later Stuarts, but national character would not have suffered as deeply as it did, nor would the stability of Roman institutions have been as seriously enfeebled.

I will mention two more singularities of the Roman Criminal System which were produced by the same theory of judicial authority. They are, the extreme multiplicity of the Roman criminal tribunals, and the capricious and anomalous classification of crimes which characterised Roman penal jurisprudence throughout its entire history. Every *Quæstio*, it has been said, whether Perpetual or otherwise, had its origin in a distinct statute. From the law which created it, it derived its authority ; it rigorously observed the limits which its charter prescribed to it, and touched no form of criminality which that charter did not

expressly define. As then the statutes which
constituted the various Quæstiones were all called
forth by particular emergencies, each of them
being in fact passed to punish a class of acts
which the circumstances of the time rendered
particularly odious or particularly dangerous,
these enactments made not the slightest reference
to each other, and were connected by no common
principle. Twenty or thirty different criminal
laws were in existence together, with exactly
the same number of Quæstiones to administer
them ; nor was any attempt made during the
Republic to fuse these distinct judicial bodies
into one, or to give symmetry to the provisions
of the statutes which appointed them and defined
their duties. The state of the Roman criminal
jurisdiction at this period, exhibited some resemblances to the administration of civil remedies
in England at the time when the English Courts
of Common Law had not as yet introduced those
fictitious averments into their writs which enabled
them to trespass on each other's peculiar province.
Like the Quæstiones, the Courts of Queen's Bench,
Common Pleas, and Exchequer, were all theoretical emanations from a higher authority, and
each entertained a special class of cases supposed
to be committed to it by the fountain of its
jurisdiction ; but then the Roman Quæstiones
were many more than three in number, and it
was infinitely less easy to discriminate the acts
which fell under the cognisance of each Quæstio,
than to distinguish between the provinces of the
three Courts in Westminster Hall. The difficulty
of drawing exact lines between the spheres of

the different Quæstiones made the multiplicity
of Roman tribunals something more than a mere
inconvenience ; for we read with astonishment
that when it was not immediately clear under
what general description a man's alleged offences
ranged themselves, he might be indicted at once
or successively before several different Commissions, on the chance of some one of them declaring
itself competent to convict him ; and, although
conviction by one Quæstio ousted the jurisdiction
of the rest, acquittal by one of them could not be
pleaded to an accusation before another.   This
was directly contrary to the rule of the Roman
civil law ; and we may be sure that a people so
sensitive as the Romans to anomalies (or, as their
significant phrase was, to *inelegancies*) in jurisprudence, would not long have tolerated it, had
not the melancholy history of the Quæstiones
caused them to be regarded much more as temporary weapons in the hands of factions than
as permanent institutions for the correction of
crime.   The Emperors soon abolished this multiplicity and conflict of jurisdiction ; but it is
remarkable that they did not remove another
singularity of the criminal law which stands in
close connection with the number of the Courts.
The classifications of crimes which are contained
even in the Corpus Juris of Justinian are remarkably capricious.   Each Quæstio had, in fact,
confined itself to the crimes committed to its
cognisance by its charter.   These crimes, however,
were only classed together in the original statute
because they happened to call simultaneously
for castigation at the moment of passing it.   They

had not therefore anything necessarily in common ;
but the fact of their constituting the particular
subject-matter of trials before a particular Quæstio
impressed itself naturally on the public attention,
and so inveterate did the association become
between the offences mentioned in the same
statute that, even when formal attempts were
mode by Sylla and by the Emperor Augustus
to consolidate the Roman criminal law, the
legislator preserved the old grouping. The Statutes
of Sylla and Augustus were the foundation of the
penal jurisprudence of the Empire, and nothing
can be more extraordinary than some of the
classifications which they bequeathed to it. I
need only give a single example in the fact that
perjury was always classed with *cutting and
wounding* and with *poisoning*, no doubt because
a law of Sylla, the Lex Cornelia de Sicariis et
Veneficis, had given jurisdiction over all these
three forms of crime to the same Permanent
Commission. It seems too that this capricious
grouping of crimes affected the vernacular speech
of the Romans. People naturally fell into the
habit of designating all the offences enumerated
in one law by the first name on the list, which
doubtless gave its style to the Law Court deputed
to try them all. All the offences tried by the
Quæstio De Adulteriis would thus be called
Adultery.

I have dwelt on the history and characteristics
of the Roman Quæstiones because the formation
of a criminal jurisprudence is nowhere else so
instructively exemplified. The last Quæstiones
were added by the Emperor Augustus, and from

that time the Romans may be said to have had
a tolerably complete criminal law. Concurrently
with its growth, the analogous process had gone
on, which I have called the conversion of Wrongs
into Crimes, for, though the Roman legislature
did not extinguish the civil remedy for the more
heinous offences, it offered the sufferer a redress
which he was sure to prefer. Still, even after
Augustus had completed his legislation, several
offences continued to be regarded as Wrongs,
which modern societies look upon exclusively as
crimes; nor did they become criminally punishable
till some late but uncertain date, at which the
law began to take notice of a new description of
offences called in the Digest *crimina extraordinaria*.
These were doubtless a class of acts which the
theory of Roman jurisprudence treated merely
as wrongs ; but the growing sense of the majesty
of society revolted from their entailing nothing
worse on their perpetrator than the payment of
money damages, and accordingly the injured
person seems to have been permitted, if he
pleased, to pursue them as crimes *extra ordinem*,
that is, by a mode of redress departing in some
respect or other from the ordinary procedure.
From the period at which these *crimina extraordinaria* were first recognised, the list of crimes
in the Roman State must have been as long as
in any community of the modern world.

It is unnecessary to describe with any minuteness the mode of administering criminal justice
under the Roman Empire, but it is to be noted
that both its theory and practice have had powerful
effect on modern society. The Emperors did not

26

immediately abolish the Quæstiones, and at first
they committed an extensive criminal jurisdiction
to the Senate, in which, however servile it might
show itself in fact, the emperor was no more
nominally than a Senator like the rest. But
some sort of collateral criminal jurisdiction had
been claimed by the Prince from the first ; and
this, as recollections of the free commonwealth
decayed, tended steadily to gain at the expense
of the old tribunals. Gradually the punishment
of crimes was transferred to magistrates directly
nominated by the Emperor, and the privileges
of the Senate passed to the Imperial Privy Council
which also became a Court of ultimate criminal
appeal. Under these influences the doctrine,
familiar to the moderns, insensibly shaped itself
that the Sovereign is the fountain of all Justice
and the depositary of all Grace. It was not so
much the fruit of increasing adulation and servility
as of the centralisation of the Empire which had
by this time perfected itself. The theory of
criminal justice had, in fact, worked round almost
to the point from which it started. It had begun
in the belief that it was the business of the collective community to avenge its own wrongs by its
own hand; and it ended in the doctrine that the
chastisement of crimes belonged in an especial
manner to the Sovereign as representative and
mandatory of his people. The new view differed
from the old one chiefly in the air of awfulness
and majesty which the guardianship of justice
appeared to throw around the person of the
Sovereign.

This later Roman view of the Sovereign's

relation to justice certainly assisted in saving
modern societies from the necessity of travelling
through the series of changes which I have illustrated by the history of the Quæstiones.   In the
primitive law of almost all the races which have
peopled Western Europe there are vestiges of
the archaic notion that the punishment of crimes
belongs to the general assembly of freemen ; and
there are some States—Scotland is said to be one
of them—in which the parentage of the existing
judicature can be traced up to a Committee of
the legislative body.   But the development of
the criminal law was universally hastened by two
causes, the memory of the Roman Empire and
the influence of the Church.   On the one hand,
traditions of the majesty of the Cæsars, perpetuated by the temporary ascendancy of the House
of Charlemagne, were surrounding Sovereigns
with a prestige which a mere barbarous chieftain
could never otherwise have acquired, and were
communicating to the pettiest feudal potentate
the character of guardian of society and representative of the State.   On the other hand, the
Church, in its anxiety to put a curb on sanguinary
ferocity, sought about for authority to punish the
graver misdeeds, and found it in those passages
of Scripture which speak with approval of the
powers of punishment committed to the civil
magistrate.   The New Testament was appealed
to as proving that secular rulers exist for the
terror of evil-doers ; the Old Testament, as laying
down that "whoso sheddeth man's blood, by man
shall his blood be shed."   There can be no doubt,
I imagine, that modern ideas on the subject of

crime are based upon two assumptions contended
for by the Church in the Dark Ages—first, that
each feudal ruler, in his degree, might be assimilated to the Roman Magistrates spoken of by
Saint Paul; and next, that the offences which
he was to chastise were those selected for prohibition in the Mosaic Commandments, or rather
such of them as the Church did not reserve to
her own cognisance. Heresy, supposed to be
included in the First and Second Commandments,
Adultery, and Perjury were ecclesiastical offences,
and the Church only admitted the co-operation
of the secular arm for the purpose of inflicting
severer punishment in cases of extraordinary
aggravation. At the same time, she taught that
murder and robbery, with their various modifications, were under the jurisdiction of civil
rulers, not as an accident of their position, but
by the express ordinance of God.

There is a passage in the writings of King
Alfred (Kemble, ii. 209) which brings out into
remarkable clearness the struggle of the various
ideas that prevailed in his day as to the origin
of criminal jurisdiction. It will be seen that
Alfred attributes it partly to the authority of
the Church and partly to that of the Witan, while
he expressly claims for treason against the lord
the same immunity from ordinary rules which
the Roman Law of Majestas had assigned to
treason against the Cæsar. " After this it happened," he writes, " that many nations received
the faith of Christ, and there were many synods
assembled throughout the earth, and among the
English race also after they had received the

faith of Christ, both of holy bishops and of their exalted Witan. They then ordained that, out of that mercy which Christ had taught, secular lords, with their leave, might without sin take for every misdeed the *bot* in money which they ordained; except in cases of treason against a lord, to which they dared not assign any mercy because Almighty God adjudged none to them that despised Him, nor did Christ adjudge any to them which sold Him to death; and He commanded that a lord should be loved like Himself."

NOTE S

ARCHAIC PROCEDURE

THE account given by Maine of the symbolism involved in the Legis Actio Sacramenti may be taken as generally correct. The Sacramentum itself, however, seems, according to the generally received modern opinion, to have had the definite and practical purpose of bringing the matter in dispute within the highest jurisdiction. Each party swears to the justice of his cause under a conventional forfeit, and thus the king, who is also chief priest, is brought in to decide which of them is perjured: "il faut au roi, chef de la religion et de la justice criminelle, chercher qui a raison." The separation of civil and spiritual jurisdiction under the Republic led to the abolition of the oath (Girard, "Manuel," pp. 13, 977). If this opinion is right, the Praetor does not represent a discreet passer-by, nor yet (as might also be conjectured) the village elders, but intervenes as the minister of the king's justice, conceived in the first instance (as it was in England in the early Middle Ages) as an extraordinary justice applicable only for special reasons. English readers hardly need to be reminded of the fictions by which the King's Bench and Exchequer extended their jurisdiction to ordinary pleas between subjects.

Maine's reference to the trial scene described in the Iliad, Σ. 497-508, as adorning the shield of Achilles, is very brief; but the whole scene is of such interest for early legal history that we may be allowed to dwell on it a little. The point specially made by Maine is that the two talents of gold are a fee for the member of the court who shall be thought to speak the law best. On this he is confirmed by Dr. W. Leaf's very careful interpretation of the passage in his notes *ad loc.*, and his earlier paper in Journ. Hell. Stud. viii. 122. There is no difficulty about the magnitude of the sum, for the Homeric talent represents only the value of one ox (Ridgeway in Journ. Hell. Stud. viii. 133). We shall now give Dr. Leaf's version.

" The people were gathered in the place of assembly, and there had sprung up a strife; two men were striving about the price of a man slain. The one averred that he had paid in full [namely by tender of the blood-fine then and there before the assembly; but Dr. Leaf's alternative in his later notes to the Iliad, Appendix I., ' claimed to pay,' is as good or better for the grammar of εὔχετο πάντ' ἀποδοῦναι, and makes better sense], and made declaration thereof to the people, but the other refused to accept aught [this is the proper idiomatic meaning of ἀναίνετο μηδὲν ἑλέσθαι: ' denied that he had received anything ' is, even apart from the context, barely admissible]; and both were desirous to take an issue at the hand of a daysman [this person, ἵστωρ, summons the council and presides, but the judgment has to be theirs; he is more like the sheriff in the old county court than a modern judge or referee]; and the people were shouting for both, taking part for either side [not unlike such glimpses as Bracton's Note Book and other sources afford us of the behaviour of medieval county courts]. And the heralds were restraining the people, and the elders sate on polished stones in the holy circle [such stones may be seen on Dartmoor to this day], and in their hands they held the clear-voiced herald's staves. With these they rose up and gave sentence in turn; and in their midst lay two talents of gold to give to him among them that spake the justest doom."

In addition to Dr. Leaf's reasons for rejecting the view formerly current that the dispute is on the mere question of fact whether a blood-fine admitted to be due has been paid or not, we may observe that such a payment would surely be made in a notorious manner and with ample witness, to say nothing of the physical difficulty of handing over some score of cattle (for such would be the most likely form of payment) as privately as modern debtors hand over cash or post a cheque.

The result is that we are confronted with an ancient Greek blood-feud in an interesting stage of transition, that in which the slain man's kindred are no longer free to accept or refuse compensation at their will, but are expected to abandon the feud, in a proper case, on receiving a sum fixed either by custom or by the judgment of the assembly. Homicide aggravated by treachery or the like would probably not fall within such a rule; and the amount of the fine, if we may judge by the practice of Iceland as described in the Sagas, might give matter enough for discussion among the wise men even if no preliminary question arose. Indications of a similar stage, though not clear enough to amount to proof if they stood alone, may be found in the Anglo-Saxon laws.

There is no question in the Homeric text of a formally compulsory jurisdiction; the parties have agreed to put themselves on the judgment of the assembly whether in all the circumstances, whatever they were, tender of the customary fine ought to be accepted. But when such voluntary references have become common practice we are near the point at which they cease to be voluntary, and the party who stands out for what formerly would have been his right incurs, at all events, public reprobation which will be an efficient sanction for most purposes.

Maine's opinion that in the infancy of criminal jurisdiction the sum paid to the king, or the State, was not penal, but a fee for hearing and determining the cause at the request of the parties, "the fair price of its time and trouble," is borne out by later researches in the antiquities of Germanic law. Such was probably at one time the *wite* of the Anglo-Saxon laws, though it is treated as penal in the earliest documents we have. If one feature in early procedure may be fixed on more than another as marking the recognition of criminal and civil responsibility as distinct in character, though one and the same act may be and quite commonly is both a wrong and an offence, perhaps it is the appearance of a special fine for breaking the peace. The development of the king's peace in England from a privilege attached to certain persons, places, and occasions, to the common right of every lawful man belongs to another and later stage.

INDEX

INDEX TO INTRODUCTION AND NOTES

Printed by Hazell, Watson & Viney, Ld., London and Aylesbury, England.